Football's Eagle & Stack Defenses

D1530203

Ron Vanderlinden

Human Kinetics

Library of Congress Cataloging-in-Publication Data

Vanderlinden, Ron.
 Football's eagle & stack defenses / Ron Vanderlinden
   p. cm
 Includes index.
 ISBN-13: 978-0-7360-7253-3 (soft cover)
 ISBN-10: 0-7360-7253-5 (soft cover)
 1. Football--Defense. 2. Football--Coaching. I. Title.
 GV951.18.V36 2008
 796.332'2--dc22

                          2008018334

 ISBN-10: 0-7360-7253-5
 ISBN-13: 978-0-7360-7253-3

Developmental Editor: Heather Healy; **Assistant Editor:** Carla Zych; **Copyeditor:** Patrick Connolly; **Proofreader:** Jacqueline Eaton Blakley; **Indexer:** Craig Brown; **Permission Manager:** Martha Gullo; **Graphic Designer:** Nancy Rasmus; **Graphic Artist:** Francine Hamerski; **Cover Designer:** Keith Blomberg; **Photographer (cover):** Ned Dishman/Getty Images; **Photo Office Assistant:** Jason Allen; **Art Manager:** Kelly Hendren; **Associate Art Manager:** Alan L. Wilborn; **Illustrator:** Tim Brummett; **Printer:** Versa Press

Human Kinetics books are available at special discounts for bulk purchase. Special editions or book excerpts can also be created to specification. For details, contact the Special Sales Manager at Human Kinetics.

Printed in the United States of America

10 9 8 7 6 5 4 3 2 1

Human Kinetics
Web site: www.HumanKinetics.com

United States: Human Kinetics
P.O. Box 5076
Champaign, IL 61825-5076
800-747-4457
e-mail: humank@hkusa.com

Canada: Human Kinetics
475 Devonshire Road Unit 100
Windsor, ON N8Y 2L5
800-465-7301 (in Canada only)
e-mail: info@hkcanada.com

Europe: Human Kinetics
107 Bradford Road
Stanningley
Leeds LS28 6AT, United Kingdom
+44 (0) 113 255 5665
e-mail: hk@hkeurope.com

Australia: Human Kinetics
57A Price Avenue
Lower Mitcham, South Australia 5062
08 8372 0999
e-mail: info@hkaustralia.com

New Zealand: Human Kinetics
Division of Sports Distributors NZ Ltd.
P.O. Box 300 226 Albany
North Shore City
Auckland
0064 9 448 1207
e-mail: info@humankinetics.co.nz

Football's Eagle & Stack Defenses is dedicated to my wife, Lisa, in appreciation of the tremendous assistance she has provided and the many sacrifices she has made to allow me the opportunity to coach the great game of college football. Lisa's counsel, help in recruiting, work in planning and preparing player dinners, enthusiasm for each of our moves, and care of our children, Chelsea and Reid, are much appreciated and valued.

This book is also dedicated to my mother and father, Pete and Mary Vanderlinden, in honor of the sacrifices they made to open the world of athletics to me at an early age and to send me to Divine Child High School, where I was exposed to a world of higher expectations, a championship football program, and outstanding coaches and educators. The lifelong example of discipline, hard work, and integrity set by my father continues to inspire me.

Contents

Foreword vi ■ Acknowledgments vii ■
Development of a Defensive System viii ■ Key to Diagrams xii

PART I Foundational Elements

1 High-Pursuit Philosophy and Tactics   2

2 Gap Designations and Role Playing   11

PART II Eagle Defense

3 Eagle Alignments   22

4 Eagle Coverage Calls   31

5 Eagle Stunt Packages   41

6 Eagle Versus Common Running Plays   61

PART III Stack Defense

7 Stack Alignments   78

8 Stack Coverage Calls   89

9 Stack Stunt Packages   101

10 Stack Versus Common Running Plays   109

PART IV   **Eagle-Stack Combos**

11   **Eagle With Stack Modifications**   **120**

12   **Stack With Eagle Modifications**   **131**

PART V   **Reads, Stances, and Techniques**

13   **Defensive Linemen**   **142**

14   **Linebackers**   **161**

15   **Defensive Backs**   **181**

PART VI   **Situational Preparation
and Execution**

16   **Goal Line Defense**   **206**

17   **Game Planning**   **211**

18   **Player Organization and Critical Situations**   **223**

Index 230 ■ About the Author 235

Foreword

I first became aware of Ron Vanderlinden when he coordinated the defenses of the 1995 and 1996 Big Ten championship teams at Northwestern. His defenses reminded me of the many great Penn State defenses we have had through the years. They had tough, disciplined, fundamentally sound players who played with tremendous desire each and every play. That's why, in 2001, when we had a chance to add Ron to our staff, I was eager to do so.

Since then Ron has played a key role on our Nittany Lion defensive staff, which coaches a unit that is consistently one of the nation's best, particularly in the most important defensive category of all: scoring defense. Such success against today's high-speed, wide-open, spread-formation offenses requires a defense that doesn't simply sit back and react to the opposition's attack; it presents a variety of looks, applies pressure from different positions and angles, and pursues the ball with great speed and enthusiasm.

This book explains how to play that kind of defense and is one of the most comprehensive on the subject. It details three popular schemes—the Eagle, Stack, and a stunt package that complements the two. The thing I especially like about the book is that in addition to all the situation- and formation-specific adjustments, it covers key defensive fundamentals needed for success as a player and a team. The drills are good too because they tie directly to the techniques and tactics and also help develop the mind-set needed to be successful in each defense. In some games, you'll need a crucial stop as the opponent threatens to score; the material in the section on the goal line defensive package will help you make the stop and prevent that touchdown.

In *Football's Eagle & Stack Defenses,* Ron has provided the blueprint and coaching insights to help you learn, teach, practice, and execute the very best defensive packages in the modern game.

Joe Paterno

Acknowledgments

The material presented in *Football's Eagle & Stack Defenses* is a culmination of my 30 years of coaching, during which I have been blessed to work with and learn from many outstanding coaches. To give due credit to each coach who has had a positive influence on my football knowledge and philosophy would add another chapter to the book, but I would like to thank the head coaches I have coached under and learned from: Dwight Wallace of Ball State; Bo Schembechler of Michigan; Gary Barnett of Northwestern; and Joe Paterno of Penn State.

I would also like to give a special note of gratitude to Bill McCartney, who was my head football coach at Divine Child High School and a successful head coach at the University of Colorado, and to Frank Joranko and Steve Beckholt, the head coach and defensive coordinator at Albion College, where I played college football. Coaches McCartney, Joranko, and Beckholt each had a tremendous influence on my decision to enter the coaching profession, for all the right reasons.

As an assistant coach at Colorado, I worked with Bill McCartney, a great head coach and an outstanding defensive mind, and with defensive coordinators Lou Tepper and Mike Hankwitz. During my nine years at Colorado, I was exposed to the Eagle defensive structure and to many of the defensive concepts and strategies that I believe in and use today.

When Gary Barnett asked me to join his Northwestern staff in 1992 as the defensive coordinator, he provided me the opportunity to continue to grow professionally. It was at Northwestern, while I was teamed with Gerry Brown, Tim Kish, and Vince O'Kruch, that a system based on blending aspects of the Stack defense with the Eagle defense took shape. Our efforts, combined with those of a great group of players, contributed to the development of the nation's number one scoring defense in 1995.

At Penn State I not only have the honor of coaching under and learning from legendary coach Joe Paterno but also the privilege of working with outstanding coaches: coordinator and corners coach Tom Bradley, defensive line coach Larry Johnson, and safeties coach Brian Norwood. As a result of our combined efforts and those of our players; our defense has ranked very high nationally in almost every defensive category over the past few years, including the most important category, scoring defense.

I would like to thank the many student-athletes I have had the pleasure of working with. The best part of every workday is the player meeting at 2:45 and the practice that follows. Thank you all for the countless wonderful moments and the many lessons I have learned from you.

Finally, I would like to extend my thanks to Ted Miller and the staff at Human Kinetics for bringing this project to life. Special thanks to Heather Healy and Carla Zych for their expertise and unfailingly positive attitudes.

Development of a Defensive System

To be successful on defense play after play and game after game, defenders must play with tremendous passion and resolve to not allow their opponent into the end zone. All 11 defenders must be aware of their assignment and responsibilities within the defense and must carry them out with determination. The front seven defenders must play with a low pad level, with their shoulders and feet square, and with great technique and awareness. The secondary defenders must keep the ball inside and in front to prevent big plays. Each defender must be an effective and sure tackler.

I strongly believe that certain principles must be followed in order to play successful defense on a consistent basis. Throughout my years in coaching, these principles have not changed. Since 1985, I have coached at four universities but have stayed with the same basic defensive system. The terminology and adjustments have varied from school to school and occasionally from season to season, but the basic structure, philosophy, and coaching points have remained constant.

Developing the Eagle and Stack

I was first introduced to the Eagle defensive system in 1983 while working as an assistant coach at the University of Colorado. That same year Lou Tepper joined the Colorado coaching staff as the defensive coordinator. Lou had previously coached at Virginia Tech under head coach Bill Dooley. Virginia Tech had been particularly strong in stopping the run.

Colorado was a member of the former Big Eight Conference. To be successful in the Big Eight during the 1980s, a team had to be able to defend the power running attack of Nebraska and the speed and finesse of Oklahoma's wishbone offense. Oklahoma State had also built a tradition of outstanding running backs that included Thurman Thomas and Barry Sanders. Dealing with these offenses was a daunting task for any defense.

From 1985 to 1991, our Colorado defense consistently ranked in the top 20 in most statistical categories. Most important, in scoring defense, we finished in the top 20 nationally six times during those years. We were able to achieve seven consecutive winning seasons, play in six bowl games, and win two straight Big Eight championships (and tie for a third). We also shared the 1990 national championship. The Colorado offense deserves a great deal of credit for our defensive success. They ran the ball with authority, shortened the game, and kept the ball away from our opponents.

In 1992, Gary Barnett was hired as the head football coach at Northwestern University. Gary had previously been the offensive coordinator at Colorado. Gary asked me to join him at Northwestern as the defensive coordinator. Northwestern had endured 20 consecutive losing seasons. Only twice in those 20 seasons did North-western win at least four games in a season. Defensively, the Wildcats had given up an average of 33 points per game the previous 5 seasons before our staff's arrival at Northwestern.

I installed the Eagle defensive package at Northwestern. My second season at Northwestern, we improved dramatically in defending the run. However, in the Big Ten Conference, more teams were using spread formations on offense to throw the football. The Eagle defense is built to stop the run and includes having a single safety deep. Wanting to play some two-deep coverage to help us defend the pass, I blended in the use of the Stack defensive front and coverage package. I used the Stack defense primarily in neutral and passing situations.

Out of a need to create pressure on the quarterback and reduce the amount of man coverage we played in pressure situations, I first developed and started using zone blitz concepts at Northwestern. Our corners and safeties didn't always match up well with opposing receivers, and our four-man pass rush was good but not great. Zone stunts allowed us to bring five defenders—and at times, six defenders—on the pass rush and drop a defensive lineman into coverage. We were also able to use both the Eagle and Stack defenses to give us the best possible setup for using our zone pressure package.

In 1995, our fourth season at Northwestern, we went undefeated in the Big Ten Conference and earned the right to represent the conference in the Rose Bowl. It was Northwestern's first bowl appearance in 46 years. Equally impressive, our Northwestern defense led the nation in scoring defense. Again, the Northwestern offense deserves a great deal of credit. They ran the ball well and rarely turned the ball over to the opponent in bad field position. In 1996, we repeated and shared the Big Ten championship.

In 2001, I joined the Penn State University coaching staff as the linebacker coach. Our defensive structure from 2001 to 2003 was the Eagle defense, and we added features of the Stack defense. In 2004, we changed our base defense to the Stack 4-4-3. We now add features of the Eagle defensive structure to create a combination defense. From 2004 through 2006, we finished 11th, 10th, and 9th nationally in scoring defense.

Lessons in Defense

Early in my career, I had the good fortune of coaching under and learning from several outstanding defensive-minded coaches. I have learned many defensive lessons over the last 30 seasons. One of the first lessons I learned back in 1983 is still imprinted on my brain and still applied in my coaching—that lesson involved the importance of practicing the fundamentals. I was coaching the defensive line at the University of Colorado. We had gone through 20 spring practices and two weeks of preseason football camp in August in preparation for the season. After warm-ups each day, I devoted a 10-minute block of time to drills that emphasized the fundamentals of defensive line play.

The first drill simulated attacking an offensive lineman, fitting in the offensive lineman's body, gaining separation from the offensive lineman, and disengaging in the direction of the ballcarrier. The players started on their hands and knees in a six-point stance. On my command, each defensive lineman delivered a blow with his hands into the breastplate and under the armpits of a simulated offensive lineman (a sled). After four reps apiece, the players would then get into a three-point stance. On my movement, they would step with their back foot, then their front foot, attacking the sled and leading with their hands. The emphasis was on the defensive lineman stepping with six- to eight-inch steps and getting both feet on the ground before making contact with the sled. I refer to this action as "winning the line of scrimmage." The defensive lineman should maintain a flat back and a perfect fit on the sled during and after contact. In this flat-back position, their body should be like a "human harpoon" that cannot be bent backward.

In the next drill, the defensive linemen paired up. One player simulated an offensive lineman who had fired off the ball and made contact with the defensive lineman. The offensive lineman was now leaning on the defensive lineman. The defensive lineman would align his body in a "perfect fit" position with his hands in the armpits of the offensive lineman (the defensive lineman must make sure to keep his hands inside the offensive lineman's hands). On my "lock out" command, the defensive lineman gained separation from the offensive lineman. The defensive lineman would violently thrust his arms out while maintaining a low pad level and a wide base with his feet. On my "separate" command, the defensive lineman shed the blocker and shuffled laterally in position to make a play on the ballcarrier.

In the middle of August, I could see improvement in these fundamentals during the live contact drills and scrimmages with the offense. I felt my players had mastered the fundamentals in this area, so I cut the 10-minute drill sequence from our practices. Two weeks later, after studying the game tape from our opening game, I was disappointed to see that my players often did not have inside hand position on the offensive lineman. Furthermore, my players were often not in good position to separate and shed the offensive lineman while in pursuit of the football. Consequently, they did not get off blocks as well as they should have and did not make as many plays as they should have.

At that point, I realized the importance of practicing key fundamentals that players need to execute repeatedly in the course of every game. Your players' ability to execute fundamentally will determine to a large extent the success of your defense. You should be able to see the drills you do in practice on your game tape. If you can't, you need to change the drills.

When I joined the Northwestern staff as the defensive coordinator and linebacker coach, I quickly identified the skills needed to be successful at the linebacker position, and I designed drills to teach those skills. I still use many of these drills today. When I was on the coaching staff at Colorado, head coach Bill McCartney wanted his football teams to be great fundamentally. He felt that if the players at each position executed their role in the defense, it would be impossible for an offense to have success play after play. When game tape showed our team's performance starting to slip, Coach McCartney would make sure the subsequent practices provided adequate time for fundamental drills that would address the areas needing improvement. The results were not always immediate; however, within a couple of weeks, the players would improve at each position and as a team.

Another lesson I've learned is the benefit of playing zone coverage in the secondary. Zone coverage gives defensive backs depth and vision on the ball, which puts them in position to front the ball up when it penetrates the line of scrimmage. Explosion plays—that is, runs and passes greater than 15 yards—win and lose games. Allow me to illustrate this point. In 2005, Penn State University won both the Big Ten championship and the Orange Bowl, and our defense finished 10th in the nation in scoring defense. During that year, the Penn State defense only gave up nine runs over 15 yards in a total of 12 games.

Several factors are essential to minimizing explosion plays. First, a defensive system must allow depth and vision in the secondary so that players can keep the ball inside and in front of them. Second, the defensive team must be great at tackling. Third, every player must know where his area of responsibility is within the framework of the defense. Most explosion plays in the running game are a result of one of two things: missed tackles at or near the line of scrimmage or a loss of containment that allows the ball to get outside the defense and on the perimeter.

Bill McCartney used to continually say, "Defenders must know where their help is." Each player should be in perfect position on every play of every practice. Practice does not make perfect. *Perfect* practice makes perfect performance. Fourth, successful defenses play with passion and a tremendous resolve to stop their opponent. They are tough minded and will play with great effort all the time. Pursuit becomes their trademark. As Winston Churchill said, "Whatever it takes, as long as it takes." Pursuit and the proper course of pursuit should be taught on every play of practice.

Finally, I often emphasize that there is a start and a finish to every play, with six to eight seconds in between. The defensive huddle, presnap information, each player's stance, the ability to execute fundamentally, and the start of the play are all vitally important. However, it is the finish of the play—when a defender meets and puts the ballcarrier on the ground or makes a play in the passing game—that is critical to the success of the defense. A defender must incorporate all of the coaching points mentioned; in addition, as he meets the ballcarrier, the defender should be in a balanced, square position, with his feet shoulder-width apart, his knees bent, and his head up. I cannot emphasize this enough.

Key to Diagrams

   x Defensive player
   ○ Offensive player
   ⊗ Center
   ◐ Side of block
   ⊗ Inside leg of noseguard aligned on outside leg of center
   ● Ballcarrier
   ⊕ Pulling lineman
 → Run
 ⊣ Offensive player blocking in a running play or defender walling out a receiver in pass coverage
 →• Run and stop
 ⌇⌇ Presnap motion
--→ Alternate route, Pass
--- Indicates man-to-man coverage responsibility
ǁor= Handoff or fake handoff
   △ Cone
   ▮ Pop-up bags

Position and personnel abbreviations
 B Linebacker
 C Corner
DE Defensive end
 E Eagle linebacker
FS Free safety
 N Noseguard
 T Defensive tackle
 R Rush end
 S Sam linebacker
SS Strong safety
BC Ballcarrier

PART I

Foundational Elements

CHAPTER 1

High-Pursuit Philosophy and Tactics

Pursuit involves an intense, all-out effort that is driven by an insatiable desire to get to the football and to put the ballcarrier on the ground. Pursuit is the essence of a good defensive football team. Visualize 11 defensive players disengaging from blocks and sprinting relentlessly to the ballcarrier on every play. That type of effort makes it very difficult for an offense to sustain a successful running attack. It also makes it difficult for an offense to break a big play. This is demoralizing to the offense.

Pursuit is not, however, a natural reaction for most football players. On plays where the ballcarrier is not going directly at them, many defensive players will first look to see if they are needed. They will then make a quick decision on whether to join in the pursuit of the play. If they decide that they are not needed, many players will simply jog in the direction of the play. Even when a defensive player makes the decision that he is needed, unbridled pursuit of the ballcarrier is often the exception rather than the rule. Therefore, you need to emphasize pursuit as a key to your defensive philosophy.

At the various universities where I have coached, one of our defensive goals for each game has been to not allow a run over 15 yards. The great defensive teams I have been a part of would not allow more than 15 runs greater than 15 yards over the course of an 11-game season. Consistent success on defense cannot occur without great team pursuit. Our 2004 Penn State defense ended the season ranked 10th in the nation in scoring defense. That defense allowed only 11 runs over 15 yards throughout the 11-game season. Our 2005 Penn State defense allowed only 9 runs over 15 yards during the course of a 12-game season. That team finished 10th nationally in scoring defense.

Principles of Pursuit

Another positive by-product of emphasizing the relentless pursuit of the football is the mental effect it will have on your defensive team. Your defensive players will take great pride in their ability to play hard on every play. This will also increase their confidence. At Northwestern University in 1995, we often used the expression "If we chase them long enough and hard enough, we will catch them and stop them." When a defense focuses on pursuit, the defensive players develop a mind-set that includes the following qualities:

1. **Accountability.** Your players will feel accountable to each other. All members of the defensive team will develop tremendous pride in the great effort that they give on every play. No player will want to be the weak link in the chain of pursuit.

2. **Respect.** Intense effort will bring about a sense of respect and accomplishment from within. This will create a bond between your players that is built on mutual respect, and these feelings will permeate through your defensive unit.

3. **Aggressive attitude.** There is no question that intense effort leads to an aggressive style of play. Your players will take tremendous pride in swarming to the football. This will have an intimidating effect on the ballcarrier. Nothing is more demoralizing to a ballcarrier than having to unpile from under five defenders after every play, with the other six defenders forming a wall around him.

4. **Confidence.** The blend of accountability, respect, and aggressive play will lead to a strong synergy within the defense. The combination of these qualities will lead to success. With success comes confidence.

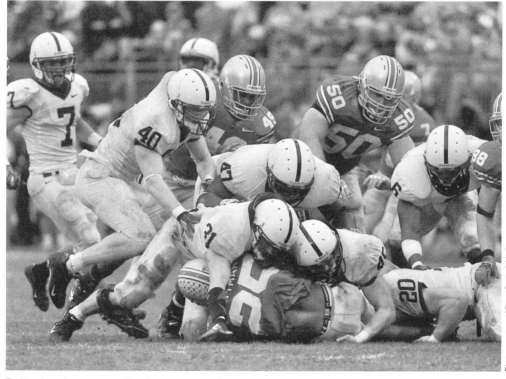

Photo courtesy of Penn State Athletics

Defensive players must develop an aggressive attitude and take pride in swarming to the football and putting the ballcarrier on the ground.

On the surface, unbridled pursuit to the football seems like a simple concept. However, pursuing is not simply running to the ball. If this were the case, speed and effort would be the only requirements for proficiency at this task. As we delve into the methods and skills involved in successful pursuit, you will discover that pursuit also requires discipline and the development of proper technique, including the technique to use when the defender regains leverage on the ballcarrier at the end of a pursuit course.

Four types of pursuit are employed by defenders:

1. Shuffle. This technique, often used by linebackers, is a controlled movement parallel to the line of scrimmage (this movement may initially feel quite unnatural). The shuffle technique begins with an 8- to 12-inch reach step with the foot in the direction of the defender's initial movement. The initial step should be low to the ground and parallel to the line of scrimmage. The other foot should slide a similar distance, also low to the ground and parallel to the line of scrimmage.

The shuffle technique allows the linebacker to easily change direction as he reacts to the ballcarrier. This technique is used when a defender has leverage on the ballcarrier, and it can be used from tackle to tackle when the ball is in the *box* (the area between the split tackle and the tight end). The following coaching points should be stressed when teaching the shuffle:

- **Stay square.** Defenders should always work to keep their shoulders square to the line of scrimmage. The football often changes direction during the course of a play, either by plan or by the broken or elusive running of an offensive back. Defenders must be in position to quickly change direction. Therefore, defenders should always keep their shoulders parallel to the line of scrimmage while moving in their shuffle.

- **Regain the shuffle.** When a defender is in his shuffle, he can react quickly with either foot. A common error for all defensive personnel is to overrun the football. When a pursuing defender gains leverage on the ballcarrier (gets within four yards of the ballcarrier), the defender should return to using the shuffle technique. This will help prevent the defender from crossing his feet over at the most critical moments—just before contact with the ballcarrier. Many missed tackles can be attributed to a defender crossing over as he meets the ballcarrier, allowing the ballcarrier to cut back across the face of the defender. Regaining the shuffle is a key in preventing overpursuit.

2. Alley. Alley pursuit begins whenever the shuffle does not allow the defender to keep pace with the ballcarrier as he gains speed. Now, the defender must turn his hips and run inside out to the ball. He must work his arms hard to keep his shoulders as square as possible. He should also maintain a low pad level. When the defender regains his leverage on the ballcarrier, he should regain his shuffle and fit inside out on the ballcarrier. This principle cannot be overstated.

3. Press. This term is used to describe a technique used by a linebacker when he has an opening to the ball. In this situation, the linebacker should press the ball, attacking the line of scrimmage in an attempt to make a minus-yardage play. This type of penetration from a linebacker is essential for creating defensive plays that have a positive impact.

4. Angle of pursuit. If the ballcarrier quickly outflanks the interior defenders and crosses the line of scrimmage, the defenders need to adjust their course to put each defender in position to intercept the ballcarrier. As an individual defender regains leverage on the ballcarrier, the defender should regain his shuffle and expect the ballcarrier to attempt to cut back.

Each defender has a responsibility within the defense called. For example, in a defense employing a three-deep coverage, the strong safety to the field (wide side) and the outside linebacker to the boundary (short side) are the contain players responsible for turning the ball back inside. The free safety who occupies the deep one third in pass defense is generally an alley defender. His run responsibility is to proceed under control to a head-up position on the football. The defensive line and linebackers provide inside-out pursuit on the football. Their responsibility is to push the ball deep and wide to the support players. They always maintain an inside-out relationship on the football until contact is made, never wanting to allow the ballcarrier to cut back inside of their position.

This is where the two principles stressed in teaching the shuffle come into play. As defenders approach the ballcarrier, they must *fit* on the ballcarrier with regard to their area of responsibility—in other words, they must approach the ballcarrier at an angle that allows them to fulfill their responsibility within the defense. The interior defenders should regain their shuffle, stay square, and fit inside out on the ballcarrier, anticipating that the ballcarrier will attempt to cut back. Alley defenders should regain their shuffle and fit on the ballcarrier head up. The contain or support players should regain their shuffle and ensure that the ballcarrier does not get outside of their position.

Regaining the shuffle puts each defender in the best possible position to make an effective tackle and drive the ballcarrier backward. Any other body position will decrease the defender's opportunity to make an effective tackle and will lead to missed tackles. The proper defensive fits should be practiced and reinforced on each play of each practice. They should also be pointed out on each play when going over game tape. In the game of football, every play has a start and a finish. The finish is critical to the success of a team. Defensively, the finish is putting the ball on the ground. To accomplish that goal, each defensive player must fit perfectly in regard to where his responsibility is within the defense.

Pursuit Drills

When big plays occur, a defensive coach should first examine whether or not he has effectively drilled the players on the various defensive schemes to prevent the big plays. Coaches are often quick to say that they have covered the play and that their defensive players should have prevented it. However, the proof of how well we have coached our players is in their performance on the field.

Teaching unbridled effort, proper courses to the ball, and a balanced tackling position in practice will carry over to your team's performance on the game field. Bill McCartney, the successful former head coach at the University of Colorado, used to constantly say, "You achieve what you emphasize." When you emphasize the importance of unbridled effort on every play, your defense will become more successful.

You can incorporate a number of effective pursuit drills into your practices to ensure that your defense will develop the skills and commitment to chase down the ball on every play. Pursuit drills can be done in three- to five-minute segments once a day during preseason practice and once or twice a week during the season. An efficient pursuit drill should only take three to five minutes to run. This type of drill can also replace postpractice conditioning.

In addition to using the pursuit drills that follow, consider designating one of the defensive coaches as the "pursuit coach" for certain segments of the team practice. For example, this could be done during the segment where your defense is working against a scout team replicating the opponent's offense. The designated pursuit coach blows the first whistle when the ballcarrier is secured. A second whistle is blown only after all 11 defensive players have fit perfectly around the football in regard to their area of responsibility. As in all drills and each play from scrimmage, every defensive player should arrive at the football in a balanced stance with a low pad level.

Angle Pursuit Drill

The pursuit drill that has the most direct application to gamelike situations is the angle pursuit drill (see figure 1.1). This drill involves a full defensive unit aligning on the ball. Cones are set up on the field at the outside edge of the numbers. The cones start at the line of scrimmage, and a cone is placed every 5 yards for a distance of 40 yards. Cones are not necessary to run the drill, but they do make the drill more effective because they keep the ballcarrier from being disrupted. A defensive coach has the football in front of the noseguard, and a ballcarrier aligns 5 yards deep in the backfield and approximately 5 yards inside of the cones. We often use our kickers and punters as ballcarriers.

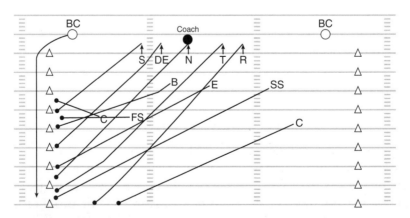

Figure 1.1 Angle pursuit drill.

The defensive coach calls a defense, and the defensive front aligns in that defense. Each member of the defensive team gets in his football stance. The coach calls out an offensive cadence and takes the ball off the ground to approximate the snap of the football. The coach then turns to either his right or his left. At that point, the entire defense does a down-up and sprints in the direction the coach has opened to. Using seat rolls in the direction the coach opens to can be a nice change from a down-up.

As the coach declares either a right or left direction, the ballcarrier starts on a path outside of the cones at approximately three-quarter speed. Each defender sprints at an angle to intercept the ballcarrier. As a defender approaches the ballcarrier, the defender should settle his hips in position to intercept the ballcarrier. At this position, the defender regains his shuffle and simulates not allowing the ballcarrier to cut back across the defender's position.

Defenders should not go beyond the plane of the cones because doing so will disrupt the ballcarrier's course. This can prevent the other defenders from learning to take the correct course to intercept the ballcarrier while pursuing with all-out intensity. During this drill, if a player takes an improper course to intercept the ball-carrier or does not give great effort, all 11 players should hustle back to the huddle, and the drill should be repeated.

The first few times you use this drill, you will likely see defensive players who do not take the proper course to intercept the ballcarrier. I constantly reinforce to our players that this drill is not a conditioning drill, nor is it punishment. The drill is simply a way to work toward our goal as a defensive football team—to put the ball on the ground. I also emphasize to our players that if their course of pursuit doesn't intercept the ballcarrier, it is wasted effort.

Another coaching point is to make sure that the chase contain player on the back side of your defense shuffles flat down the line of scrimmage until he has cleared the possibility of a bootleg or a reverse (these plays are his responsibility). The chase contain player should then proceed on a course downfield to intercept the ballcarrier. This player has to be convinced that the play-side corner will turn the ball back inside to him. That intersection usually occurs 35 to 45 yards downfield. As you do this drill repeatedly throughout the season, your chase contain player will develop good habits on the back side of a perimeter play. As a result, this player will undoubtedly make some key pursuit plays for your defense during games.

To reinforce all-out effort during pursuit to the football, you can use a variation of this drill by placing a coach 25 yards downfield on each sideline. A coach remains over the football, gives the cadence, and simulates the ball being hiked. As the ball is hiked, the players do a down-up, then sprint to the coach. When the players approach the coach, they should come to a balanced position with their feet pumping until the coach releases the group with a "ready break" command (or any type of break or buzz word that reinforces your defensive philosophy).

Interception Pursuit Drill

The interception pursuit drill is designed to incorporate the principles of pursuit into the passing game (see figure 1.2). The coach aligns in the middle of the formation with a football. The coach simulates taking a snap from center, drops back seven yards, and sets up as a quarterback ready to throw the football. As the ball is snapped, the four defensive linemen do a down-up out of their stance and then accelerate to the quarterback. They stop just short of the quarterback and assume a balanced position.

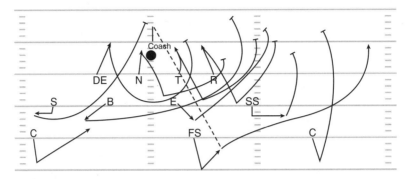

Figure 1.2   Interception pursuit drill.

The linebackers and defensive backs execute their pass drops. The linebackers should drive for depth with their head on a swivel (being able to see both the quarterback and a potential receiver in their pass coverage zone). As the quarterback completes his drop, the linebackers should settle their hips and square up. This puts them in a position to drive on the football as the quarterback turns his shoulders and releases the football. The defensive backs stay in their backpedal until the ball is thrown.

The coach who is acting as the quarterback turns his shoulders and throws the ball to 1 of the 7 defenders dropping into coverage (the coach should throw the ball to the area above the defender's head and shoulders). When the ball leaves the quarterback's hands, all 11 defenders must break full speed to the ball. All 11 defensive players should yell out "pass" as the quarterback takes his drop. They should yell out "ball, ball, ball" as the ball leaves the quarterback's hands. Defenders should attack the ball while moving forward when possible. The defender should catch the ball in his hands when the ball is at its highest point. As the interception occurs, the defender intercepting the ball should communicate and inform teammates that a defender has intercepted the ball. *Oskie, bingo,* and *fire* are the most common terms used to inform teammates that an interception has occurred. After the interception, all defenders should turn and escort the ballcarrier into the end zone.

A variation of this drill is to have three or four coaches simulate offensive players covering the interception; these coaches stand between the line of scrimmage and the goal line, five to eight yards downfield. The defenders escorting the ballcarrier should "fit up" on the coaches and become blockers.

Coaching points such as "Remember, never block below the waist, and never block behind the football" should be emphasized during this drill. You should also teach the defender who intercepts the football to sprint to the nearest sideline as he heads toward the goal line. Taking the interception to the nearest sideline allows the blockers to anticipate where the defender with the ball is headed. It also gives the defender the best opportunity to avoid and outrun most of the opposing team. Furthermore, many defensive players are not accustomed to carrying a football and can be more easily stripped of the football. However, when the player advances the ball down the sideline, the ball will often be knocked out of bounds if it does become dislodged, allowing the defense to maintain possession on the turnover.

The final coaching point in this drill is to make sure the defensive players escorting the ballcarrier into the end zone celebrate a great defensive play. When our staff arrived at Northwestern University in 1992, the Wildcats football program had endured several continuous years of losing. One of the many lessons that our football team needed to learn was to expect good things to happen. We wanted to teach our players to play with emotion and enthusiasm—and to celebrate the great plays.

Screen Pursuit Drill

The purpose of the screen pursuit drill is to teach defenders the importance of their fit in their area of responsibility within the defense called. For this drill, three pop-up bags (or any bags that will stay upright) are placed five yards downfield on both sides of the field (see figure 1.3). Each bag simulates an offensive lineman who has released to block on a screen pass. On each side of the field, a ballcarrier stands with a football two yards behind the middle bag. The ballcarriers, who will act as receivers of a screen pass, begin with a ball in hand to ensure that they don't drop a pass or have it batted down, which would disrupt the drill.

The coach aligns in the middle of the formation with a football. He simulates the ball being snapped and a quarterback's pass drop to a depth of seven yards. He then continues to drift backward, simulating a quarterback executing a screen pass. The defensive linemen do their down-up and then sprint to the quarterback. When the defense recognizes that the quarterback is starting to drift backward, taking an abnormally deep drop, they should be aware that a screen pass is being set up by the offense. The defensive linemen should turn and find the eligible receiver in the backfield preparing to catch the screen pass. The defensive lineman closest to the quarterback could continue his pursuit of the quarterback.

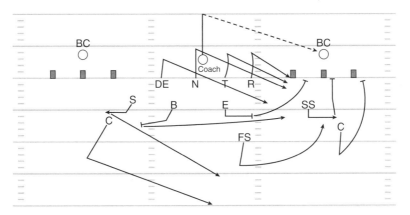

Figure 1.3 Screen pursuit drill.

As the quarterback starts to drift three or four steps beyond his normal seven-yard drop, the seven defenders taking their pass drops should react to defend the screen pass. All defenders should be yelling "screen, screen." An important coaching point is to have the support player in the defense take on the bag farthest to the outside with his inside arm, keeping the ball to his inside and maintaining outside leverage on the ballcarrier. As with all defenders, this player should fit square and come to a balanced position as he closes on the ball. The pass defender responsible for the curl to the side of the screen pass should accelerate and fit square on the middle bag, holding the middle to outside edge of the bag. These two fits are critical in stopping the screen play. The other defenders pursuing from the inside should fit inside out on the football. The inside-out players should each keep the ball on their outside arm as they pursue and fit on the ballcarrier. They must not allow the ballcarrier to cut back across the defense.

When you run this pursuit drill, be sure to sometimes change your defensive call, which changes the player responsible for containment. For example, in a three-deep coverage, the strong safety or outside linebacker would contain, and the inside line-backer or free safety would be the curl defender. In a two-deep coverage, the corner would contain, and the outside linebacker would be the curl defender, fitting on the middle bag. Through the course of two-a-day practices, and periodically throughout the season, you should call your variation defenses to change who the contain and curl players are.

Competitive Pursuit Drill

The competitive pursuit drill (figure 1.4) teaches defensive players to give unbridled effort. This drill should only be used a few times during the course of a season. Start with five players in four-point stance at midfield. The coach faces the players on a knee. The players perform grass drills, varying from bear crawls to seat rolls, based on the coach's instructions. Four pop-up bags are placed about 20 to 30 yards downfield, five yards apart from each other on the numbers.

After giving three or four commands, the coach points in the direction of the bags, and the players immediately convert from the grass drill to a pursuit course. The players should lay out and tackle the pop-up bag when they reach it. Since there are five defenders and only four bags, the defender who is last to a bag has

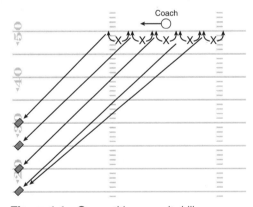

Figure 1.4 Competitive pursuit drill.

to hustle back in line and repeat the drill. Anything less than full speed brings about negative consequences for the player who comes up short. This drill is extremely competitive and will get the players' attention. The drill emphasizes the importance of giving great effort on every play.

CHAPTER 2

Gap Designations and Role Playing

Each defensive system needs organization and a common defensive language so coaches can communicate with each other and with the players when describing the various defensive alignments, techniques, and gap responsibilities. This chapter presents the identification of the offensive line gaps and how they correspond to the front seven defensive players' alignments and gap responsibilities. The chapter then covers the requirements and responsibilities of each of the 11 defensive positions as well as the physical characteristics needed to excel at each. Appropriately assigning your personnel to the various defensive positions is critical to individual player and team success.

Offensive Line Gap Designations

My system of gap identification differs from most programs. Most coaches describe the center-guard gap as the A gap, the guard-tackle gap as the B gap, and the tackle-tight end gap as the C gap. I think it is more logical to number the gaps. The center-guard gap is the 1 gap. The guard-tackle gap is the 3 gap. The tackle-tight end gap is the 5 gap. The area outside the tight end is the 7 gap and is also referred to as *the alley*.

In most cases, the numbered gaps correspond with a player's alignment, technique, and gap responsibility. The noseguard is aligned in a 1 alignment, and he is described as a 1 technique. He is responsible for the 1 gap. The defensive tackle is aligned in a 3 alignment, and he is described as a 3 technique. He is responsible for the 3 gap. The defensive end is aligned in a 5 alignment, and he is responsible for the 5 gap.

The exceptions are the 0, 2, and 4 techniques. The 0 alignment is head up on the center, and depending on the defensive call, a defender in this alignment could be responsible for either the front-side or back-side 1 gap. The 2 alignment is on the inside shoulder of the offensive guard, and a defender in this alignment is responsible for the 1 gap. A 4 eye alignment is on the inside shade of the offensive tackle, and a defender in this alignment is responsible for the 3 gap. In the Eagle defense, I have rarely used a 4 eye alignment.

Numbering the gaps is also helpful in describing the linebackers' gap responsibilities. For example, I will refer to the inside linebacker in our base Eagle defense as a 32 technique. The first number describes this player's gap responsibility when the backfield flow is to him. The second number describes his gap responsibility when the backfield flow is away from him. When the inside linebacker is a 32 technique, he knows that there is not a 2 gap on the other side of the center. Therefore, the number 2 tells the linebacker that he does not have a gap that he is responsible for on the other side of the center. He can stay on the back hip of the ballcarrier and be in position to play the cutback.

Linebackers must be aware of the gap responsibilities for each member of the defensive front seven. Numbering the gaps helps all of the front seven defenders learn how each defender's alignment and technique will directly correspond to his gap responsibility. When using stunts—either up front, with the linebackers, or both—attaching a number to each gap makes it easier for the defenders to learn each stunt and to learn where each defender fits.

Another example of numbering a linebacker's gap responsibilities is demonstrated when a stunt is called that requires the defensive front to slant toward the tight end. The inside linebacker's gap responsibility would be described as a 50 (see figure 2.1). This linebacker would be responsible for the 5 gap when the backfield flow is at him. When the backfield flow starts away from his side of the ball, the inside linebacker is responsible for the

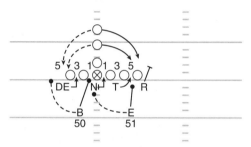

Figure 2.1 Inside linebacker's 50 gap responsibility.

0 gap. The 0 gap is the near 1 gap. Referring to the near 1 gap as the 0 gap provides a way to differentiate between the 1 gap on his side of the ball and the 1 gap on the other side of the ball.

Role Playing Your Defensive Personnel

The concept of "role playing" your personnel refers to matching the individual players in your program with the specific positions in the Eagle defense. Many of the same principles also apply when selecting personnel to play the various positions in the Stack defense. Role playing involves identifying individual players with the unique physical characteristics needed to excel at each defensive position. Few teams are blessed to have several players who are perfectly suited physically to play the same position. For example, few teams have two linebackers who are 6 feet 2 inches tall, weigh 225 to 230 pounds (with 7 percent body fat), can run the 40-yard dash in 4.6 seconds, have the ability to change direction quickly, and can vertical jump over 30 inches. A team may have one linebacker with some of these traits. The team's second linebacker, who might actually be the most productive and instinctive player, may be 5-10 and weigh 200 pounds. The Eagle defensive structure is perfect for these two players—with one playing the inside linebacker position and one playing the eagle linebacker position. In this defense, your two best linebackers may differ from each other in size, speed, and the ability to stun and separate from a blocker.

The **inside linebacker** is in a 3 alignment, which is on the outside edge of the offensive guard. The inside linebacker has to be a tough, physical player. He is responsible for the 3 gap on plays to his side of the ball. To control the 3 gap, this linebacker will frequently have to take on and defeat an offensive guard. The inside linebacker will also see many fullback lead plays run at him.

The **eagle linebacker,** on the other hand, can be a smaller, active player with a nose for the football. The eagle linebacker sits in the "nest" and is protected by the noseguard and the defensive tackle, whose job includes keeping the offensive guard off of the eagle linebacker. Because the eagle linebacker is unblocked much of the time, he should be a quick, active player who can get to the football.

When I coordinated the Northwestern University defense in the mid-1990s, I had two very productive linebackers who were different in their physical characteristics. Both players excelled in their roles within the Eagle defense but would have been challenged to play the other's position. My inside linebacker was Pat Fitzgerald. Pat was 6-3 and weighed 235 pounds. He ran the 40-yard dash in 4.8 seconds. However, Pat was the definition of tough, and he was very disciplined. He had great instincts for finding the football. Pat was well equipped to play over and take on offensive guards, a task required at the inside linebacker position. Pat Fitzgerald's size, physical stature, and other qualities made him the prototype inside linebacker. Pat went on to be first-team All-American, All-Big Ten, and the college football player of the year for two consecutive years. The eagle linebacker was Danny Sutter. At 6-2 and 210 pounds, Danny didn't have the physical stature to take on guards play after play. However, he was a quick and active player with a nose for the ball—just the type of player needed at the eagle linebacker position.

Paul Posluszny was an All-American at Penn State and the college defensive football player of the year in 2005 and 2006. When Paul was a freshman weighing only 215 pounds, he started at the eagle

Two-time winner of the Bednarik and Nagurski Awards, Pat Fitzgerald had the toughness and instincts needed to be an outstanding inside linebacker.

Photo courtesy of Northwestern University Athletics

linebacker position. As a true freshman, Paul was far from the complete player he would develop into, but he was fast and aggressive and had great instincts to find the football. Paul eventually grew, and by his senior season, he had developed into an inside linebacker.

The **Sam linebacker,** when aligned to a tight end, positions on the line of scrimmage with his inside foot aligned with the outside foot of the tight end. From this position, he must be able to defeat a reach block. He must also be physical enough to take on a kick-out block from a fullback or a pulling guard. The Sam's pass responsibility is the curl zone to the flat zone. The Sam does not need to diagnose blocking schemes and play as quickly as the eagle and inside linebackers. His potential blockers and reads are straightforward, and the ball takes longer to reach the Sam. He does have to be a smart player and be able to adjust to various formations. The Sam linebacker must also be able to play in a walk position, approximately four yards off the line of scrimmage and four yards outside of the defensive end. The Sam linebacker should have better-than-average coverage skills.

To me, the Sam is the easiest of the three linebacker positions to play because the reads, the potential blockers, and the area of responsibility are clearly defined. In addition, it takes the ball longer to get to the Sam linebacker. With that said, the ability to play on a tight end and to walk off the line of scrimmage when aligned to a split end surface (when there is an offensive guard and tackle but no tight end) requires a unique player.

Players of various body types excel at the Sam linebacker position. This player is often an oversized strong safety who is very tough but may be a little lacking in the hips and in speed to play at the strong safety position; this type of player is better than most linebackers in coverage. To play the Sam linebacker position, a player must be able to play over and defeat a tight end on the line of scrimmage. I have found that size is not the most important factor in defeating a tight end on the line of scrimmage. Some players have a natural hip roll, punch, and physical toughness to go with their quickness advantage, allowing them to hold up quite well against most tight ends.

Tim Scharf and Derrick Wake both played and excelled at the Sam linebacker position. Tim was on the Northwestern Big Ten championship teams in 1995 and 1996, and Derrick was on our 2002 Penn State team, which finished 9-3. Both of these players differed from the oversized strong safety type. Both players were about 6-2 or 6-3 and weighed 235 to 240 pounds. Derrick and Tim had the size to play the inside linebacker position. Both players also possessed the speed and athletic ability to play any of the three linebacker positions. Because of their size, we tried both players at the inside linebacker position. However, neither player felt comfortable inside with blockers coming at him from every angle. When moved outside to the Sam linebacker position, they both turned in several outstanding performances.

The **rush end** is another position that can be played effectively by players with various body types. The rush end can play in a two- or three-point stance, depending on which stance is most comfortable for the player. I have used undersized but active defensive linemen and oversized linebackers with good hip rotation and shock at this position. The rush end must be able to defeat a tight end from a head-up, an inside, or an outside shade alignment. This defender must be physical enough to maintain the line of scrimmage, but he must also be athletic enough to play cat and mouse with the quarterback on an option play. The rush end needs to be a good edge pass rusher. On occasion, he will also be involved in pass coverage, primarily dropping into the boundary flat when a zone stunt is called.

Before the start of the 2006 season at Penn State, we moved our starting inside linebacker, Tim Shaw (who is 6-2 and weighs 238 pounds), to the rush end position because we needed to replace Tamba Hali at the position. Tamba (who was 6-1 and 270 pounds) was an All-American the previous season and a first-round draft pick. Moving Tim to the rush

Photo courtesy of Penn State Athletics

Tim Shaw, who sacrificed by moving from linebacker to rush end to make our defense stronger overall, went on to play linebacker in the NFL.

end position also allowed us to get our best 11 defenders on the field. Tim played in a two-point stance and had an outstanding season, leading our team in quarterback sacks.

The **noseguard** is often a short, quick, and tough player. Most teams have this type of player in their system. A short, undersized player can be effective at this position because the noseguard has the advantage of lining up just inches from the football. In this alignment, the noseguard is tilted slightly in toward the center. Versus a scoop block, the noseguard must squeeze the center and keep him from releasing up to the inside linebacker. The noseguard must also be able to defeat the center on a reach block.

My first All-Big Eight noseguard at the University of Colorado was Kyle Rappold. Kyle was 5 feet 11 inches tall and weighed 245 pounds. Kyle was quick with his first step. He was tough and played with great leverage. He became very proficient at squeezing the center versus a scoop block, then penetrating into the backfield. Kyle was also great at beating a reach block and penetrating into the backfield. As a result of his success, Kyle became known as the "Trash Compacter." A section of the Colorado fans even started coming to games wearing garbage bags. Kyle once referred to himself and his role in our defense as "being a fire hydrant in

Photo courtesy of University of Colorado Athletics

Third-Team All-American Kyle Rappold demonstrated the toughness needed to be a great noseguard.

a dog show." Team morale, leadership, and chemistry are built with players who have the type of unselfish—but somewhat animated—attitude demonstrated by Kyle Rappold.

My last noseguard at Colorado was Joel Steed. Joel was 6-2, 300 pounds. Joel was a dominant player who excelled in every area. He often attacked and drove the center into the quarterback before the quarterback had a chance to clear the line of scrimmage and start the execution of a play. Joel went on to play nine seasons for the Pittsburgh Steelers. A player like Joel only comes around once in a coach's career.

The **defensive tackle** is your biggest and most physically tough defensive lineman. This player often doesn't have the same quickness as the other three interior defensive linemen, but he must be able to control and push the line of scrimmage. At the very least, he must be able to maintain the line of scrimmage. The tackle must always attack and control the line of scrimmage versus a base or reach block. Versus a scoop block, the defensive tackle should squeeze the offensive guard into the front-side 1 gap, not allowing the guard to release cleanly through to the eagle linebacker.

The **defensive end** is typically a tall, athletic lineman who may not have the bulk to play inside like the defensive tackle. He should be athletic enough to contain the quarterback on a sprint-out pass and to play cat and mouse with the quarterback on an option play. He should also be a good edge pass rusher. The defensive end must be physical enough to attack an offensive tackle and defeat a base or reach block, maintaining the line of scrimmage. He needs to be strong enough to squeeze an offensive tackle who releases inside and tough enough to cross arm a pulling guard versus a trap block. (See chapter 13 for more on the cross arm technique.)

The **free safety** should be your best overall safety. He must possess the coverage skills to be a deep-one-third defender versus the pass. The free safety will be in the middle of the offense's passing attack; he should have good ball skills and football awareness. The free safety must also be a sure tackler. On a good defensive team, the free safety is often the third leading tackler for the season (the eagle and inside linebacker are usually the two leading tacklers on the team).

Our most recent free safeties at Penn State—Calvin Lowry and currently Anthony Scirrotto—are exactly what you would look for in a free safety. They are both smart players who are able to make all of the defense's alerts and coverage adjustments. Calvin, who currently plays safety in the NFL, and Anthony are both ball hawks. If the ball is in the air, they believe it belongs to them. They are also able to play man-to-man coverage on the number two receiver. Equally important, they are both strong, sure tacklers, yet neither player is particularly big—both players are right at 6 feet tall and 200 pounds.

Photo courtesy of Penn State Athletics

Calvin Lowry (#10), an All-Big Ten player at Penn State, is now enjoying a fine NFL career at safety and special teams.

The **strong safety** needs to have the tackling skills of the free safety but doesn't have to be as good in pass coverage. The strong safety must be able to take on and defeat a blocker on the perimeter. His main responsibility in coverage is the curl and flat zones. In man coverage, he is most often matched up with the tight end, and he is frequently the blitzer when the defense brings pressure. The strong safety is the big, physical defensive back that a coach likes to have in the running game but would make a coach nervous if playing as a deep defender in the passing game. This position is often the easiest to fill because there are many good players with the physical qualifications needed.

In most cases, the **corners** are deep-one-third or deep-one-half defenders. They are seldom primary support players versus the run. This is particularly true in the Eagle defense. Size is not a primary factor when choosing a corner. Corners need to be sure tacklers, but they are not nearly as involved in stopping the opponent's run game as the safeties are. Corners have to be athletic and possess the speed to cover the opponent's best receivers on deep pass routes. Because the corners are often matched up against the opponent's best and fastest athletes, they must be highly competitive and must have confidence in their ability to make plays in open space.

Corners must also have a short memory if they are responsible for giving up a big play. The corner's competitive nature should enable him to embrace the challenge of the next play. Coaches need to be encouraging and understand that every defensive back, no matter how talented, gives up a big play from time to time. In this situation, you should review the play with the defensive back, making corrections if possible, and help him to develop the mind-set that the next time the ball is in the air, it belongs to him. In the run game, though, I am intolerant of players who turn down or miss tackles. A player who misses a tackle must at least force the ballcarrier back inside to his teammates. Making open-field tackles depends on the defender's body position, knowing where his teammates are, and possessing a strong desire to put the ballcarrier on the ground.

In addition to matching player qualifications with specific positions, role playing your personnel provides other benefits. It limits the blocking schemes that each player will face and therefore reduces the number of schemes that each player must practice against. This allows more time to do drill work and improve on the fundamentals required at each position. For example, a defensive tackle is always in a 3 alignment. He never aligns on the offensive center, just as the noseguard is never in a 3 alignment. When the defense is practicing for an opponent, the plays that are run to the defensive tackle do not have to be duplicated and run to the noseguard. The defensive tackle has to work against the following types of blocks:

- A reach block and base block by the offensive guard
- A scoop block by the guard releasing inside and up to the eagle linebacker
- A double-team block where the offensive guard uses a base block on the defensive tackle while the offensive tackle blocks down on the defensive tackle

- A play that involves the offensive tackle blocking down on the defensive tackle, with the offensive guard pulling to the outside
- A play that involves the offensive guard pulling across the formation, with the center blocking back on the defensive tackle
- Any trap-blocking schemes that the defensive tackle will face

This is a lot of blocking schemes for the defensive tackle to practice against. If you play your two interior defensive linemen left and right (using two defensive tackles instead of one defensive tackle and a noseguard), both of these players will have to practice facing the same blocking schemes. That will double your practice time and limit the amount of time the defensive tackle will have to perfect his technique and reaction time against the various blocking schemes.

The noseguard, on the other hand, will see a reach, base, scoop, and double-team block. As mentioned earlier, his alignment is much different from the defensive tackle's. The noseguard is aligned over the center and is tilted slightly in toward the center. In this alignment, the noseguard is inches from the football and the center. Playing the blocks mentioned is different when in the noseguard's alignment.

The same kinds of differences in alignment and responsibilities exist between the rush end and the defensive end, and between the inside linebacker and the eagle linebacker. If you decide to implement the Eagle defense, you will see that the plays and blocking schemes will vary greatly when run to the call side compared to when run away from the call side. The differences in the roles of the free safety and the strong safety in the Eagle defense also allow their practice time to be spent more efficiently.

PART II

Eagle Defense

CHAPTER 3

Eagle Alignments

I have coached in the Eagle defensive system since 1983, when I was an assistant coach at the University of Colorado. I believe in this system for several reasons. It is a gap control defense that has eight and often nine defenders close to the line of scrimmage. Each member of the defense has a clearly defined gap responsibility versus the run. There is very little gray area in each defender's read and responsibility. And this system provides a coach with versatility and flexibility in aligning his defensive front and in his stunt selection.

The flexibility in the system lies in being able to place the call side to the field, into the boundary, to the split side of the offensive formation, to the strength of the formation, or to the weak side of the formation. (In this system, the strong side refers to the passing strength of the offensive formation.) Because of the flexibility, a coach can present a variety of alignments to challenge an offense; however, the reads, techniques, and responsibilities at most positions remain the same for each defender. When players are comfortable in their assignments, they play with confidence, allowing them to play fast, aggressive football.

Placement Calls and Position Alignments

The eagle linebacker, defensive tackle, rush end, and strong safety all align to the placement call, which is referred to as the *call side*. The placement of these players on the call side is also referred to as the *reduction*, where the defensive tackle is aligned over the offensive guard. The inside linebacker, noseguard, defensive end, and Sam linebacker travel together away from the placement call. The free safety aligns to the field or in the deep middle third. The corners align right and left. You can also have a boundary and a field corner. If a corner is a significantly better tackler but is not as good in coverage, take advantage of that corner's strength by always aligning him into the boundary; if a corner is not a good tackler but excels in coverage, make him the field corner so that he is the farthest from the action.

Each defensive structure begins with a placement call, which is where the reduction is set, followed by the front, then any stunts or blitzes being used, followed by the coverage (see table 3.1). Field and Strong placements have an odd-numbered coverage, and Short and Weak placements have an even-numbered coverage. (Eagle coverages are discussed in chapter 4. Eagle stunts are presented in chapter 5.) When any of these placement calls is made, the coverage is predetermined and does not change regardless of the offensive formation. A Split placement has a dual coverage call—an even coverage (Cover 4) when the call side is away from the free safety and an odd coverage (Cover 5) when the call side is to the free safety.

TABLE 3.1 **Eagle Defensive Structure**

Placement	Front	Stunt or blitz*	Coverage
Field	Eagle	Fin	5
Strong	Eagle	Gopher	3
Short	Eagle	Lightning	4
Weak	Eagle	Lightning	4
Split	Eagle	Shoot	4-3, 4-7, or 4-5

*Each front can be played with or without a stunt or blitz.

The free safety always aligns to the field. A logical way to teach the coverage system to the free safety is to explain it as follows: Any time the placement call is to the same side as the free safety, an odd coverage is used. Any time the placement call is away from the free safety's alignment, an even-numbered coverage is used. Therefore, the free safety knows that an odd coverage is used whenever the placement call is to the field. When the ball is in the middle of the field, the free safety is always aligned to the strength of the offensive formation. When the ball is in the middle of the field, the free safety knows that an odd coverage is used if the placement call is to his side of the field. Another way to explain the coverage system is that if the strong safety is on the same side as the free safety, an odd coverage is called. If the strong safety is away from the free safety, an even coverage is called.

I have always liked having the ability to get the defense lined up without regard to the offensive formation, shifts, or motions. Once the placement is called and the front is set, the front does not move. The secondary is responsible for any adjustments that take place, which are minimal. Because our defense only makes limited and simple adjustments to offensive shifts and motions, we usually see very few tight end shifts from one side of the formation to the opposite side. I am always amazed when I watch defenses that have to move several defenders each time a tight end shifts from one side of the formation to the other.

When identifying an offensive formation on the field, our defenders use a system to count the receivers so that the defenders can align properly. This system also helps each secondary defender identify which receiver he will be reading or keying, and it assists the defenders with pass route recognition. We number the receivers from the outside in, starting from the strong side of the formation and moving to the weak side of the formation. (In zone coverage, we count receivers at the snap of the ball because formations often change with motions and shifts. In man coverage, we count receivers at their original alignment.)

Against a pro formation, for example, we label the widest receiver to the strong side of the formation the number one receiver. The second widest receiver, which in this formation would be the tight end, is the number two receiver. Either running back could potentially be the number three receiver if he releases out of the backfield to the strong side of the formation. To the weak side of the formation, the widest receiver would be the number one receiver. Either running back could be the number two receiver if he releases out of the backfield to the weak side of the formation.

In general, we use the Field Eagle placement call most often. A Field placement (see figure 3.1), which is played with Cover 5, aligns the reduction to the wide field. Cover 5 is an overshifted coverage (see figure 3.2). The free safety is the key player in the secondary. The free safety is aligned to the field, over the number two receiver. The free safety is responsible for a deep fourth of the field versus the passing game. The free safety lines up 8 to 10 yards off the line of scrimmage when aligned over a tight end. He will line up 10 yards off the line of scrimmage when aligned over a wide receiver. For his run-pass read, the free safety keys the number two receiver. If the number two receiver releases vertically, the free safety locks on and covers him man to man. If the number two receiver releases flat, the free safety looks to the number one receiver to the field.

We usually instruct the free safety to first help defend the post route by the number one receiver, then react to the

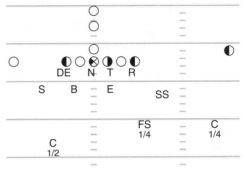

Figure 3.1 Field Eagle Cover 5 aligned against a pro formation.

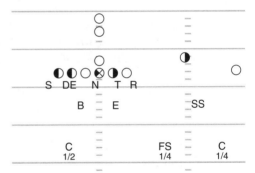

Figure 3.2 Field Eagle Cover 5 aligned against a twin formation.

curl. Some teams choose to have the free safety "rob" the number one receiver—that is, play the curl route first, then help with a post route from an underneath position. Playing from an underneath position forces the ball to be thrown high, allowing the corner to play the post route through the upfield shoulder of the receiver. Although this alternative can be effective, I prefer to first take away the deep threat. Big plays lead to points scored, which leads to defeat.

If the tight end crosses the formation, the free safety works back to the deep middle third. Some teams have their free safety look to help defend the number one receiver either to the field or to the boundary, depending on the game plan. Most of the secondary coaches I have coached with have preferred playing the free safety as a deep-middle-third defender when the tight end crosses the formation or versus a play-action pass. However, many other coaches ask their free safety to first rob the curl and square-in routes when the tight end releases to the flat or across the formation. More passes are thrown to the underneath zones than are thrown deep.

Playing the free safety as a robber allows the defense to have an extra defender in the curl and square-in zones. Both philosophies are effective.

If the number two receiver blocks, the free safety bounces and looks to support the run. His area of responsibility is the alley, or the area just outside of the rush end and inside of the strong safety. The run support that the free safety provides in the alley is one of the benefits of this coverage. It allows the eagle linebacker to press the first open gap (moving inside out) to the ballcarrier versus a perimeter running play.

The risk in playing this coverage is that the free safety is occasionally caught flat-footed on a hard run fake. Because of this risk, both corners should play with inside leverage on the wide receivers, and they must be prepared to defend the post route without help. The boundary corner lines up 12 yards off the line of scrimmage and 4 yards outside of the college hash mark (or 2 yards outside of the high school hash mark). The boundary corner is responsible for defending the deep one half of the field on the boundary side. The field corner is positioned 8 to 10 yards off the line of scrimmage, depending on his ability and the ability of the receiver he is aligned over. The field corner should be aligned 1 yard inside of the wide receiver. Both corners must be prepared to defend the streak (or takeoff route) and the post route. Versus any play-action pass, the free safety should accelerate to defend the deep middle of the field in an attempt to avoid giving up a big play.

As mentioned earlier, the strong safety aligns to the call side. In a Field placement, the call side is to the field. Versus the run, the strong safety is the contain player to the field. As the contain player to the field, he is also responsible for the pitch versus an option play.

His pass responsibility is to defend the curl to flat zones. Against a two-by-two formation (where two receivers are on the line of scrimmage on both sides of the football) or a trips formation, if the number two receiver releases vertically, the strong safety should sink and carry the number two receiver. As the strong safety sinks with a vertical release, communication from the other pass defenders is critical. In addition, the strong safety must keep his head on a swivel, allowing him to have vision on the receiver in his area, a receiver who may be entering his area, and equally important, on the quarterback. This will assist the strong safety in knowing when he should come off of a vertical route by the number two receiver.

The eagle linebacker aligns to the field and is stacked behind the defensive tackle in a 3 alignment. For his run-pass read, the eagle linebacker keys the helmet of the offensive guard he is aligned over. The eagle linebacker is responsible for the 1 gap. If the offensive guard's helmet attacks the outside shoulder of the defensive tackle, and there is a threat to the 1 gap, the eagle linebacker should attack the 1 gap. If the running backs are on a wide path and there isn't a threat to the 1 gap, the eagle linebacker should press the first open seam to the ballcarrier, maintaining inside-out leverage on the ballcarrier.

If the offensive guard pulls to the outside, the eagle linebacker should yell "out" and should accelerate through the first open seam, moving inside out to the ballcarrier. If the offensive guard's helmet releases inside on a scoop course, the eagle linebacker should shuffle toward the center. If the 1 gap is open, the eagle linebacker should step up into the 1 gap and close it. He should take on the offensive guard with his outside arm. If the offensive guard pulls across the formation, the eagle linebacker should call out "pull." He should follow the guard across the ball and press the first open gap on the other side of the ball.

Versus the pass, the eagle linebacker is a hook to curl defender. If you decide to have your free safety rob the curl route to the field, then your eagle linebacker can sit in the hook area versus the pass. Being in the hook area puts the eagle linebacker in position to respond quickly to the running back delay route, the draw play, a screen pass, or a quarterback scramble.

The rush end also aligns to the call side, which is to the field. When a tight end is aligned to the field, the rush end aligns in an inside shade on the tight end. When aligned to a split end surface, the rush end is aligned in a wide 5, with his inside foot on the outside foot of the offensive tackle. The rush end is responsible for the 5 gap.

When my teams have had a dominant rush end, we have lined him up in a 6 alignment, which is head up on the tight end. In a 6 alignment, the rush end is still responsible for the 5 gap. Being in a 6 alignment puts the rush end in a more advantageous position to widen the alley versus a perimeter play when the tight end blocks the rush end. It also disrupts the tight end's release from the line of scrimmage on a passing play. The downside to playing the rush end in a 6 alignment is that he is more susceptible to getting cut off by the tight end from the 5 gap on a play that starts on the other side of the football. Most years we have played our rush end in a 7 alignment, which is an inside shade on the tight end.

Versus a pass, the rush end is the edge rusher to his side and is responsible for containing the quarterback. Versus an option play, the rush end is responsible for the quarterback. Over the years, my teams have faced some powerful option attacks, including the Oklahoma wishbone option attack and Nebraska's I option attack in the 1980s, the Air Force spread option attack in the 1990s, and recently the North-western spread option attack. I can say without question that the best way to defend an option attack is for the rush end to stay on the line of scrimmage and "slow play" the quarterback, forcing the quarterback to pitch the football. The rush end should then flatten down the line of scrimmage (in the alley), buying time for the strong safety to defeat his blocker and contain the ballcarrier. This will also buy time for the free safety and the other defenders to pursue the pitchback inside out. The rush end will often end up making the tackle on the pitchback.

The inside linebacker aligns away from the call side and into the boundary. He is in a 3 alignment with his inside leg splitting the crotch of the offensive guard. The inside linebacker keys the offensive guard's helmet for his run-pass read. He is responsible for the 3 gap when the play is to him. When the inside linebacker reads the offensive guard's helmet reaching for his outside shoulder, the inside linebacker should shuffle with width and then step up and stun the offensive guard, maintaining control of the 3 gap with his outside arm. If the offensive guard pulls to the outside, the inside linebacker should yell "out" and should press the first open seam outside of the defensive end. The noseguard should be able to beat the center's reach block and play through from the 1 to the 3 gap, which will allow the inside linebacker to press and penetrate to the ballcarrier outside of the defensive end. When either the inside or eagle linebacker calls "out," this tells the other linebacker that the ballcarrier is headed to the perimeter, and that the linebacker should fast flow to the football.

Versus the pass, the inside linebacker drops down to the hash on the boundary side. He is responsible for defending the hook, square-in, and curl routes. On most square-in routes that are run into the boundary, the ball is caught on or near the hash. The inside linebacker should try to get approximately 10 yards deep, on or near the hash.

The Sam linebacker aligns away from the call and into the boundary. He is the contain player to the boundary. His alignment is dependant on the offensive formation. Versus a pro formation, he is in a walk alignment, four yards off the line of scrimmage and four yards outside of the offensive tackle. For his run-pass read, the Sam linebacker keys the offensive tackle. He should not take a step up toward the line of scrimmage until he is sure of the intent of the play. Stepping up toward the line of scrimmage versus a pass or a play that is not right at the linebacker's position, will take him away from the play and out of position. The Sam linebacker is responsible for a reverse, so he must stay behind the ball versus any running play that cuts back. He must also be in position to defend the boundary flat versus a bootleg pass.

Versus a twin formation when the Sam linebacker has a tight end aligned to his side of the field, the Sam linebacker is in a 9 alignment on the line of scrimmage, with his inside foot over the outside foot of the tight end. Versus a one-back formation with two receivers (a tight end and a wide receiver) aligned to the boundary, the Sam linebacker is in a walk alignment, four yards off the line of scrimmage and two yards outside of the tight end. Against a strong run offense, I play the Sam linebacker in a 9 alignment on the line of scrimmage. Versus a formation with two wide receivers aligned into the boundary, the Sam linebacker should align five yards off the line of scrimmage, on the outside edge of the number two receiver. He is now in position to contain the ballcarrier and defend the flat. He is also in position to take the pitch versus an option. Both the strong safety and the Sam linebacker would run with a receiver who goes through their flat zone and turns upfield on a wheel route.

The defensive tackle aligns to the call side. He is in a 3 alignment with his inside foot splitting the crotch of the offensive guard. On the snap of the ball, the defensive tackle should take a six- to eight-inch power step with his inside foot. His key is the helmet of the offensive guard. Versus a base or reach block when the offensive guard's helmet attacks his outside arm, the defensive tackle should attack and press the offensive guard into the backfield, keeping his outside arm free or driving the offensive guard into the 3 gap. The defensive tackle is responsible for the 3 gap when the play is to him. When the offensive guard's helmet releases inside, this indicates that he is attempting to execute a scoop block on the eagle linebacker. The defensive tackle should squeeze the offensive guard into the 1 gap to close the 3 gap and keep the offensive guard from getting to the eagle linebacker.

The noseguard aligns away from the call side. He is in a 1 alignment with his inside foot on the outside foot of the offensive center. The noseguard's body is tilted slightly in toward the center. The noseguard keys the center's helmet. On the snap of the ball, the noseguard attacks the center with a six- to eight-inch power step directly at the V of the center's neck. This power step must be straight ahead. If the noseguard steps underneath himself or steps across the center, he is very susceptible to being blocked.

Versus a reach block, the noseguard reads the center's helmet flattening to attempt to reach his outside shoulder. On his initial power step, the noseguard will flatten the center's body. The noseguard should then lock his arms out and flatten to the ballcarrier. Versus a scoop block on a play away from the noseguard, the noseguard's power step puts him in great position to squeeze the center into the far 1 gap and then pursue to the ballcarrier.

The defensive end aligns away from the call side in a 5 alignment. He is responsible for the 5 gap versus a reach or base block. When the defensive end is aligned into the boundary (as he is in Field Eagle Cover 5), he should line up with his inside foot aligned with the crotch of the offensive tackle. When the defensive end is aligned to the field (as he would be in a Short placement call), he should line up with his inside foot on the outside foot of the offensive tackle. Staying on the outside edge of a reach block is more important when the defensive end has a lot of field to defend. The defensive end keys the offensive tackle's helmet.

Versus a reach block into the boundary, the defensive end should press through the V of the offensive tackle's neck. Doing so will turn the offensive tackle's body parallel to the line of scrimmage, which will allow the defensive end to press the offensive tackle into the backfield. Versus a veer block, the defensive end should disrupt the offensive tackle's inside release and should close hard inside to fill the 3 gap. Versus the pass, the defensive end is the edge rusher and is responsible for containing the quarterback.

Placement Call Strategy

Field Eagle Cover 5 is the placement call that many defenses will use most often. When the ball is in the middle of the field, the complement to a Field placement call would be a Strong placement call. A Strong placement sets the call side to the passing strength of the formation. Because the free safety is aligned in a more centered position in the middle of the field, Cover 3 is a more balanced coverage than Cover 5. One concern with playing Cover 3 is that the free safety cannot provide the quick support in the alley versus the perimeter run game as quickly as he does in Cover 5. Because Cover 3 gives the defense three deep defenders when the ball is aligned in the middle of the field, Cover 3 is the smart, safe call.

The opposite of a Field placement call would be a Short placement call, which places the call side into the boundary and is played with Cover 4. The strong safety is now aligned into the boundary. Through the years, we have played the strong safety in one of two alignments. The first alignment is in the boundary flat (cloud position); the strong safety lines up five to seven yards off the line of scrimmage, on the outside edge of the number one receiver. When aligned in a cloud position, the strong safety is responsible for containment versus the run. Versus the pass, his responsibility is to funnel the number one receiver inside and to defend the boundary flat. The other alignment for the strong safety would be the deep-one-half defender into the boundary.

Depending on where you decided to play the strong safety, the boundary corner would play the other position. Versus the pass, the free safety and the field corner would play the same techniques as they play in Cover 5. The only difference is that the free safety's responsibility for run support is now inside of the tight end (instead of in the alley outside of the tight end).

A Split placement call sets the reduction to the split side of the formation. The strong safety, rush end, defensive tackle, and eagle linebacker align away from the tight end. As noted in table 3.1, a Split placement call requires a double-digit coverage call. The coverage combinations I have used, in order of frequency, are 4-3, 4-7, and 4-5. If the strong safety is aligned to the boundary, an even-numbered coverage is called (Cover 4). If the strong safety is aligned to the field, an odd coverage is called (Cover 3, 7, or 5).

Each placement provides a coach with various options in game planning. For example, a Field placement presents the offense with nine defenders close to the football. Depending on the offensive formation, the defense may be in a tight or a split defensive front, each presenting the offense with a different surface and blocking adjustments. The same is true of a Short placement call—the defensive alignment is predetermined, and the offense won't be able to predict the defense surface they will face. The call side and reduction are set into the boundary.

CHAPTER 4

Eagle Coverage Calls

The variety of formations used by today's offenses dictates that defensive packages must be sound in structure and must enable the defense to adjust easily to all formations. In the Eagle defense, each defensive front is determined by the placement call, and the front is coordinated with the coverage played. This coordination between the placement call setting the front and the coverage package played behind the front is designed in a logical way that makes it easy for players to learn. The coverage should also be easy to adjust when the offense aligns in one formation and then changes the strength of the formation from one side of the ball to the other.

Coverage Adjustments

This section provides an overview of the coverage that is played with each placement call, as well as the coverage adjustments that are commonly made against one-back formations. It also describes the coverage adjustments made when the offense puts the formation into the boundary or uses an unbalanced formation.

Field Eagle Cover 3

Field Eagle Cover 5 versus a two-running-back formation is described in detail in chapter 3. Versus any formation with just one running back, the coverage checks to Cover 3. When two receivers are aligned on each side of the football, we refer to that formation as a *two-by-two set.* When three receivers are aligned on one side of the football, we refer to that as a *three-by-one set* or a *trips formation.* Cover 3 allows the defense to continue to outnumber the offense at the line of scrimmage versus the run game. The three linebackers always remain in close-support position to defend the run. Playing Cover 3 also balances your coverage and run support. In addition, Cover 3 is the best way to defend the bubble screen, where the number two receiver flares and the number one receiver blocks for him.

The downside to playing Cover 3 against a one-back, two-by-two formation is trying to defend four vertical routes in the passing game. We use two methods to defend four vertical passing routes. One way is to have the strong safety sink and carry the number two receiver to the field. As the strong safety sinks, he should have vision on what is in front of him and on the quarterback. The strong safety should try to slow the number two receiver's vertical release with a collision on the receiver if possible. If any of the receivers run any route other than a vertical route, the strong safety should come off the vertical route by the number two receiver and should expand to the flat zone. Communication by the other defenders is essential in helping the strong safety know when to come off the vertical release of the number two receiver.

The second way to defend four vertical routes in Cover 3 is to have the inside linebacker sink down the boundary hash when the number two receiver into the boundary releases vertically. The inside linebacker does not have to sprint for depth. He should open to the number two receiver, who is typically a tight end, and start to wall out the receiver and defend a potential tight end option route. As the inside linebacker reads the vertical release of the number two receiver, he should turn back inside, regaining vision on the quarterback but continuing to sink and stay on the back hip of the tight end. If the quarterback does throw to the tight end, he should have to throw a high, lofting pass over the inside linebacker. This will allow the free safety to break on the throw and arrive at the tight end when the ball does.

When the boundary corner recognizes a two-by-two formation and a vertical alert, he should play a deep one third with inside leverage on the number one receiver into the boundary. This will allow him to break on the number two receiver if a deep pass is thrown to him. By having the strong safety carry the number two receiver to the field, the defense is vulnerable to the out route to the field but this situation will not turn into an explosion play. When the receiver makes a catch on an out route, he usually catches the ball and runs out of bounds. In addition, not many quarterbacks can consistently throw an out route from the hash to the field. Just the opposite is true with a vertical route from an inside receiver. The vertical pass to a number two receiver is an easier throw to make, and the consequences of the defense giving up a vertical pass are often devastating and frequently lead to points being scored.

As a general rule, the free safety should always make a vertical alert call to the defense any time the offense is aligned in a two-by-two formation. This call should alert both the strong safety and the inside linebacker of the four receivers on the line of scrimmage. To reinforce the alert, the inside linebacker and the Sam linebacker should communicate with each other to ensure that one or both linebackers disrupt and carry the number two receiver on a vertical release. When the Sam linebacker has a tight end to his side versus a one-back, two-by-two formation, the Sam is in a walk alignment. The Sam will make a "wide" call to the defensive end, who will widen his alignment to an inside shade on the tight end (see figure 4.1). The defensive end will communicate to the noseguard that he should widen to an inside shade on the guard. Making a wide call and adjustment will balance the defensive front and put the Sam linebacker in a better position to provide coverage help underneath on the receiver into the boundary.

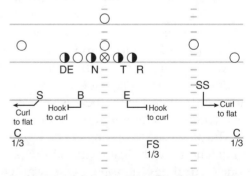

Figure 4.1 Field Eagle Cover 5 checks to Cover 3 against a one-back, two-by-two formation.

If the opponent is a dominant running team and an average passing team, I prefer not to make a wide call. In this situation, I prefer to keep the defensive end in the 5 alignment and keep the noseguard in the 1 alignment. I would also leave the Sam linebacker on the line of scrimmage in a 9 alignment. This arrangement makes the defense stronger versus an inside running play.

Versus a trips formation, the underneath coverage should flood the coverage to the field (see figure 4.2). The strong safety should continue to sink with the number two receiver if he reads both the number two receiver and the number three receiver pushing vertically. The strong safety should read the number three receiver through the number two receiver by backpedaling on the snap of the ball with his eyes on the number three receiver while feeling the number two receiver he is aligned over.

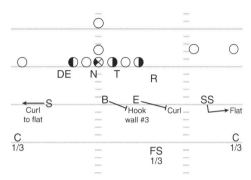

Figure 4.2 Field Eagle Cover 5 checks to Cover 3 versus a trips formation, and it checks "flood."

If either receiver is not pushing vertically, the strong safety should expand to the flat. The eagle linebacker should expand past the number three receiver to the curl zone. The inside linebacker should open with vision to the number three receiver and defend the hook zone to the field. Flooding the coverage to the field will take away an offense's passing attack to the field. If the number three receiver releases vertically, climbing toward the boundary hash, the inside linebacker should carry the number three receiver, maintaining an inside relationship. The inside linebacker should maintain vision on the quarterback. If the ball is thrown to the number three receiver, the throw will have to be a high, lofting pass to clear the inside linebacker. This will give both the boundary corner and the free safety an opportunity to break on the pass. If the tight end or any of the receivers from the trips side cross the formation to the one-receiver side, the formation turns into a two-by-two set. In this situation, the inside linebacker calls out the crossing route and gets depth down the boundary hash in position to defend a square-in route by the boundary receiver.

Versus a trips pro formation (the tight end is to the trips side of the formation), the eagle linebacker checks to a Stack defensive alignment. Checking to a Stack front instructs the rush end to widen his alignment to a 9. The rush end is now the alley defender versus a run and the player responsible for the quarterback versus an option. The eagle linebacker now aligns in a 5 and is responsible for the 5 gap. The inside linebacker aligns in a 1 and is responsible for the 1 gap. The Sam linebacker stays in his hip alignment. Versus a running play at the Sam linebacker, he should shuffle up to the depth of the heels of the offensive lineman. Keeping his outside arm free, the Sam linebacker should be in position to tackle the ballcarrier if the ballcarrier penetrates through the 3 gap. The Sam linebacker should also contain the ballcarrier if the ballcarrier bounces outside the defensive end.

Versus a trips formation with the tight end aligned into the boundary, the eagle linebacker has to widen his alignment to the inside edge of the number three receiver.

The eagle linebacker should not widen farther than five yards outside of the outside leg of the defensive end. If the eagle linebacker does widen past three yards, he can call a "G" stunt for the defensive tackle, instructing the tackle to rip into the 1 gap. The eagle linebacker is now responsible for the 3 gap, which is much closer to his walk alignment. The coverage will still check to flood.

Short Eagle Cover 4

Figure 4.3 shows Short Eagle Cover 4 versus a pro formation with two running backs. The Short placement call sets the call side and the reduction to the short side of the field (into the boundary). The same rules apply with each of the placement calls. The eagle linebacker, defensive tackle, rush end, and strong safety travel to the call side. The inside linebacker, noseguard, defensive end, and Sam linebacker align away from the call (for a Short placement call, this is to the field). Some coaches use a Short placement call because they like to put the reduction into the boundary and have the Sam linebacker be the support player to the field. This would place the Sam linebacker over the number two receiver versus a twin formation. In general, I prefer to have the strong safety aligned to the field and have the Sam linebacker into the boundary. Therefore, I have used a Short placement call primarily

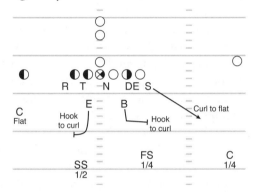

Figure 4.3 Short Eagle Cover 4 versus a pro I formation.

to stunt from. As a change-up placement call against a two-back attack, I have always liked to use a Split placement alignment. The Split placement call puts the noseguard in a 1 alignment, the defensive end in a 5 alignment, and the Sam linebacker in a 9 alignment on the line of scrimmage, on the outside edge of the tight end.

Cover 4 is known in the football world as *quarter-quarter-half coverage.* In Cover 4, the field corner has the same alignment and the same responsibility as in Cover 5. If Cover 4 is played with the strong safety in a cloud position and the boundary corner as the deep-one-half defender, the boundary corner has similar alignment and responsibility as in Cover 5. The free safety uses the same alignment as in Cover 5 and gets his run-pass read off the number two receiver. Versus the pass, his responsibilities remain the same as in Cover 5. Versus the run, his fit is now off of the Sam linebacker. The Sam linebacker is the support player to the field. If the Sam linebacker contains the ballcarrier, the free safety will fit the run inside of the Sam linebacker. If the Sam linebacker loses containment, then the free safety will fit outside of the Sam linebacker. In football terms, the free safety "makes the Sam linebacker right." The strong safety continues to align to the call side, which is now into the boundary. He is the deep one-half player into the boundary. The boundary corner, shown in figure 4.3 in a cloud alignment, is the contain player to his side of the field, and he defends the curl and flat zones versus the passing game.

Cover 4 can be played two different ways into the boundary. At Colorado, we played a cloud technique with the strong safety rolled up on the receiver into the boundary. The strong safety is aligned 1 to 2 yards outside of the receiver (depending on the receiver's split) and 5 yards off the line of scrimmage. Versus the pass, the strong safety funnels the receiver to the boundary corner, who is aligned on the hash, 12 yards deep. Our front seven defenders at Colorado were talented versus the run, and our free safety to the field became our eighth defender versus the run.

At Northwestern, we felt that we needed to play the strong safety in a sky position into the boundary. The boundary corner would be positioned in his Cover 5 alignment, which is 4 yards off the college hash (or 2 yards off the high school hash) and 12 yards deep—I refer to this as a *cheated half position.* Having the strong safety in a sky position gives the defense nine players in the *box* (the area opposite the offensive linemen and relatively close to the line of scrimmage) versus a two-back pro formation (see figure 4.4). The strong safety's alignment and responsibilities are the same as when he is aligned to the field in a Cover 5 alignment. Playing the strong safety in a sky position also gives the defense another physical player close to the line of scrimmage. Because the strong safety's alignment is close to the formation and into the boundary, it provides an excellent disguise when the strong safety stunts.

When a Short Eagle Cover 4 placement call has been made versus a twin formation (see figure 4.5), the free safety aligns inside of the number two receiver and continues to read the release of the number two receiver. The Sam linebacker aligns between the number two receiver and the offensive tackle. For his run-pass key, the Sam linebacker reads the offensive tackle. His pass responsibility is the curl to flat zones. The Sam linebacker will only expand to the flat if the number three receiver expands to the flat. If the

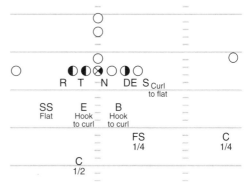

Figure 4.4 Short Eagle Cover 4 (sky) versus a pro formation.

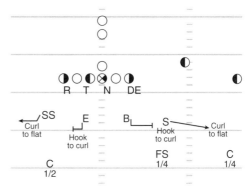

Figure 4.5 Short Eagle Cover 4 versus a twin formation.

number two receiver releases to the field-side flat at a depth of five yards or less, the field corner, who reads the number two receiver through the number one receiver as he backpedals, should break up on the number two receiver in the flat. A wheel route by the number two receiver would be impossible for the Sam linebacker to cover. The combination of a skinny post by the number one receiver and a wheel route by the number two receiver is a challenge for Cover 4. For this reason, the field corner and the free safety stay in their respective deep-one-fourth zones, and they would exchange a skinny post by the number one receiver and a wheel route by the number two receiver.

Short Eagle Lightning, (see the figures on page 43) is an example of a stunt being run from the boundary versus a two-back formation. Bringing the strong safety on a stunt from the boundary is effective because it enables the defense to bring pressure and cancel the inside running lanses without voiding the flat zone to the field. From this formation, many offenses will attack the field-side flat with the passing game. Seldom does a team design a passing attack into the boundary. The only two conceivable passing plays would be the bootleg into the sideline and a power pass with the fullback releasing into the boundary. In both cases, the eagle linebacker would be responsible for defending the boundary flat. Because of the strong safety blitzing off the edge and applying pressure on the quarterback, the pass play will declare itself quickly, allowing the eagle linebacker to react to a pass in the flat. On a Short Eagle Lightning stunt, the eagle linebacker does not have an immediate gap to fill and should be able to defend the boundary flat.

Strong Eagle Cover 5 or 3

A Strong placement call puts the call side and the reduction to the strength of the offensive formation. In this case, I refer to passing strength, which is the two-receiver side. I have primarily used a Strong call when the ball is in the middle of the field. In this situation, the defenders play Cover 3, which is a three-deep coverage (see figure 4.6). A Split placement call can also be used when the ball is in the middle of the field (with Cover 4-3).

When the ball is in the middle of the field, playing Cover 5 can make a defense vulnerable to passes on the weak side of the formation. Cover 5 is an overshifted coverage to the field, putting the free safety and the strong safety in a strong position to provide run support. When the ball is on the hash, the boundary corner can play a cheated half position. However, when the ball is in the middle of the field, there is too much area for the weak-side corner to cover from a cheated half position. Cover 3 allows both corners to play a deep third, with post help in the middle. Versus a pro set, the free safety aligns over the strong-side guard, 10 to 12 yards deep. He aligns over the strong-side tackle versus a twin

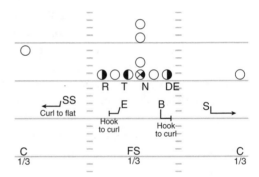

Figure 4.6 Strong Eagle Cover 3 versus a pro formation.

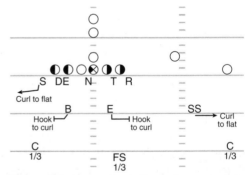

Figure 4.7 Strong Eagle Cover 3 versus a twin formation.

formation (see figure 4.7). Cover 3 puts the free safety in a better position to provide alley support to either side of the formation versus the run; however, it does slow his alley pursuit to the strength of the formation. Versus the pass, the free safety is the deep-middle defender. Cover 3 is a more conservative coverage versus both the run and the pass. Having a true center fielder helps prevent big runs and big passes.

I have also used a Strong call versus a flanker formation, which has two tight ends, two backs, and one wide receiver (see figure 4.8). This offensive set is generally used as a power running formation. Because there is not a detached receiving threat away from the overshifted coverage, Cover 5 allows the defense to have 10 players within nine

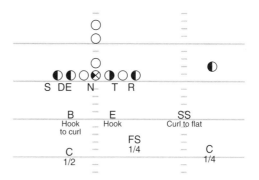

Figure 4.8 Strong Eagle Cover 5 versus a flanker formation.

yards of the line of scrimmage. This coverage can be used on the hash and in the middle of the field. If the wide receiver motions from one side of the formation to the other, the free safety checks the coverage to Cover 4. In this case, the free safety shifts over to the tight end on the opposite side.

Weak Eagle Cover 4

A Weak placement call puts the reduction to the weak side of the offensive formation. The weak side is away from the passing strength of the formation. I have used a Weak placement call in two situations. One is when the ball is in the middle of the field and I want to be assured of playing Cover 4, which is a quarter-quarter-half coverage scheme. The other situation is when I want to use a stunt versus a flanker formation. A Weak placement allows the defense to stunt off the edge of the formation on the side where there is not a detached receiver to be concerned about. An example of this is Weak Eagle Lightning Cover 3.

Split Eagle Cover 4-5, 4-3, 4-7, or 2-7

A Split placement call places the reduction to the split side of the formation, or away from the tight end (see figures 4.9 and 4.10). Because the offensive formation could put the tight end to the field or to the boundary, or to the strong or weak side of the formation, a double-digit coverage call is needed. Versus a pro set with the tight

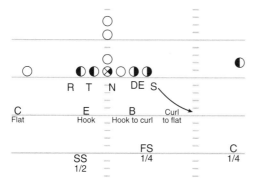

Figure 4.9 Split Eagle Cover 4-3 versus a pro I formation.

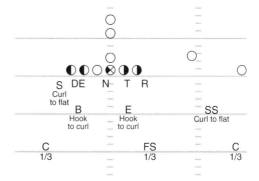

Figure 4.10 Split Eagle Cover 4-3 versus a twin I formation.

end to the field, an even coverage is played. Versus a twin formation with the tight end into the boundary, an odd coverage is played.

A Split placement call allows a defensive coach to dictate the defensive front to the offense. A Split placement sets the noseguard in a 1 alignment, the defensive end in a 5 alignment, and the Sam linebacker in a 9 alignment on the line of scrimmage, all to the tight end side of the ball (away from the call side). On the call side, which is the split side of the ball, the defensive tackle is in a 3 alignment, and the rush end is aligned in a 5.

A defense could have success without ever deviating from playing Cover 4, Cover 5, and Cover 3. Cover 2 and 7 are coverage change-ups. Cover 2, as mentioned, has two deep defenders on the hashes and five underneath defenders and would be used versus a pro formation where the free safety and the Sam linebacker are aligned on the same side. Cover 7 is a variation of a two-deep coverage with the strong safety aligned to the field; it is another way to play a two-deep passing shell against a twin formation, putting three defenders over two receivers (see figure 4.11).

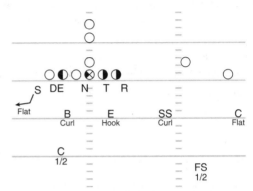

Figure 4.11 Split Eagle Cover 2-7 (Cover 7) versus a twin formation.

In a running or neutral situation, I have most often played Split Eagle Cover 4-3. In passing situations, I have mixed in Cover 2-7. When playing conservatively, most often in run or neutral situations (such as on first and 10 or on second and 5), I would play Split Eagle Cover 4-3.

Formation Strength to the Boundary

When a Field, Split, or Weak placement call is made and the offense aligns in a flanker formation into the boundary with two backs in the backfield, I have used two adjustments. The adjustment that I'm most comfortable with is to check to Cover 3 (see figure 4.12). The Sam linebacker aligns on the tight end. From this alignment, the Sam linebacker remains the contain player. The free safety should adjust his position from aligning over the field offensive tackle to aligning over the field offensive guard. From this alignment, he can still cover the deep middle third versus the pass, and he is now in a better position to provide alley support versus a running play into the boundary.

The second adjustment is to play Cover 4 into the boundary. The free safety would align over the tight end into the boundary. His reads and responsibilities for the run

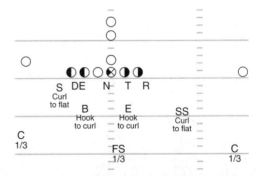

Figure 4.12 Field Eagle Cover 5 versus a pro I formation with the strength into the boundary checks Cover 3.

and pass are the same as if he were to the field versus a pro formation to the field. Playing Cover 4 into the boundary will provide immediate run support into the boundary. The weakness of playing Cover 4 into the boundary is in defending the deep middle of the field versus the pass. The field corner must align 10 yards deep and 2 to 4 yards inside the wide receiver to the field. His pass responsibility is to defend the takeoff and post routes. The post corner route to the field is a problem when playing Cover 4 into the boundary. However, the post corner route is a difficult and low-percentage pass to throw. If defending the run is the top priority, Cover 4 is a good adjustment.

When two quick receivers are aligned into the boundary (see figure 4.13), we always check to Cover 3. If the placement call is a Field or Weak placement, and the Sam linebacker is aligned into the boundary, he will align over the number two receiver, five yards deep. From this alignment, he remains the support player versus the run and the flat or curl defender versus the pass. If a Split or Strong placement call is made, the strong safety will be aligned to the boundary over the number two receiver. In this case, the Sam linebacker is aligned to the field in a 9 alignment on the tight end.

When the placement call places the strong safety into the boundary, for example when a Short call is made (but any placement call could put him there), I have always checked to Cover 3, regardless of the formation. The strong safety is the support player versus the run and the flat defender versus the pass.

Versus any form of trips formation to the boundary, we check to Cover 3 (see figure 4.14). When the strong safety is to the field and the offense puts a trips formation into the boundary, the free safety will snap down over the number two receiver. When doing so, the free safety will say "I'm here," notifying the Sam linebacker to now align over the number three receiver. The strong safety then rotates back to the deep middle third. The corner to the field must give a call to the eagle linebacker to widen approximately four yards outside of the rush end and provide underneath coverage help to the field corner. The eagle linebacker should read the offensive tackle for his run-pass read.

When a Short or Strong placement call is made, the strong safety will be aligned to the trips side of the formation when it is into the boundary. The coverage rules for the free safety and strong safety are applied. These rules dictate that the cover-

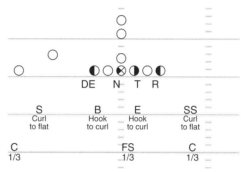

Figure 4.13 Field Eagle Cover 5 versus a twin formation to the boundary checks to Cover 3.

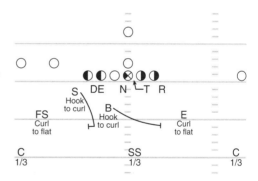

Figure 4.14 Field Eagle Cover 5 checks to Cover 3 when the formation is trips to the boundary.

age should check to Cover 3 because there is one running back in the backfield. Cover 3 is also called for because the strong safety is aligned into the boundary with the formation strength into the boundary. The strong safety is the contain and flat defender into the boundary, and the free safety is the deep-middle-third defender. The Sam Linebacker would be in a walk alignment to the field against a single detached wide receiver. If the single receiver to the field is a tight end, the Sam Linebacker would align in a 9 on the line of scrimmage.

Unbalanced Line

When a Field or Strong placement call is made that places the reduction to the field and places the Sam linebacker to the boundary, the Sam linebacker is the adjuster to an unbalanced formation to the field. The corner to the nub side of the unbalanced line and the Sam linebacker are responsible for identifying that there is an unbalanced formation. The Sam linebacker then hustles to the field and aligns two yards outside of the rush end on the line of scrimmage. The free safety can stay in Cover 5 or check to Cover 3. Through the years, I have coached on staffs that have preferred both of these options. I favor playing Cover 3, putting the free safety in the best position to provide run support versus an inside or outside run to either the field or the nub side of the formation.

Offenses often align in an unbalanced line to see if the defense will adjust properly. Many times the offense will run an inside isolation play or a power play to see if the defense has adjusted. Offenses will also attempt to attack the defense with a sweep to the field, an option to the field, or a sprint-out pass to the field. Option teams will also be prepared to run an option play into the nub side of the formation.

Bringing the Sam linebacker over to the unbalanced side of the formation will provide the defense with an alley player to the field versus a sweep play, a contain player versus a sprint-out pass, and an unblocked player to take on the quarterback versus the option. Keep in mind that the strong safety is still in a support position over the number two receiver. This position allows the strong safety to play the pitch versus an option play.

Playing a three-deep coverage puts the free safety in position to front the ball up if it penetrates through the defensive front. He is also in position to defend the alley versus the run to both the field and the boundary.

If the Sam linebacker is already aligned to the field—such as when a Split, Short, or Weak placement call is made—the free safety will snap down over the number two receiver to the field. The free safety will be the contain player and the defender of the curl and flat zones to the unbalanced side of the formation. The strong safety will rotate to the deep one third. The Sam linebacker can tighten his alignment to a tight 9 and add to the rush if the quarterback drops back or sprints out.

If a team puts the unbalanced line to the boundary and the Sam linebacker is already aligned into the boundary, the free safety snaps the coverage and rotates down into the boundary over the number two receiver. The strong safety will rotate to the deep middle third of the field. This adjustment is the same as when an offense puts a trips formation into the boundary.

CHAPTER 5

Eagle Stunt Packages

During a game, there may be times when a coach recognizes that his defensive players are not playing as aggressively as he would like. One way a coach can increase the players' aggressiveness is to call a stunt or a blitz. A big play by the defense can ignite the entire team. When using the Eagle defense, a variety of stunts and blitzes can be incorporated into your game plan. This chapter provides details on stunts and blitzes that can be used in conjunction with zone coverage as well as those commonly used with man coverage.

Bringing pressure is an effective way to set an offense back and create long-yardage situations. Stunts and blitzes are often good calls in neutral situations. When the offense is ahead in down and distance—for example, on second down and five—the offense has the advantage, but a well-conceived stunt or blitz can stop the offense for no gain or minus yardage.

Pressure on the quarterback is the most important aspect in defending a passing attack. Hitting the quarterback early and often usually pays dividends for the defense. A well-designed stunt and blitz package will enable the defense to attack the offense's protection and exploit any weaknesses in the offensive personnel. Stunts and blitzes can also be used to take away an offense's best running plays. Figure 5.1 on page 42 provides a checklist that will help you ensure that your stunts place the maximum amount of pressure on the offense.

Zone Coverage Stunts

Because the Eagle defense enables the coach to set the call side and the reduction to the boundary or to the field, this defensive structure sets up well for executing a zone stunt package. Since the placement call predetermines the call side, the defenders' assignments remain constant when executing various zone stunts, regardless of the offensive formation. When deciding which stunts to install in your defensive package and whether to use stunts with zone or man coverage, you should consider the three key points detailed at the top of page 43:

FIGURE 5.1   Defensive Pressure Checklist

❑ **Make sure each stunt is draw-, screen-, and option-proof (if the offense you are playing against runs the option).**

Each player should know his responsibilities.

❑ **Practice your stunt package from the start to the end of the season.**

In most cases, the defense should stay within their system. When your players know their assignments and the adjustments to all formations, they will perform with confidence, allowing them to play fast, aggressive football. It will also give the defensive coordinator a strong working knowledge of each stunt's strengths and weaknesses and the confidence to call each stunt in the appropriate situation.

❑ **Require second-level players to be at or near the line of scrimmage at the snap.**

I refer to this as players being close to their work. In the passing game, the defense has only 1.6 to 2.3 seconds to get to the quarterback. If the defender stunting is 4 yards from the line of scrimmage when the ball is snapped, it will take him 1 second just to get to the line of scrimmage.

❑ **Blitz your best rushers.**

Certain players have a knack for blitzing and making plays; others don't. Make sure you blitz your playmakers.

❑ **Evaluate the offense's quarterback before pressuring the passing game.**

The following questions will help you evaluate the quarterback:

1. How effective is the quarterback versus pressure? How quickly does he get rid of the football?
2. What pass does the quarterback check to? Does the offense throw the ball short (slants or hitches) or do they throw deep (streak, corner, or post routes)?
3. What is the quarterback's success percentage against pressure?
4. How good is the quarterback at escaping pressure?

❑ **Use all-out pressure versus the passing game when playing man coverage.**

I like to bring seven defenders and spy a defensive lineman on the running back. In most cases, the running back is tied into the protection and won't be able to release on a pass route. If the running back is part of the blitz control and flare releases out of the backfield, the contain rusher peels and covers the flare route. This principle is true in all man and zone pressures and should be practiced regularly.

   The purpose of spying a defensive lineman on the running back is twofold. I usually choose to spy the nose guard or defensive tackle on the running back. In most cases they are not going to get to the quarterback. This forces an offensive lineman to block a player who is not rushing. That will allow the seventh rusher to blitz untouched to the quarterback. Slip screens are always a concern versus pressure. Spying a defensive lineman will prevent the offense from executing a slip screen. It is critical that whoever is spying the running back closes up to the running back as quickly as possible.

1. Playing zone coverage behind a stunt enables the defense to always have 11 sets of eyes on the ball, allowing all 11 defenders to break on the ball against both the run and passing game. This is the most important reason for using zone coverage behind a stunt. When playing man coverage, the defenders responsible for defending receivers in the passing game must keep their eyes on the receiver they are covering. These defenders can easily lose vision on the ball.

2. Playing zone coverage behind a stunt minimizes the risk involved if the offense does execute effectively against the stunt.

3. In most cases, defensive pressure is the last thing an offense wants to see. Applying pressure by using a stunt in conjunction with zone coverage gives the defense aggression and penetration while minimizing the risk of giving up a big play (this risk is increased when playing man-to-man coverage).

Short Eagle Lightning Cover 3

This stunt is used primarily in run or neutral situations. The strong safety travels to the call side, aligning into the sideline in an invert position. On this stunt, the strong safety blitzes off the boundary edge. As the safety blitzes off the edge, he should "take a picture" as he crosses the line of scrimmage. He must instantly determine if the play is a run and whether the play is to him or away from him.

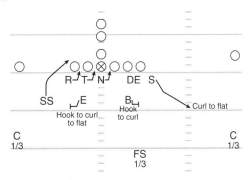

Short Eagle Lightning versus a pro formation.

Versus an option play to the strong safety, the strong safety has pitch responsibility. Versus an inside or off-tackle run, he should settle his hips, stay square, and squeeze and constrict the play. The strong safety is the contain player and should hold the edge. Versus a run away from the strong safety, he should "squeeze smart," staying square and shuffling down the line of scrimmage. Squeezing smart will put him in position to play a reverse, a naked bootleg, or a cutback by the running back.

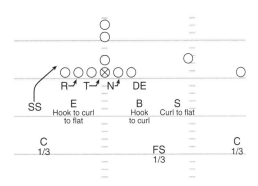

Short Eagle Lightning versus a twin formation.

The Short placement call puts the rush end and the defensive tackle into the boundary and puts the noseguard and the defensive end to the field. The front four defenders execute a Gopher stunt, which commands the rush end, defensive tackle, and noseguard to execute a rip technique toward the field. When the defensive end has a tight end aligned outside of him, he also executes a rip technique to the outside.

The eagle linebacker aligns in a 3 versus a nontight end surface and in a 5 versus a tight end surface. Versus a run to the eagle linebacker, the eagle linebacker should press tight off the butt of the rush end. (When I refer to a linebacker being "tight off the butt" of a lineman, I mean that the linebacker must not allow any seam to open up that a ballcarrier could get through.) Versus a run away, the eagle linebacker should shuffle slowly, staying behind the rush end and anticipating that the ballcarrier will cut back. Versus a pass, the eagle linebacker is a "hook to curl to flat" defender. He should only expand to the flat if the flat is threatened.

A Short placement call sends the Sam linebacker to the field. When aligned to a tight end, the Sam linebacker is in a 9 technique on the line of scrimmage, outside of the tight end. He is responsible for containment versus a run, and he is a curl to flat defender versus a pass.

The inside linebacker aligns in a wide 3 alignment. Versus a run to him, the inside linebacker is responsible for the 3 gap. Versus a pass, he is a middle hook defender. He should wall out any hook threat. The free safety and both corners play a three-deep coverage.

Versus a twin formation, the Sam linebacker aligns five yards deep and one yard inside of the number two receiver. He remains a flat defender; however, he will only expand to the flat if the flat is threatened.

Versus a trips formation, the secondary snaps to a three-deep coverage with the strong safety coming out of the blitz and rotating back to the deep-middle-third position; the free safety rotates down to an invert position over the number two receiver to the field. The Sam linebacker aligns over the number three receiver. The Sam linebacker is now a hook to curl defender versus the pass, and he is an alley defender versus a running play. Rotating the safeties to the trips side of the formation (to the field) makes the defense stronger and balanced versus a run or pass to the trips side.

With the offense in a trips formation, the defensive line continues to execute a rip technique to the field. The eagle and inside linebackers continue to execute the same as they would if the strong safety continued to stunt off the boundary edge. Many teams continue to leave the stunt on versus a trips formation. In this case, the Sam linebacker would walk out on the number two receiver as he does versus a twin formation. The inside linebacker would now align over the number three receiver, and the eagle linebacker would align over the ball.

Short Eagle Blast Cross 3 Hole

This is an effective stunt against running plays that use man blocking schemes, such as isolation and power plays. A Short placement call aligns the defensive reduction into the boundary. The noseguard, defensive tackle, and rush end execute a rip technique to the boundary. The rush end is responsible for containing the ball versus a run, and he has the pitch versus an option. Versus a pass, the rush end is the flat defender into the boundary.

The defensive end aligns in a wide 5 alignment and attacks straight ahead on the snap of the ball. The defensive end is responsible for containment versus a pass, and he has the quarterback versus an option.

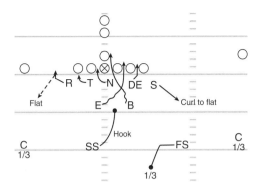

Short Eagle Blast Cross 3 Hole versus a pro formation.

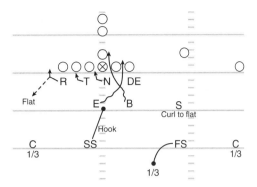

Short Eagle Blast Cross 3 Hole versus a twin formation.

The inside linebacker aligns in a 3 alignment at a depth of three yards. On the snap of the ball, he blitzes the near 1 gap. He should take on all blockers with his outside arm. If the guard attacks the inside linebacker, the inside linebacker should cross the guard's face and penetrate the 1 gap. If the guard blocks down on the noseguard, the inside linebacker should accelerate off the guard's butt and should cross the face of the first blocker to show (often the fullback or a pulling guard).

The eagle linebacker should align in the boundary 1 gap at a depth of four yards. On the snap of the ball, the eagle linebacker blitzes tight off the butt of the inside linebacker. Aligning four yards off the ball will help disguise the stunt, and it will give the eagle linebacker a better angle to blitz off the butt of the inside linebacker.

The strong safety travels to the call side and aligns in a two-deep alignment into the boundary. On the snap of the ball, the strong safety stems down over the ball at a depth of approximately seven yards from the line of scrimmage. The strong safety will be unblocked on most running plays, and he will be in position to front the ball up if it penetrates through the line of scrimmage. Versus a perimeter run, the strong safety should pursue the ball inside out. Versus a pass, he is the middle hook defender. The free safety and both corners play a three-deep coverage.

Short Eagle Shoot Cover 4

This stunt is best suited to attack a two-back offense and is a good call when an inside run is expected. A Short placement call aligns the defensive reduction into the boundary. The eagle linebacker blitzes through the 1 gap. The defensive tackle and the rush end widen their alignment and attack straight ahead. The noseguard and the defensive end play their normal alignments and assignments in a Short Eagle defense.

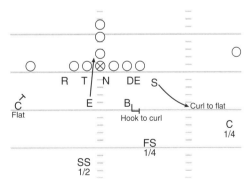

Short Eagle Shoot versus a pro formation.

As a change-up, the defensive tackle can execute a rip technique in the 1 gap. The eagle linebacker would then blitz through the 3 gap.

Cover 4 is a quarter-quarter-half coverage. The field corner and the free safety both play quarter coverage. The strong safety aligns on the boundary hash and is responsible for his deep one half of the field. The boundary corner aligns in a cloud position. He is responsible for the flat versus a pass and for containment versus a run. The inside linebacker is the middle hook defender. The Sam linebacker is responsible for the curl and flat zones to the field.

Versus a twin-receiver, two-back formation, the coverage stays Cover 4. As mentioned, this stunt is designed to stop an inside running attack from a two-back formation. Versus a one-back formation, several adjustments can be made. I believe the best adjustment is to simply not have the eagle linebacker blitz.

Depending on the offensive tendencies, you can also blitz the inside linebacker through the 3 gap with the same coverage rules.

Short Eagle Brave Cover 3

A Short placement call aligns the defensive reduction into the boundary. On this stunt, the front four defenders execute a rip technique toward the boundary. The rush end is responsible for containment versus the run and for the pitch versus an option. Versus a pass, he is responsible for the boundary flat. Versus a running play away, the rush end should fold and play the cutback.

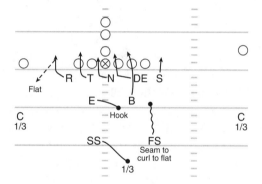

Short Eagle Brave versus a pro formation.

The defensive tackle will rip across the face of a down block. He has the contain responsibility versus a pass. He must clear a naked bootleg by the quarterback before pursuing a running play away. The noseguard rips across the face of the center. The defensive end executes a long rip technique, which will take him all the way to the 1 gap.

The eagle linebacker aligns to the call side. When aligned to a split end surface, the eagle linebacker aligns in the 1 gap. When aligned to a tight end surface, he is in a 5 alignment. Versus an off-tackle or inside run at him, the eagle linebacker should sit, and the ball should be forced back inside

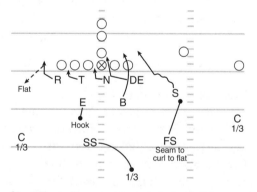

Short Eagle Brave versus a twin formation.

to him. Versus a run away, the eagle linebacker should flow to the ball. In most cases, he will be unblocked. Against a pass, he is responsible for the middle hook.

When two quick receivers are aligned into the boundary, the eagle linebacker makes a "gut" call to the rush end and exchanges pass drop responsibilities with him (a gut call is made in this situation for all of the zone stunts where the rush end is responsible for the boundary flat). When the eagle linebacker makes a gut call, he is then responsible for the flat, and the rush end drops into the middle hook area. The main threat with two quick receivers into the boundary is a wheel route by the number two receiver. The eagle linebacker is better equipped to handle the wheel route and other route combinations that can be run by two quick receivers. A gut call is also made when a single receiver is aligned to the boundary and a running back is aligned offset into the boundary.

The inside linebacker blitzes tight off the butt of the defensive end. Versus a running play to the inside linebacker, he should spill the ball outside to the free safety, who is spinning down to the outside. Versus a running play away, the inside linebacker should change direction and close quickly to the ball. Versus a pass, he should rush the quarterback inside out.

When aligned to a tight end surface, the Sam linebacker is in a 9 alignment. He is in a walk alignment when twin receivers are to his side of the field. On the snap of the ball, the Sam linebacker blitzes off the edge. He is responsible for containment. As the Sam blitzes off the edge, he should "take a picture" as he crosses the line of scrimmage. He must instantly determine if the play is a run and whether the play is to him or away from him. Versus an option play to him, he has the pitch. Versus an inside or off-tackle running play, the Sam should settle his hips, stay square, and squeeze and constrict the play. The Sam is the contain player and should hold the edge. Versus a run away from him, the Sam linebacker should "squeeze smart," staying square and shuffling down the line of scrimmage for a possible reverse, naked bootleg pass, or cutback. The Sam linebacker does not want to continue upfield.

The free safety aligns as if he is playing Cover 4. On the snap of the ball, he rotates down to a position inside of the number two receiver. Versus a running play to his side, the free safety will be at linebacker depth when the running back gets to the line of scrimmage. He will fit on the ball, keeping it on his inside arm. Versus a pass, the free safety will "seam" the number two receiver, which means he will carry a vertical route and will expand through the curl zone to the flat versus a nonvertical route.

The strong safety aligns as if he is playing Cover 4—that is, he aligns as a half defender into the boundary. Just before the snap of the ball, he will rotate to the deep middle third. Both corners are also deep-one-third defenders.

Short Eagle Flame Roll

A Short placement call aligns the defensive reduction into the boundary. The front four defenders execute a rip technique toward the boundary. The rush end is responsible for containment versus the run and for the pitch versus an option. Versus a pass, he is responsible for the boundary flat. Versus a running play away, the rush end should fold and play the cutback.

The defensive tackle will rip across the face of a down block. He has the contain responsibility versus a pass. He must clear a naked bootleg by the quarterback before pursuing a running play away. The noseguard rips across the face of the center. The defensive end executes a long rip technique, which will take him all the way to the 1 gap.

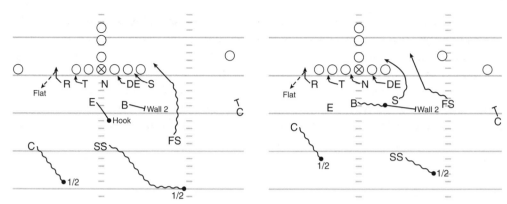

Short Eagle Flame Roll versus a pro formation.   Short Eagle Flame Roll versus a twin formation.

When aligned to a split end surface, the eagle linebacker is in the 1 gap. When aligned to a tight end surface, he is in a 5 alignment. Versus an off-tackle or inside run at him, the eagle linebacker should sit, and the ball will be forced back inside to him. Versus a run away, he should flow to the ball. In most cases, he will be unblocked. Versus a pass, the eagle linebacker is responsible for the middle hook.

When two quick receivers are aligned into the boundary, the eagle linebacker makes a "gut" call to the rush end and exchanges pass drop responsibilities with him (a gut call is made in this situation for all of the zone stunts where the rush end is responsible for the boundary flat). When the eagle linebacker makes a gut call, he is then responsible for the flat, and the rush end drops into the middle hook area. The main threat with two quick receivers into the boundary is a wheel route by the number two receiver. The eagle linebacker is better equipped to handle the wheel route and other route combinations that can be run by two quick receivers.

The Sam linebacker executes a rip technique inside. Versus a run to him, he should cross the face of all blockers and spill the ball outside. Versus a run away, he should flatten and look for the cutback. Versus a pass, the Sam linebacker must rush inside of all blockers.

Versus a run to him, the inside linebacker scrapes tight off the butt of the Sam linebacker. Versus an inside run away from him, the inside linebacker shuffles slowly, expecting the ballcarrier to cut back. Versus a pass, the inside linebacker is a curl defender, building a wall on the number two receiver.

The free safety aligns as if he is in Cover 4. Just before the snap of the football, he rotates to linebacker depth and then blitzes off the edge. As the free safety blitzes off the edge, he should "take a picture" as he crosses the line of scrimmage. He must instantly determine if the play is a run and whether the play is to him or away from him. Versus an option play to him, the free safety has the pitch. Versus an inside or off-tackle run, the free safety should settle his hips, stay square, and squeeze and constrict the play. The free safety is the contain player and should hold the edge. Versus a run away, the free safety should "squeeze smart," staying square and shuffling down the line of scrimmage for a possible reverse, naked bootleg, or cutback.

Most zone stunts are run with a three-deep coverage behind the stunt; however, Short Eagle Flame is played with a change-up coverage that is referred to as *Roll*. This is a two-deep coverage to the field, with three underneath defenders. Roll coverage gives the offense a different read on who the support player will be versus a bubble screen, a play that many offenses run when anticipating pressure.

The strong safety aligns into the boundary in a Cover 4 alignment. Just before the snap of the football, he rotates his alignment to the field hash. He is responsible for the deep-one-half zone to the field.

The boundary corner aligns in a Cover 4 alignment. Just before the snap of the ball, he backpedals to a depth of 12 yards, 2 yards outside of the hash. He is responsible for the deep one half of the field into the boundary.

The field corner aligns at a depth of 7 yards and 1 yard outside of the receiver. On the snap of the ball, the field corner squats and plays a cloud technique. He is responsible for the flat. Having the field corner play a cloud technique takes away flat and curl combinations and takes away the three-step passing game to the field.

Short Eagle Bingo Cover 3

A Short placement call aligns the defensive reduction into the boundary. The rush end, defensive tackle, and noseguard execute a rip technique toward the boundary. The rush end is responsible for containment versus the run and for the pitch versus an option. Versus a pass, he is responsible for the boundary flat. Versus a running play away, the rush end should fold and play the cutback.

The defensive tackle will rip across the face of a down block. He has the contain responsibility versus a pass. He must clear a naked bootleg by the quarterback before pursuing a running play away. The noseguard rips across the face of the center.

When aligned to a split end surface, the eagle linebacker is in the 1 gap. When aligned to a tight end surface, he is in a 5 alignment. Versus an off-tackle or inside run at him, the eagle linebacker should sit, and the ball will be forced back inside to him. Versus a run away, he should flow to the ball. In most cases, he will be unblocked. Versus a pass, the eagle linebacker is responsible for the middle hook.

When two quick receivers are aligned into the boundary, the eagle linebacker makes a "gut" call to the rush end and

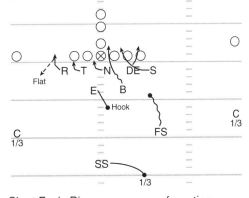

Short Eagle Bingo versus a pro formation.

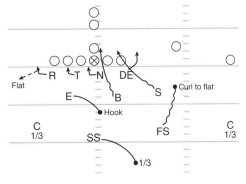

Short Eagle Bingo versus a twin formation.

exchanges responsibilities with him (a gut call is made in this situation for all of the zone stunts where the rush end is responsible for the boundary flat). The eagle linebacker now has the flat, and the rush end drops into the middle hook area. The main threat with two quick receivers into the boundary is a wheel route by the number two receiver. The eagle linebacker is better equipped to handle a wheel route and other route combinations that can be run by two quick receivers.

The inside linebacker aligns at a depth of three yards in a 3 alignment. On the snap of the ball, he blitzes the near 1 gap. He should take on all blockers with his outside arm.

The defensive end aligns in a wide 5 alignment. On the snap of the ball, he executes a rip technique in the 5 gap. Versus a down block by the tight end, the defensive end should rip across the face of the tight end. The defensive end has the quarterback versus an option, and he has the contain responsibility versus a pass. The defensive end must beat a reach block by the offensive tackle.

The Sam linebacker takes an 8- to 12-inch flat step with his inside foot. His second step should be with his outside foot off the butt of the defensive end, simultaneously ripping his outside arm to clear any potential blocker. He should penetrate the line of scrimmage on his second step, moving a yard deep into the offensive backfield. His third step should be with his inside foot to square and balance his shoulders. As with all seven positions on the defensive front, the Sam linebacker must maintain a low body position.

Versus a running play away, the Sam linebacker should flatten down the line of scrimmage and look for the cutback. Versus a running play at the Sam linebacker, he should make the tackle or take on the blocker with his outside arm while staying square. He wants to force the ballcarrier to deviate radically to one side or the other. Versus a pass, the Sam linebacker should take an inside path to the quarterback when he encounters a blocker.

The free safety aligns as if he is playing Cover 4. On the snap of the ball, he rotates down to a position inside of the number two receiver. Versus a running play to his side, the free safety will be at linebacker depth when the running back gets to the line of scrimmage. He will fit on the ball, keeping it on his inside arm. Versus an option, the free safety has the pitch. Versus a pass, the free safety will "seam" the number two receiver, which means he will carry a vertical route and will expand through the curl zone to the flat versus a nonvertical route.

The strong safety aligns on the boundary hash as if he is playing Cover 4. Just before the snap of the ball, he will rotate to the deep middle third. Both corners are also deep-one-third defenders.

Short Eagle Bingo can also be run with the free safety blitzing instead of the Sam linebacker. The Sam linebacker would then seam the number two receiver versus a pass and would take the pitch versus an option play.

Man Coverage Stunts

Every defensive game plan has a place for six- or seven-man pressure with man-to-man coverage. I often use blitzes that require man-to-man coverage to pressure an opponent's running attack. Man coverage stunts allow defenders to fill every run gap. Versus a two-running-back offense, these stunts can turn six-man pressure into a nine-man defensive front. When the offense is in a two-back formation, the defenders responsible for man coverage on the tight end and the running backs are close to the line of scrimmage; therefore, they are in position to quickly support the run when their man either blocks or carries the football.

Mixing in a run blitz with man-to-man coverage to stop the run is also effective when the offense throws a play-action pass in run situations. In using the play-action pass, the offense is trying to catch the defense in zone coverage and trying to get the underneath coverage to react up to the play-action run fake. A blitz in this situation can surprise the offense when they are expecting zone coverage and a four-man pass rush. Six-man pressure can harass or sack the quarterback. At the very least, it forces the quarterback to execute under pressure. It also provides tight coverage on the receivers.

Blitzing an offense in a passing situation such as third and long can change the momentum of the game and can force the offense into a mistake and a negative play. Well-executed blitzes can change the tempo and rhythm of the game. In most cases, a blitz is the last thing an offense wants to see in a passing situation.

However, an offense with an efficient quarterback and a well-conceived passing attack can create big plays in the passing game when the defense is playing man-to-man coverage. I often communicate to our players that when we blitz and bring all-out pressure, we are putting the defense at a maximum risk. The defenders must have a great sense of urgency to get to the quarterback or the ballcarrier. If the offense does execute, we have to minimize the damage defensively with great pursuit effort, proper angles to the ballcarrier, and great tackling.

Field Eagle Thunder Cover 0

This stunt should be used against a two-back offensive formation. Field Eagle Thunder Cover 0 is an effective blitz versus a run or a play-action pass. A Field placement call aligns the defensive reduction to the field. In a running situation, the defensive linemen should attack their gaps and play the run first. In a passing or neutral situation, the defensive linemen should execute a pass rush move into the gap they are aligned in. When signal-

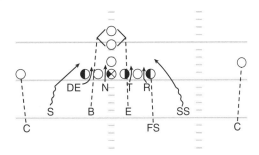

Field Eagle Thunder Cover 0 versus a pro formation.

ing the call for this stunt into the defensive huddle, the coach can add a "rush" call to indicate that the defensive line should key the football and execute a pass rush technique on the snap of the ball.

Cover 0 is man-to-man coverage. Each corner has the number one receiver to his side of the field. The free safety has the number two receiver to the field. The eagle linebacker has the number three receiver to the field, and the inside linebacker has the number two receiver to the boundary.

The strong safety blitzes off the edge to the field, and the Sam linebacker blitzes off the edge to the boundary. As the strong safety and the Sam linebacker blitz off the edge, they should "take a picture" as they cross the line of scrimmage. They must instantly determine if the play is a run and whether the play is at or away from them. When the play is at him, the strong safety or the Sam linebacker should settle his hips no more than one yard across the line of scrimmage, squeezing and constricting the hole inside of him. He should take on the widest blocker with his inside arm, keeping his outside arm free and maintaining containment of the football. In this situation, the strong safety or the Sam linebacker cannot let the ball get outside of him. Versus an option play to his side of the field, the strong safety or the Sam linebacker has the pitch.

When the play is away from him, the strong safety or the Sam linebacker should squeeze smart and shuffle down the line of scrimmage, staying in position to play a reverse, a naked bootleg, or a cutback by the running back. Versus a pass, the strong safety and the Sam linebacker are edge or contain rushers. The free safety is responsible for providing man-to-man coverage on the number two receiver to the field. Both corners are responsible for providing man-to-man coverage on the number one receiver to their side of the field.

This stunt can also be run with a Short placement call. Short Eagle Thunder would put the call side and the reduction into the boundary. The strong safety would now blitz from the boundary, and the Sam linebacker from the field. If a Split Eagle Thunder call is made, this would place the reduction and the strong safety to the split side of the formation, and it would place the Sam linebacker to the tight end side of the formation. Regardless of the placement call (Field, Short, Split, Strong, or Weak), the stunt remains the same, only the placement of the reduction changes.

Field Eagle Double Shoot

On this stunt, the inside and eagle linebackers blitz the gaps they are responsible for. In a running situation, the defensive linemen should attack their gaps and play the run first. In a passing or neutral situation, the defensive linemen should execute a pass rush move into the gap they are aligned in. The coach signaling the defensive calls into the huddle can control the defensive line's execution by signaling a "rush" call, which would command them to execute a pass rush stunt.

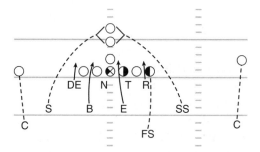

Field Eagle Double Shoot versus a pro formation.

The strong safety is responsible for covering the first back out of the backfield to his side of the field (or the number two receiver to the field versus a trips formation). The free safety covers the number two receiver to the field man to man (or the number three receiver versus a trips formation). The strong safety is in a sky alignment to the field, and the free safety is aligned over the number two receiver (or the number three receiver to the field verses a trips formation). These are the same alignments that the safeties show when playing Cover 5, the base Field Eagle coverage. Therefore, their alignment helps disguise the blitz.

The Sam linebacker is responsible for covering the first back out of the backfield to his side of the field. The corners are responsible for providing man-to-man coverage on the number one receiver to their side of the formation. This stunt can also be run with a Split placement call.

Defensive Line Movement Package

We enter each season with a stunt package that is twofold: our zone and man coverage stunt package and our defensive line movement stunt package. The zone and man coverage stunt package involves the defensive front, the linebackers, and the secondary. In this package, the coverage is almost always altered by the stunt. The line movement stunts involve the defensive front and linebackers only. These stunts do not affect the coverage. (Even when the linebackers are not directly involved in the stunt, the defensive line movement will affect their gap responsibilities.)

Movement by the defensive front allows your defensive line to have a "three-way go," which is the ability to attack straight ahead or to execute a rip technique to the right or to the left. When offensive linemen have to be concerned with the possibility of lateral movement by the defensive linemen, it slows the offensive linemen's charge off the ball and creates indecision in their minds. As a result, they will be less confident and less aggressive.

When a coach calls a line stunt, he is controlling the execution for the players involved in the stunt (the same is true with pass rush stunts). The stunt tells the defensive lineman or linebacker what foot to step with and where to go. When a player is executing a stunt, he becomes, or should become, more aggressive and assertive. Defensive linemen generally look forward to the opportunity to stunt and penetrate into a gap. They realize that the stunt may free them up and create an opportunity for a minus-yardage play.

The defensive line movements presented here were created to provide each player with the three-way go, and they can be used with the Eagle defensive structure, the Stack defensive structure (see chapters 7 through 10), or either of the combinations of Eagle and Stack (see chapters 11 and 12). A coach must also be able to adjust his defense by canceling gaps that the offense is attempting to run into. Defensive line movement forces the offense to adjust to movement on the snap of the ball and to be athletic in their attempt to handle the movement. It will also force the offensive line and the running backs to be mentally sharp. Line movement forces them to adjust their blocking schemes and running lanes.

As with any aspect of defense, flawless execution is the key to being successful. Any time a defensive lineman moves from one gap to another, the technique used is referred to as a *rip technique*. The defensive lineman involved in the stunt should key the ball for his initial movement. His first step should be lateral, or parallel to the line of scrimmage. On his second step, his trail leg and arm should rip through simultaneously. His arm should be low enough to grab grass as it rips through the surface of the offensive lineman, simultaneously protecting the defensive lineman's trail leg from the headgear of the offensive lineman trying to block him. A complete description of the rip technique and the defensive linemen's reads and reaction to various blocking schemes can be found in chapter 13.

When a line movement is called, it should have a purpose. Generally, we will call a line stunt only when it is needed to help stop a particular running play. However, an occasional line stunt will help slow down the charge of the offensive line. Coaches should make sure that the stunt called does not put their team at a disadvantage. This is accomplished through thorough game planning, which gives a coach the most information in his stunt selection.

A defensive team should repeatedly practice against plays that are run to and away from each defensive line movement so that each player knows where his particular fit is within each defensive line movement called. Early in practice, we rehearse the defensive line movements being used that week using agility bags or garbage cans to replicate an offensive formation. Players must be able to execute each movement at full speed with perfect technique and a low pad level.

In practice, I act as the quarterback and have a running back behind me. I instruct the running back what he should do each play. For example, I will have the running back take an inside and an outside running path on each side of the offensive formation and defensive line movement. I also run an option play to each side of the movement to make sure each defender correctly executes his option responsibility. I will also drop back for a pass to ensure that each defender executes his pass rush or pass drop responsibility. The running back should occasionally flare release to make sure the contain rusher peels and covers the flare release. In an 8- to 10-minute period, we can get in a multitude of repetitions while coaching proper technique and assignments.

For each of the line movements, I have included an explanation that describes my philosophy on how the stunt is best used; however, far more uses exist for each defensive line movement. Your philosophy and the offense you are defending may be different from the application described, so you can and should use the line movements according to the particular needs of your team and the offense you are facing.

Stunts From the 3–Technique Side

Most of the defensive line movements that involve the defensive tackle, who is usually in a 3 alignment, begin with the letter G. Generically, in football terminology, a G alignment places the defensive lineman in an inside shade of the offensive guard. Once this concept is taught, it helps the defensive tackle become alert to any defensive line movement beginning with the letter G, knowing it affects him.

Because most offenses generally run more plays to the tight end side than to the split end side of their formations, the defensive line movements are usually executed from a Split placement alignment and usually move the specified linemen toward the tight side of the formation. If a defense is expecting an inside running play—for example, on third down and one with the offense in a two-tight-end, two-running-back offense—a Field or Short placement call can be used. In this type of situation, Field or Short Gopher is an effective call, commanding the rush end, defensive tackle, and noseguard to all execute a rip technique away from one of the tight ends (toward the inside of the offensive formation). This cancels the offense's inside running lanes to the side of the stunt and moves the defenders toward the other tight end, which makes a Gopher stunt effective versus an inside running play on both sides of the ball.

Split Eagle G Cover 4-7

A Split placement call places the rush end, defensive tackle, and eagle linebacker to the side of the offensive formation away from the tight end. On this stunt, the defensive tackle executes a rip technique in the 1 gap. The letter *G* designates that the tackle is moving to a G alignment. The

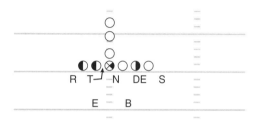

eagle linebacker is now a 32 technique, and he is responsible for the 3 gap when the play is run at him.

This is an effective stunt when the offense runs an isolation play to either the tight end or the split end side of the formation. When the isolation play is run to the split end side of the formation, this stunt allows the inside linebacker to fast flow to the 3 gap. He should stay tight off the butt of the defensive tackle, who is executing a rip technique into the 1 gap. When the defensive tackle rips into the 1 gap, this prevents the running back from cutting back.

When the offense runs an isolation play to the tight end side of the formation, the defensive tackle often beats the offensive guard into the 1 gap and forces the running back to widen his intended path or to cut back to an unblocked rush end or eagle linebacker. At the very least, the defensive tackle should squeeze the offensive guard into the 1 gap, closing the 1 gap with the guard's body and preventing him from getting up to the eagle linebacker. The eagle linebacker is then free to stay on the back hip of the ballcarrier and play for the cut back. The eagle linebacker may also pursue across the ball to the ballcarrier if the ballcarrier's path stays on the opposite side of the football.

Split Eagle G is also a good defensive line movement versus a team that traps the defensive tackle. On any off-tackle or wide play to the defensive tackle, the offensive guard will often overreach the defensive tackle, and the defensive tackle will rip into the 1 gap and flatten back to the ball—untouched. In general, Split Eagle G is a safe, low-risk line movement.

Split Eagle Go Cover 4-7

This line movement is similar to Split Eagle G. The defensive tackle (who is aligned to the call side) executes a rip technique in the 1 gap. In addition, the noseguard also rips away from the call, into his 1 gap. The eagle linebacker is now a 32 technique and is responsible for the 3 gap versus a play at him. Since the defensive tackle and

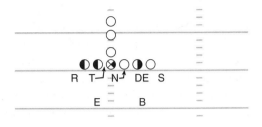

the noseguard are both ripping toward the tight end, this stunt is effective against any running play to the tight end side.

The downside to the noseguard ripping away from the center is when the play starts to the split end side of the formation (versus most offenses, this happens far less often than running plays to the tight end side of the formation). Versus running plays to the split end side, Split Eagle Go gives the center an unobstructed path to the inside linebacker, and the noseguard is more susceptible to being scooped by the offensive guard.

Split Eagle Game Cover 4-7

In this stunt, the defensive tackle, nose-guard, and defensive end all execute a rip technique away from the call. This stunt is effective against most plays run to the tight end, particularly the power, sweep, and option plays to the tight end. The eagle linebacker is now a 32 technique,

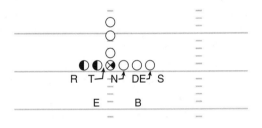

which makes him responsible for the 3 gap when the play is at him. A disadvantage of this stunt is that it widens the 3 gap to the tight end side of the formation against an isolation play at the inside linebacker.

Split Eagle Gopher

The rush end, the defensive tackle, and the noseguard all execute a rip technique away from the call side. The *Go* in *Gopher* tells the defensive tackle and the noseguard their assignment, and the *R* in *Gopher* tells the rush end that he is also involved in the movement. The word association helps the players learn each

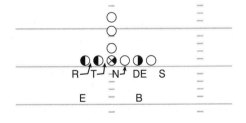

defensive line movement without simply memorizing words that mean nothing to the players. The eagle linebacker is now in a 52 technique. Versus a play to the split end side of the formation, the eagle linebacker provides support tight off the butt of the rush end. This stunt is also effective when the placement is to a tight end. Gopher closes the inside running lanes when the play is run to the call side, forcing the ballcarrier to bounce outside. It closes the cutback lanes when the ballcarrier starts away from the call side. I have used this defensive line movement effectively in short-yardage situations and also against a big running back who runs well between the tackles but doesn't have the speed to consistently bounce to the outside. Versus a pass, the noseguard will contain late on the split end side of the formation.

Field Eagle Gopher Cover 5

This is the same defensive line movement as Split Eagle Gopher, except the line movement is run with a different placement call. A Gopher can be run from any placement and is commonly run from a Field or Short placement call versus a two-tight-end formation.

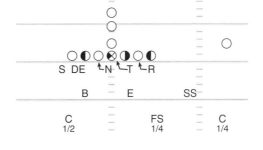

Regardless of the placement call, when a Gopher stunt is called, the rush end, defensive tackle, and noseguard all rip away from the call side. The advantage to running this defensive line movement is that it closes the inside running lanes and forces the ball to be bounced to the outside. Versus a two-tight-end, two-running-back formation, we often call Field Gopher Cover 5 because of the quick run support provided by the eagle linebacker, the strong safety, and the free safety, particularly in short-yardage situations and versus an inside running attack. A risk in calling Field Gopher Cover 5 is the possibility of losing containment to the field versus a passing play. The noseguard is still responsible for providing late containment, but this can be a challenge against an athletic quarterback.

When a coach wants to cancel every gap on both sides of the football, he can add the term *Blast,* which commands the inside linebacker (who is aligned away from the call side) to stunt through the 3 gap. This combination of defensive line movement and inside linebacker stunt is particularly strong versus an isolation play at the inside linebacker, and it would eliminate the running back's opportunity to cut back.

Field Eagle Shoot Cover 5

Shoot is a term that tells the eagle linebacker to blitz through the 1 gap. The eagle linebacker should take on the fullback or center with his inside arm. If the guard blocks the eagle linebacker, the eagle linebacker should take on the guard with his outside arm. This stunt can be used with any placement call. The

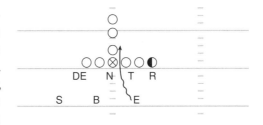

placement call should be determined by the offense and the play tendencies you are attempting to stop.

Field Eagle Shoot Cover 5 is an effective zone stunt versus a passing play when the offense is in a two-back, one-tight-end offense. The eagle linebacker is usually matched up against a running back assigned to block him. The eagle linebacker should win that matchup. Cover 5 provides an overshifted coverage (as described in chapter 4). The inside linebacker's pass drop is altered. He now drops to the middle hook area, and he has to wall out and defend the tight end versus an option route. The reason I classify the Eagle Shoot as a defensive line movement is that it does not involve a defensive lineman dropping into coverage, nor does it alter the Cover 5 responsibilities of the four defensive backs. As with all zone stunts, this stunt should force the quarterback to throw the ball quickly—under real or perceived pressure.

This stunt can also be used with a G movement call (Field or Split Eagle G Shoot). When an Eagle G Shoot is called, the defensive tackle and the eagle linebacker exchange gaps. The defensive tackle rips into the 1 gap, and the eagle linebacker stunts through the 3 gap. This is an effective change-up to use against a team that runs isolation plays to the defensive tackle. It forces both the offensive guard and the fullback to adjust their courses after the play has started.

Split Eagle Blast Cover 4-7

As mentioned, *Blast* is a term that tells the inside linebacker to stunt through the 3 gap. A Blast stunt is most often called with a Split placement, which will have the inside linebacker stunting through the 3 gap to the tight end side of the formation.

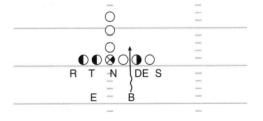

When a linebacker stunts, that linebacker should not show the offense he is stunting until the last possible moment. He should time up the quarterback's cadence and accelerate quickly to the line of scrimmage, exploding across the line of scrimmage when the ball is snapped. When you blitz a linebacker directly into a play, this can be very disruptive to the offense. However, when you blitz a linebacker away from the direction a play starts, you can lose depth in your defense and lose a second-level defender to pursue the ballcarrier. That is the risk in blitzing a linebacker.

Let me give an example of where I have effectively used a Blast stunt. We were playing an opponent that used a two-tight-end, two-back formation and had a strong tendency to run either a power play to the field or a dive option to the boundary. On third down and one, I called a Field Eagle Gopher Blast Cover 5. The Gopher stunt was called to close off the power play to the field. The Blast was called to defeat the dive option to the boundary. As we all know, the offense has the advantage in a short-yardage situation. In this particular situation, the inside linebacker stunted through the 3 gap and tackled the quarterback for a loss, stopping the offensive drive.

Stunts From the 5–Technique Side

Defensive line movements that take place away from the call side involve the defensive end (who is in a 5 alignment), the noseguard, and the inside and Sam linebackers. Many of these defensive line movements start with the letter *F*, which designates that the stunt is to the defensive end's side of the defense (the letter *F* representing the *five* in the defensive end's 5 alignment). Any placement call can be used with these defensive line movements; however, I have most often used a Field placement call, which places the stunting players into the boundary, with the movement going to the field.

Field Eagle Fin Cover 5

A Field placement puts the defensive end into the boundary. A Fin stunt tells the defensive end (who is aligned as a 5 technique) to rip inside the 3 gap. The word *Fin* stands for "five, in." The inside linebacker is now a 52 technique. He is responsible for the 5 gap when the play is to him, and he should support tight off 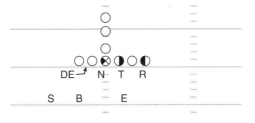 the defensive end's butt, taking on all blockers with his outside arm. Versus an isolation play at him, the inside linebacker should take on the fullback with his outside arm and should spill the ballcarrier to the Sam linebacker. The inside linebacker is responsible for the cutback when the play starts away.

Field Eagle Fin is a good stunt versus any inside play to either side of the formation. Versus an isolation play at the defensive end, this stunt forces the offensive tackle and the fullback to adjust their paths after the play has started. Versus a play that starts away from the defensive end, the defensive end is in good position to squeeze the 3 gap and take away the cutback. Whenever a tight end is aligned on the same side as the defensive end, the inside linebacker will check the stunt off. I don't like to have the defensive end rip away from the tight end. In this situation, the stunt makes the 5 gap too wide for the inside linebacker and the Sam linebacker, who now has a blocker on him (the tight end). However, many teams do leave the Fin stunt on in this situation. Your decision should be based on whether your opponent is an inside or perimeter running team. Versus a pass, the noseguard is responsible for late containment into the boundary.

Field Eagle Fill Cover 5

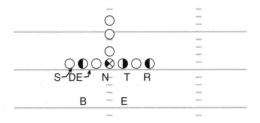

The *F* in *Fill* designates that this stunt takes place to the 5 (five) technique—that is, to the defensive end's side of the defense. The defensive end and the Sam linebacker both execute a rip technique inside toward the call side. They should cross the face of all blockers. As the defensive end and Sam linebacker rip inside, they close and cancel the 3 and 5 gaps, forcing the ball to spill to the outside.

This is an effective stunt versus a two-back offense and is equally effective versus a two-back, two-tight-end formation. When using a Field placement call, you can also add a Shoot stunt, which tells the eagle linebacker to blitz the 1 gap to the field. Field Eagle Shoot Fill closes the inside gaps from the offensive tackle to the tight end, forcing the ballcarrier to the outside.

This stunt is the same concept as a Field Eagle Gopher Blast, which has the rush end and defensive tackle (who are positioned on the call side) ripping inside and has the inside linebacker (who is aligned away from the call side) stunting through the 3 gap away from the call side. Field Eagle Fill Shoot has the defensive end and the Sam linebacker ripping inside (from their alignment away from the call side) and has the eagle linebacker stunting through the call-side 1 gap. Both defensive line movements and linebacker stunts cancel all of the inside gaps and should force the ballcarrier to the outside. The difference between Field Eagle Gopher Blast and Field Eagle Fill Shoot is in the side of the football that is ripping inside and the linebacker that is stunting.

CHAPTER 6

Eagle Versus Common Running Plays

After covering the philosophy, placement calls, alignments, and responsibilities in the Eagle defensive structure, we can now move on to discussing the practical application of the defensive system in defending common running plays. Let's first review a couple of key components that make the Eagle defense structured to stop the run.

The placement calls give the Eagle defense flexibility in where to place the reduction (or the call side). The rush end, defensive tackle, eagle linebacker, and strong safety all travel together to the call side. Consequently, the noseguard, defensive end, and inside and Sam linebackers travel together away from the call. This system enables the defensive coach to control the front that the offense is aligned against, and regardless of where you set the placement call in the Eagle structure, each defender's technique and gap responsibilities stay the same.

Defending the Run

Your defense will see a variety of running plays in the course of a season. The most important aspect of defense is being able to defend these different types of running plays in your base defense. As a coaching staff, after we have studied our upcoming opponent, the first step in our game-planning process is to make sure we have adjusted our base defense to defend the opponent's running plays. Then, as we begin our practice preparation on Monday, we are careful not to use any stunts or blitzes. Instead, we have the players stay in our base defense until we are sure they are prepared to stop the opponent's running attack.

This section provides diagrams of various running plays being defended with the Eagle defense, along with descriptions of each defender's read and responsibility against those plays. The diagrams include plays run with the tight end to the call side and away from the call side. The illustrations in this section will provide you with a basic understanding of each defender's role and fit in the Eagle defense versus common running plays.

■ Field or Strong Eagle Cover 5 Versus an Isolation Play to the Tight End Side

The **strong safety** is aligned in a five-by-five relationship outside of the rush end. He is responsible for containing the football. When the strong safety recognizes that the play is starting at him, he should bounce in place and remain in position to tackle the ballcarrier if the ballcarrier bounces to the outside.

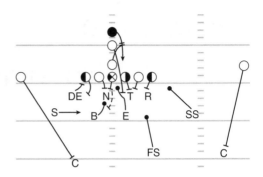

The **free safety's** read is the number two receiver to the field—in this case, the tight end. As he reads the tight end blocking the rush end, the free safety should bounce in place and start to shuffle to a stacked position over the tight end. He wants to make sure he doesn't get closer than six or seven yards from the line of scrimmage. He should then fit where needed.

As the **rush end** reads the tight end's helmet attacking his inside arm, he should attack the tight end and drive him backward about a yard. The rush end should lock his arms out and control the 5 gap, keeping his inside arm free.

The **defensive tackle** should attack the offensive guard's base block. As he feels the double team by the offensive tackle, the defensive tackle should grab the offensive guard and perform a seat roll into the offensive tackle's legs, creating a three-man pile in the 3 gap.

The **eagle linebacker** will read the offensive guard attacking the defensive tackle's outside shoulder. At the same time, he will feel full flow into the 1 gap. He should attack the 1 gap, attempting to penetrate the line of scrimmage and make contact with the fullback on the fullback's side of the line of scrimmage. The eagle linebacker should attack the fullback's outside shoulder, which will give the tailback a cutback read. Just before contact, the eagle linebacker should rip his outside arm across the fullback's body. This will put the eagle linebacker in position to make the play on the tailback, or it will force the tailback to radically change his path to the outside. If the tailback is forced to the outside, the unblocked free safety and strong safety will be in position to tackle the tailback.

The **noseguard** should squeeze the center's scoop block, keeping the inside linebacker free to play the cutback or pursue the tailback.

The **inside linebacker's** initial read is the offensive guard. The guard's flat helmet placement will take the inside linebacker to a stack position behind the noseguard.

The **defensive end** should squeeze the offensive tackle's cutoff block, lock his arms out, shed the offensive tackle, and pursue the football.

The **Sam linebacker** should pursue the football, making sure to clear any possibility of a bootleg pass, a reverse, or the tailback cutting all the way back to the Sam linebacker's original alignment.

■ Field or Strong Eagle Cover 5 Versus an Isolation Play Away From the Tight End Side

The **strong safety** is aligned in a five-by-five relationship outside of the rush end. He is responsible for containing the football. When the strong safety recognizes that the play is starting away from his alignment, he should shuffle and be in position to tackle the ballcarrier if the ballcarrier cuts back. The strong safety should always clear the bootleg pass, a reverse, and a possible cutback. He should maintain an outside-in relationship on the ballcarrier.

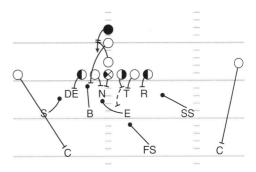

The **free safety's** read is the number two receiver to the field—in this case, the tight end. As he reads the tight end attempting to cut off the rush end from the 5 gap, the free safety should bounce in place and then start to shuffle to a stacked position over the tight end. He should make sure he doesn't get closer than six or seven yards from the line of scrimmage. He should then fit where needed.

The **rush end** is in a 7 alignment, which is an inside shade on the tight end. He is responsible for controlling the 5 gap. His read is the tight end. When the tight end's helmet releases inside and the tight end attempts to cut off the rush end, the rush end should attack, lock out, and maintain inside arm control in the 5 gap.

The **defensive tackle** is in a 3 alignment, which is an outside shade on the offensive guard. He is responsible for controlling the 3 gap. When the offensive guard's helmet releases inside, the defensive tackle should attack the offensive guard with his inside foot and arm, squeezing the offensive guard into the 1 gap. This should prevent the offensive guard from scooping up to the eagle linebacker.

The **eagle linebacker** is in a 3 alignment. As he reads the offensive guard's helmet releasing inside of the defensive tackle and feels full flow away, the eagle linebacker should fast flow to the football, keeping the ballcarrier on his inside arm.

The **noseguard** is in a 1 alignment. The noseguard should attack the center with his inside foot. As the noseguard feels the center attacking him, he should defeat the center's base block. When the noseguard feels the offensive guard block down on him, he should grab the center and perform a seat roll into the legs of the offensive guard, creating a three-man pile in the 1 gap.

The **inside linebacker** is in a 3 alignment. As he reads the offensive guard blocking down on the noseguard and reads the full flow at him, the inside linebacker should attack the fullback with his inside arm, turning the ballcarrier back toward the eagle linebacker, free safety, and strong safety. The inside linebacker wants to penetrate the line of scrimmage and attack the fullback as deep into the backfield as possible.

The **defensive end** is in a 5 alignment and is responsible for the 5 gap. As he reads the offensive tackle's base block, the defensive end should attack the 5 gap.

He should squeeze the offensive tackle into the 3 gap, maintaining outside arm control of the 5 gap.

The **Sam linebacker** is in a hip alignment, four yards deep and two yards outside of the defensive end. The Sam linebacker reads the offensive tackle for his run-pass key. When he reads the inside helmet placement of the offensive tackle and full flow into the 3 gap, the Sam linebacker should shuffle toward the line of scrimmage, and stack behind the defensive end, keeping his outside arm free and prepared to react if the ballcarrier bounces to the outside.

■ Field or Strong Eagle Cover 5 Versus a Trap Play to the Defensive Tackle

The **strong safety** is aligned in a five-by-five relationship outside of the rush end. He is responsible for containing the football. The strong safety should shuffle up to the line of scrimmage and be in position to fold and fit inside. He must also be in position to contain to the outside if the ballcarrier bounces to the outside.

The **free safety's** read is the number two receiver to the field—in this case, the tight end. As he reads the tight end attempting to cut off the rush end from the 5 gap, the free safety should bounce in place and start to shuffle to a stacked position over the tight end. He should make sure he doesn't get closer than six or seven yards from the line of scrimmage. He should then fit where needed.

The **rush end** is in a 7 alignment, which is an inside shade on the tight end. He is responsible for controlling the 5 gap. His read is the tight end. When the tight end's helmet releases inside and the tight end attempts to cut off the rush end, the rush end should attack, lock out, and maintain inside arm control of the 5 gap.

The **defensive tackle** is in a 3 alignment, which is an outside shade on the offensive guard. Versus a veer release by the offensive guard, the defensive tackle should attack, jam, and disrupt the guard's release. Doing so will prevent the offensive guard from getting a clean block on the inside linebacker. As the defensive tackle closes to the inside, he should stay square and work across the face of the pulling guard, putting himself in position to tackle the ballcarrier or force the ballcarrier to deviate from his path. Most coaches would instruct the defensive tackle to turn his shoulders and work across the face of the pulling guard. I have found that the defensive tackle is so close to the intended path of the ballcarrier (the 1 gap) that he can close too quickly and go by the 1 gap. Staying square puts him more in control and makes it easier for him to see the ballcarrier. However, versus a trap block on a defensive end who is in a 5 alignment, the defensive end should squeeze the veer release of the offensive tackle, turn his shoulders, and trap the trapper. Turning the shoulders is proper in this situation because of the distance inside that the defensive end has to cover to close the 3 gap.

The **eagle linebacker** is in a 3 alignment. The eagle linebacker will read the offensive guard's helmet release inside, and he will feel the defensive tackle squeeze and close the 1 gap. The Eagle linebacker should also hear a pull call from the inside linebacker. After the read and call, the eagle linebacker should step up tight off the butt of the defensive tackle.

The **noseguard** is in a 1 alignment. The noseguard should attack the center with his inside foot. As the noseguard feels the center blocking back on him, he should work to drive the center back into the far 1 gap while controlling the 1 gap.

The **inside linebacker** is in a 3 alignment. On this play, the inside linebacker will read the offensive guard pulling across the formation, and he will feel the downhill path of the fullback. The inside linebacker should shuffle quickly in the direction the guard is pulling and attack the first open gap to the fullback. The defensive tackle will try to close the 1 gap with the guard's body, which will free up the inside linebacker to make the play on the trap.

The **defensive end** is in a 5 alignment and is responsible for the 5 gap. As he reads the offensive tackle's inside helmet placement and cutoff block, the defensive end should squeeze the offensive tackle's body into the 3 gap, working to stay on the line of scrimmage. The defensive end should be aware of a potential reverse or bootleg pass. After quickly clearing those two threats, he should spill across the face of the offensive tackle.

The **Sam linebacker** is in a hip alignment, four yards deep and two yards outside of the defensive end. The Sam linebacker will read the offensive tackle releasing inside on a cutoff block, and he will feel the downhill path of the fullback. When this occurs, the Sam linebacker should shuffle and stay on the back hip of the ballcarrier for a possible cutback.

■ Field or Strong Eagle Cover 5 Versus a Sweep Play to the Tight End Side

The **strong safety** is aligned in a five-by-five relationship outside of the rush end. He is responsible for containing the football. As the strong safety reads the outside path of the running back, he should accelerate to the line of scrimmage, constricting the running lane outside of the rush end. He should stay square and keep his outside arm free, attempting to turn the ballcarrier inside.

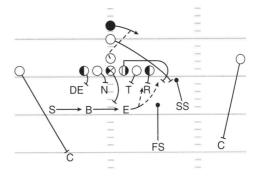

The **free safety** is aligned nine yards from the line of scrimmage, over the tight end. His key is the tight end. When the tight end blocks, the free safety should initially bounce in place. When the free safety reads both backs on a full-flow path to the outside, he should approach the line of scrimmage until he is at linebacker depth off the butt of the rush end. This will put the free safety in position to fill the void in the alley outside of the rush end and inside of the strong safety.

The **rush end** is in a 7 alignment, which is an inside shade on the tight end. He is responsible for controlling the 5 gap. His read is the tight end. When the tight end blocks down on the rush end, the rush end should attack the tight end, lock his arms out, and drive the tight end into the alley, maintaining inside arm control. At the last moment, the rush end should shed the tight end to the inside and get to the ballcarrier. However, he should not cross the face of the tight end prematurely; doing so will cause him to overlap the free safety's fit and open up the 5 gap.

The **defensive tackle** is in a 3 alignment. He is responsible for controlling the 3 gap. As the defensive tackle attacks the offensive guard and reads him pulling to the outside, the defensive tackle will instantly know that the offensive tackle will be blocking down on him. The defensive tackle should play the down block one of two ways. He can try to beat the down block with speed, penetrating the line of scrimmage underneath the down block and flattening to the ball. His other alternative is to club over the top of the down block, working across the offensive tackle's face. If he works over the top of the down block, the defensive tackle needs to be careful not to get driven back off of the line of scrimmage. Doing so will interfere with the inside linebacker's pursuit of the ballcarrier.

The **eagle linebacker** is in a 3 alignment. As the eagle linebacker reads the offensive guard pulling to the outside, he should yell "out," which tells the inside linebacker that the ball is headed to the perimeter of the defense. The eagle linebacker should accelerate and press the first open gap, moving inside out to the ballcarrier.

The **noseguard** is in a 1 alignment. The noseguard should attack the center with his inside foot. As the noseguard feels the center releasing up to the inside linebacker on a scoop block, the noseguard should squeeze and disrupt the center. Different from an inside running play, the center's path will be wider, which will make it more difficult for the noseguard to squeeze the center. It will also make it more difficult for the offensive guard to scoop the noseguard, who should flatten down the line of scrimmage in pursuit of the ballcarrier.

The **inside linebacker** is in a 3 alignment. When he reads the scoop release of the offensive guard, feels the outside path of the running back, and hears an "out" call, the inside linebacker should begin an alley pursuit to the ballcarrier. He should work over the top of the center's attempted block. As he approaches the ballcarrier, the inside linebacker should stay on an inside-out course, not allowing the ballcarrier to cut back across his face.

The **defensive end** is in a 5 alignment. As he reads the offensive tackle's inside helmet placement and cutoff block, the defensive end should squeeze the offensive tackle's body into the 3 gap. He must work to stay square and to stay on the line of scrimmage. The defensive end should be aware of a potential reverse or bootleg pass. After quickly clearing those two threats, he should spill across the face of the offensive tackle and take a deep pursuit course to the ballcarrier.

The **Sam linebacker** is in a hip alignment, four yards deep and two yards outside of the defensive end. On this play, the Sam linebacker will read the offensive tackle releasing inside on a cutoff block, and he will feel both backs on a wide full-flow path away from him. The Sam linebacker should initially shuffle and clear a possible reverse or bootleg pass. He should then take a deep pursuit course.

■ Field or Strong Eagle Cover 5 Versus a Power Play to the Tight End Side

The **strong safety** is aligned in a five-by-five relationship outside of the rush end. He is responsible for containing the football. As the strong safety reads the outside path of the fullback, he should accelerate to the line of scrimmage, constricting the running lane outside of the rush end. He should stay square and keep his outside arm free. If the tight end uses an arch block on the strong safety, the strong safety should squeeze the tight end back into the hole, staying square and keeping his outside arm free.

The **free safety** is aligned nine yards off the line of scrimmage, over the tight end. His key is the tight end. When the tight end blocks, the free safety should initially bounce in place. The free safety should then approach the line of scrimmage until he is at linebacker depth off the butt of the rush end. This will put the free safety in position to make the tackle inside of the strong safety and off of the butt of the rush end. If the tight end blocks out on the strong safety and the fullback attempts a kick-out block on the rush end, the free safety must be aware of the potential for a pass. In this situation, he should initially honor the potential release of the tight end and should clear the pass before supporting the run and fitting where needed.

The **rush end** is in a 7 alignment. He is responsible for controlling the 5 gap. His read is the tight end. As the rush end feels a base block from the tight end, he should attack the tight end and lock his arms out, gaining separation from the tight end. Feeling an inside path from the tailback, the rush end should maintain control of the 5 gap. If the tight end blocks out on the strong safety, the rush end should get his eyes and head back inside and look to squeeze and constrict the first blocking threat (this will most likely be the fullback).

The **defensive tackle** is in a 3 alignment. As the defensive tackle attacks the offensive guard, he will feel a double team from the offensive guard and the offensive tackle. The defensive tackle should shock the offensive guard, grab him, and perform a seat roll into the legs of the offensive tackle, creating a three-man pile in the 3 gap.

The **eagle linebacker** is in a 3 alignment. As the eagle linebacker reads the double team on the defensive tackle (by the offensive guard and offensive tackle), hears a "pull" call, and feels the full-flow path by both backs at him, he should press tightly off the butt of the defensive tackle.

The **noseguard** is in a 1 alignment. The noseguard should attack the center with his inside foot. As the noseguard feels the center blocking back on him, he should work to drive the center back into the far 1 gap while controlling the near 1 gap.

The **inside linebacker** is in a 3 alignment. As the inside linebacker reads the offensive guard on his side of the ball pulling across the formation, he should call out "pull." As the inside linebacker feels the downhill path of the tailback, the inside linebacker should shuffle in the direction of the pulling guard, staying on the back hip of the ballcarrier. He will be in position to attack the far 1 gap if the ballcarrier's path is toward the 1 gap or to pursue the ballcarrier if he takes a wider path.

The **defensive end** is in a 5 alignment. As he reads the offensive tackle's inside helmet placement and cutoff block, the defensive end should squeeze the offensive tackle's body into the 3 gap and work to stay on the line of scrimmage. The defensive end should be aware of a potential reverse or bootleg pass. After quickly clearing those two threats, he should spill across the face of the offensive tackle.

The **Sam linebacker** is in a hip alignment, four yards deep and two yards out-side of the defensive end. On this play, the Sam linebacker will read the offensive tackle releasing inside on a cutoff block, and he will feel the downhill path of the tailback. The Sam linebacker should shuffle and stay on the back hip of the ballcarrier for a possible cutback. He should maintain an outside-in relationship on the ballcarrier.

■ Field or Strong Eagle Cover 5 Versus an Inside Zone Play

The **strong safety** is aligned in a five-by-five relationship outside of the rush end. He is responsible for containing the football. As the strong safety reads split flow from the running backs and reads the tight end arch blocking out on him, he should keep his shoulders parallel to the line of scrimmage and shuffle to the tight end, jamming the tight end back inside. He should keep his outside arm free until he is sure where the ball is headed.

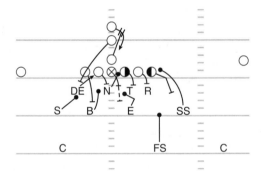

The **free safety** is aligned nine yards off the line of scrimmage, over the tight end. His key is the tight end. When the tight end blocks out on the strong safety, the free safety should initially bounce in place and honor the potential release of the tight end for a pass. As the free safety sees the tight end make contact with the strong safety and feels the split flow of the running backs, he should bounce in place until he is sure where the ball is headed. Then he should fit where needed.

The **rush end** is in a 7 alignment, which is an inside shade on the tight end. He is responsible for controlling the 5 gap. His read is the tight end. As the rush end feels the tight end blocking out on the strong safety, the rush end should immediately get his eyes and body back inside, attacking the offensive tackle and constricting the 5 gap. The rush end should stay square to the line of scrimmage and keep his outside arm free.

The **defensive tackle** is in a 3 alignment. As the defensive tackle feels the guard attacking his outside arm, he should attack the guard and control the 3 gap.

The **eagle linebacker** is in a 3 alignment. On this play, the eagle linebacker will read the offensive guard's helmet attacking the outside arm of the defensive tackle, and he will feel the split flow in the backfield. The eagle linebacker should stack behind the defensive tackle and be ready to press the 1 gap.

The **noseguard** is in a 1 alignment. The noseguard should attack the center with his inside foot. As the noseguard feels the center release to the eagle linebacker on a scoop block, the noseguard should squeeze the center into the front-side 1 gap for two counts, keeping him off the eagle linebacker. The noseguard should then proceed to the football.

The **inside linebacker** is in a 3 alignment. As the inside linebacker reads the scoop block of the offensive guard and feels the split flow by the offensive backs, he should step and stack behind the noseguard. The inside linebacker should be prepared to press the near 1 gap or to fit off of the butt of the defensive end who will be closing off the butt of the offensive tackle.

The **defensive end** is in a 5 alignment and is responsible for the 5 gap. As he reads the offensive tackle's veer release inside to the inside linebacker, the defensive end should squeeze the offensive tackle's body into the 3 gap. He should then cross the face of the next inside threat (the fullback).

The **Sam linebacker** is in a hip alignment, four yards deep and two yards outside of the defensive end. On this play, the Sam linebacker will read the offensive tackle releasing inside on a cutoff block, and he will feel the split flow of the backs. The Sam linebacker should shuffle to the inside, staying on the back hip of the ballcarrier for a possible cutback, reverse, or a bootleg passing play, which is often run off an inside zone fake. He should maintain an outside-in relationship on the ballcarrier.

■ Split or Field Eagle Cover 7 Versus an Isolation Play to the Split End Side

Versus a twin formation, the **strong safety** aligns five yards off the ball and splits the distance between the number two receiver and the offensive tackle. The strong safety should never align wider than five yards outside of the offensive tackle. The strong safety is now an alley player. He should read through the offensive tackle to the ball. As the strong safety reads the offensive tackle's base block on the rush end, he should shuffle toward

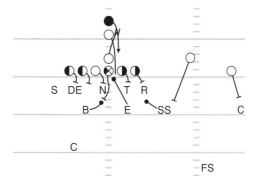

the ball, maintaining an inside-out relationship on the ballcarrier. The strong safety should not let the number two receiver cut him off.

The **free safety** is aligned 12 yards deep, on the outside edge of the number two receiver (not wider than the hash). The free safety is responsible for the deep one half of the field and provides secondary run support off the strong safety's butt.

The **rush end** is in a wide 5 alignment. He is responsible for controlling the 5 gap. His read is the offensive tackle. As the rush end feels a base block from the offensive tackle, he should attack the offensive tackle and lock his arms out, gaining separation and controlling the 5 gap.

The **defensive tackle** is in a 3 alignment. As the defensive tackle attacks the offensive guard and reads a base block by the offensive guard, the defensive tackle should attack the guard, stop his charge, lock him out, and gain separation. He should maintain control of the 3 gap.

The **eagle linebacker** is in a 3 alignment. On this play, the eagle linebacker will read the offensive guard attacking the outside number of the defensive tackle, and he will feel a full-flow path by both backs in the 1 gap. The eagle linebacker should attack the 1 gap and attempt to make contact with the fullback on the offensive side of the ball. As the eagle linebacker presses the line of scrimmage, his downhill course should attack the outside two thirds of the fullback, giving the tailback the illusion that he will have an inside path. Just prior to contact, the eagle linebacker should adjust his course and place his helmet on the inside hip of the fullback. The eagle linebacker should make the play on the tailback or alter his intended path.

The **noseguard** is in a 1 alignment. The noseguard should attack the center with his inside foot. As the noseguard feels the center releasing inside on a scoop block, the noseguard should squeeze the center into the front-side 1 gap for two counts. He should then flatten to the football.

The **inside linebacker** is in a 3 alignment. As the inside linebacker reads the offensive guard attempting to scoop block the noseguard, he should step and stack behind the noseguard. This puts the inside linebacker in position to work across the ball or shuffle to the back side if the ballcarrier cuts back.

The **defensive end** is in a 5 alignment and is responsible for the 5 gap. As he reads the offensive tackle attacking his inside shoulder and attempting to execute a cutoff block, the defensive end should squeeze the offensive tackle's body into the 3 gap and work to stay on the line of scrimmage. The defensive end should be aware of a potential reverse or bootleg pass. After quickly clearing those two threats, he should spill across the face of the offensive tackle and pursue the football.

The **Sam linebacker** is in a 9 alignment, which is an outside shade on the tight end. The Sam linebacker is responsible for containment to his side of the ball. As he reads the tight end's inside release to cut off the Sam linebacker's pursuit to the football, the Sam linebacker should squeeze the tight end into the 5 gap. The Sam linebacker should stay square and clear a potential reverse, bootleg pass, or cutback by the tailback. The Sam linebacker should then cross the face of the tight end and pursue the football.

■ Split or Field Eagle Cover 7 Versus an Isolation Play to the Tight End Side

Versus a twin formation, the **strong safety** aligns five yards off the ball and splits the distance between the number two receiver and the offensive tackle. He should never align wider than five yards outside of the offensive tackle. The strong safety is now an alley player. The strong safety should read through the offensive tackle to the ball. As the strong safety reads the offensive tackle executing a scoop block on the defensive tackle, he should

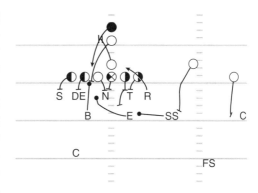

shuffle toward the ball, maintaining an inside-out relationship on the ballcarrier. The strong safety should not let the number two receiver cut him off.

The **free safety** aligns 12 yards deep, on the outside edge of the number two receiver (not wider than the hash). The free safety is responsible for the deep one half of the field versus a pass and has secondary run support outside of the strong safety.

The **rush end** is in a wide 5 alignment. He is responsible for controlling the 5 gap. His read is the offensive tackle. As the rush end reads the tackle attempting a scoop block on the defensive tackle, the rush end should squeeze and flatten off the butt of the offensive tackle. If the offensive tackle attacks the rush end's inside arm in an attempt to cut off the rush end, the rush end should attack the offensive tackle, lock him out, and spill across his face in pursuit of the ball. The rush end should always clear a reverse, bootleg pass, or cutback before he spills and pursues the ball.

The **defensive tackle** is in a 3 alignment. The defensive tackle should attack the guard with his inside foot. As he reads the guard releasing through his inside shoulder on a scoop block, the defensive tackle should squeeze the guard into the front-side 1 gap for two counts, disrupting the guard's course. He should then flatten to the football. If the offensive guard attacks the defensive tackle's inside arm in an attempt to execute a base block, the defensive tackle should attack the guard, lock him out, and spill across his face in pursuit of the ball.

The **eagle linebacker** is in a 3 alignment. On this play, the eagle linebacker will read the offensive guard's helmet attacking the inside shoulder of the defensive tackle, and he will feel a full-flow path away by both backs. The eagle linebacker should fast flow and press the far 1 gap, tight off the butt of the noseguard.

The **noseguard** is in a 1 alignment. He should attack the base block by the center. As the noseguard feels the down block by the offensive guard, he should instantly realize that he is being double-teamed. The noseguard should shock the center, grab him, and perform a seat roll into the legs of the guard, preventing the guard from working up to the eagle linebacker.

The **inside linebacker** is in a 3 alignment. On this play, the inside linebacker will read the offensive guard blocking down on the noseguard, and he will feel a full-flow path by both backs in the 3 gap. The inside linebacker should attack the 3 gap and attempt to make contact with the fullback on the offensive side of the line of scrimmage. He should attack the outside two thirds of the fullback, keeping his outside arm free. The inside linebacker should either make the play on the tailback or make the ballcarrier deviate radically from his intended path.

The **defensive end** is in a 5 alignment and is responsible for the 5 gap. The defensive end will attack the offensive tackle and read the offensive tackle attacking him. When this occurs, the defensive end should stop the offensive tackle's charge, lock him out, and gain separation. He should maintain control of the 5 gap and only spill across the face of the offensive tackle when the ballcarrier has clearly declared his path inside.

The **Sam linebacker** is in a 9 alignment, which is an outside shade on the tight end. The Sam linebacker is responsible for containment to his side of the ball. As he reads the tight end's helmet attacking his outside shoulder, the Sam linebacker should attack the tight end. He should stay square, maintain the line of scrimmage, and squeeze the tight end into the 5 gap, constricting the hole. The Sam linebacker should maintain outside arm control.

■ Split or Field Eagle Cover 7 Versus a Sweep Play to the Tight End Side

Versus a twin formation, the **strong safety** aligns five yards off the ball and splits the distance between the number two receiver and the offensive tackle. He should never align wider than five yards outside of the offensive tackle. The strong safety is now an alley player. He should read through the offensive tackle to the ball. As the strong safety reads the offensive tackle's scoop block on the rush end, he should shuffle toward the ball,

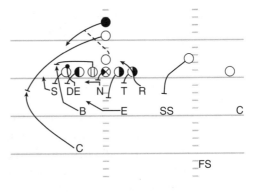

maintaining an inside-out relationship on the ballcarrier. The strong safety should not let the number two receiver cut him off. He also has to be aware of a possible bootleg pass to the field.

The **free safety** aligns 12 yards deep, on the outside edge of the number two receiver (not wider than the hash). The free safety is responsible for the deep one half of the field.

The **rush end** is in a wide 5 alignment. As the rush end reads the offensive tackle releasing flat and inside on a scoop block, the rush end should squeeze and flatten off the butt of the offensive tackle. He should stay square and shuffle down the line of scrimmage until he clears the bootleg.

The **defensive tackle** is in a 3 alignment. The defensive tackle should attack the guard with his inside foot. As he reads the guard releasing through his inside shoulder on a scoop block, the defensive tackle should squeeze the guard into the front-side 1 gap for two counts, disrupting the guard's course. He should then flatten to the football.

The **eagle linebacker** is in a 3 alignment. On this play, the eagle linebacker will read the offensive guard taking an inside release, and he will feel a full flow away by both backs on a wide path. The eagle linebacker should fast flow, maintaining an inside-out position on the ball. He should also hear an "out" call from the inside linebacker, which tells the eagle linebacker that the ball is headed to the perimeter. An "out" call should also communicate to the eagle linebacker that he needs to fast flow and work over the top of all blockers.

The **noseguard** is in a 1 alignment. The noseguard should attack the center with his inside foot. As the noseguard feels the center trying to execute a reach block on him, he should flatten down the line of scrimmage and pursue the football.

The **inside linebacker** is in a 3 alignment. As the inside linebacker reads the offensive guard pulling to the outside, he should yell "out." The inside linebacker should fast flow to the football, pressing the first open gap beyond the 5 gap.

The **defensive end** is in a 5 alignment and is responsible for the 5 gap. As he reads the offensive tackle's helmet and feels the tackle trying to execute a reach block on him, he should attack and press the offensive tackle's body into the backfield. The defensive end should attempt to defeat the reach block, but most important, he should press the line of scrimmage and allow the inside linebacker to press off of his position.

The **Sam linebacker** is in a 9 alignment, which is an outside shade on the tight end. The Sam linebacker is responsible for containing the football. As the Sam linebacker reads the tight end trying to execute a reach block on him, he should step for width with his outside foot and press the line of scrimmage with his inside foot. Doing so will turn the shoulders of the tight end and put the Sam linebacker in position to defeat the tight end's reach block. The Sam linebacker must contain the ballcarrier without widening too far.

■ Split or Field Eagle Cover 5 Versus a Power Play to the Tight End Side

Versus a twin formation, the **strong safety** aligns five yards off the ball and splits the distance between the number two receiver and the offensive tackle. He should never align wider than five yards outside of the offensive tackle. The strong safety is now an alley player. He should read through the offensive tackle to the ball. As the strong safety reads the offensive tackle taking a flat release inside, he should shuffle toward the ball, maintaining an inside-out relationship on the

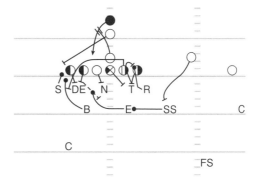

ballcarrier. The strong safety should not let the number two receiver cut him off. He also has to be aware of a possible bootleg pass to the field.

The **free safety** aligns 12 yards deep, on the outside edge of the number two receiver (not wider than the hash). The free safety is responsible for the deep one half of the field.

The **rush end** is in a wide 5 alignment. As the rush end reads the offensive tackle taking a flat inside release and setting inside, the rush end should squeeze the 5 gap, staying square. The offensive tackle's high, flat release often invites the rush end upfield on a pass rush path, which takes the rush out of the play and opens a possible cutback lane. The rush end should attack the offensive tackle, lock his arms out, and spill across the face of the offensive tackle to the ball.

The **defensive tackle** is in a 3 alignment. As the defensive tackle attacks the guard and reads the guard pulling across the formation, he should look inside to the center and jam the center back into the 1 gap. The defensive tackle should stay square and locate the football. He should cross the face of the center only when the ballcarrier has clearly declared his path on the other side of the ball. The ballcarrier will often cut back into the defensive tackle's 1 gap.

The **eagle linebacker** is in a 3 alignment. As the eagle linebacker reads the offensive guard pulling across the formation, he should call out "pull." The eagle linebacker should shuffle to the ball, staying on the back hip of the ballcarrier and looking to press the first open gap to the ball.

The **noseguard** is in a 1 alignment. The noseguard should attack the center with his inside foot. As the noseguard reads the center's back block, he should immediately step to the down block of the offensive guard and jam him into the hole. The flat course by the offensive guard will often create an opportunity for the noseguard to cross the face of the guard. The noseguard should take this opportunity if it arises and then penetrate the line of scrimmage to the ballcarrier.

The **inside linebacker** is in a 3 alignment. When the inside linebacker reads the offensive guard blocking down on the noseguard, feels full flow at him by the running backs, and hears a "pull" call, he should fast flow and press the 5 gap tight off the butt of the defensive end.

The **defensive end** is in a 5 alignment and is responsible for the 5 gap. The defensive end should attack the offensive tackle. He should stop the tackle's base block, staying on the line of scrimmage. As the defensive end feels a down block from the tight end, the defensive end should grab the offensive tackle and perform a seat roll into the tight end, creating a three-man pile in the 5 gap.

The **Sam linebacker** is in a 9 alignment, which is an outside shade on the tight end. The Sam linebacker is responsible for containing the football. As the Sam linebacker reads the tight end blocking down on the defensive end, he should close inside, staying square and closing the 5 gap. By staying square, the Sam linebacker can close the 5 gap but still be in position to flatten to the outside if the ballcarrier bounces to the outside. Many coaches believe in having the Sam linebacker turn his shoulders and cross arm the fullback's kick-out block, spilling the ball outside. In my opinion, that trades one defender for one blocker, and it eliminates the Sam linebacker from making a play on the ballcarrier. It also makes it difficult for the Sam linebacker to react to the outside and drop into coverage versus a bootleg pass. Versus a team that runs the option, if the Sam linebacker turns his shoulders when facing a down block by the tight end, this will make it impossible for the Sam linebacker to slow play the quarterback.

■ Split or Field Eagle Cover 7 Versus an Inside Zone Play

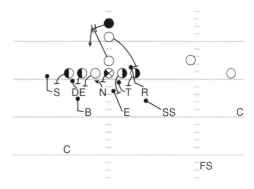

Versus a twin formation, the **strong safety** aligns five yards off the ball and splits the distance between the number two receiver and the offensive tackle. He should never align wider than five yards outside of the offensive tackle. The strong safety is now an alley player. He should read through the offensive tackle to the ball. As the strong safety reads the offensive tackle taking a flat release inside, he should shuffle toward the ball, maintaining an inside-out relationship on the ballcarrier. Split flow by the running backs should tell the strong safety that the ballcarrier may cut back and get outside of the rush end. The strong safety should stack outside on the outside edge of the rush end. This will put him in position to make the tackle if the ballcarrier does cut back. He also has to be aware of a possible bootleg pass to the field.

The **free safety** aligns 12 yards deep, on the outside edge of the number two receiver (not wider than the hash). The free safety is responsible for the deep one half of the field.

The **rush end** is in a wide 5 alignment. He is responsible for controlling the 5 gap. As the rush end reads the tackle attempting a scoop block on the defensive tackle, the rush end should squeeze and flatten off the butt of the offensive tackle. He should work across the face of the fullback's cutoff block.

The **defensive tackle** is in a 3 alignment. The defensive tackle should attack the guard with his inside foot. As he reads the guard releasing through his inside shoulder on a scoop block, the defensive tackle should squeeze the guard into the front-side 1 gap, disrupting the guard's course. He should then locate and attack the ballcarrier.

The **eagle linebacker** is in a 3 alignment. On this play, the eagle linebacker will read the offensive guard attacking the inside number of the defensive tackle, and he will feel split flow by the running backs. The eagle linebacker should press the 1 gap if it's open. If the defensive tackle closes the 1 gap, the eagle linebacker should stack behind the defensive tackle.

The **noseguard** is in a 1 alignment. He should attack the center with his inside foot. The noseguard will feel the center trying to execute a reach block on him, and he will feel a tight path by the running back. When this occurs, the noseguard should lock out, maintain control of the 1 gap, and penetrate into the backfield, forcing the ballcarrier to bounce the ball outside or to cut back deep into the backfield.

The **inside linebacker** is in a 3 alignment. As the inside linebacker reads the offensive guard taking a flat zone step, he should step and stack behind the defensive end, maintaining control of the 3 gap.

The **defensive end** is in a 5 alignment. As he reads the offensive tackle's helmet moving toward his outside shoulder on a reach block, the defensive end should attack and press the offensive tackle's body into the backfield. The defensive end should attempt to defeat the reach block, but most important, he should press the line of scrimmage and allow the inside linebacker to press off his leverage on the offensive tackle.

The **Sam linebacker** is in a 9 alignment, which is an outside shade on the tight end. The Sam linebacker is responsible for containing the football. As the Sam linebacker reads the tight end trying to execute a reach block on him, he should step for width with his outside foot and press the line of scrimmage with his inside foot. Doing so will turn the shoulders of the tight end and defeat his reach block.

■ Split or Field Eagle Cover 7 Checks to Cover 3 Versus a Zone Play From a One-Back Twin Pro Formation

This play should be fit the same way as the two-back zone play. The only exception is that versus a twin pro formation, the Sam linebacker should make a wide call to the defensive end and should walk to a hip alignment. He is still responsible for containment.

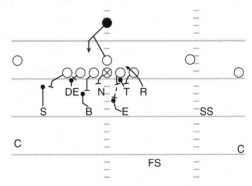

PART III

Stack Defense

CHAPTER 7

Stack Alignments

The Stack defense is a 4-3-4 or a 4-4-3 defensive alignment. Variations of this defensive alignment have been used through the years at every level. The 4-3-4 alignment grew in popularity in the mid-1980s with the success of the University of Miami program under Coach Jimmy Johnson and defensive coordinator Dave Wannstedt. Their success with the 4-3-4 defensive structure continued when Coach Johnson became the head football coach of the Dallas Cowboys.

Versus a two-running-back offense, the 4-3-4 defensive alignment puts nine defenders in the box (see figure 7.1), and the 4-4-3 alignment puts eight run defenders close to the line of scrimmage (see figure 7.2). Both the 4-3-4 and the 4-4-3 defensive structures should be very difficult to run the ball against. I have always liked the 4-4-3 defensive structure because it is played with a three-deep coverage behind the 4 defensive lineman, 3 linebackers, and the strong safety who is at linebacker depth. Having three defenders in the deep zones helps minimize the number of big plays a defense gives up in both the running and the passing game.

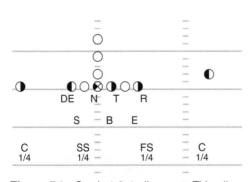

Figure 7.1 Stack 4-3-4 alignment. This alignment is quarters coverage to both the field and the boundary.

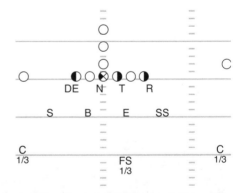

Figure 7.2 Stack 4-4-3 alignment. This alignment has three deep defenders.

The Tampa Bay Buccaneers in the late 1990s and early 2000s used the 4-4-3 alignment very effectively. They did a great job of disguising their coverage. They would show a two-deep coverage, and just before the snap of the ball, one of the two safeties would spin down either to the tight end side or the split end side of the offensive formation (see figure 7.3). The low-level safety would play like an outside linebacker. The other safety would rotate to the deep middle. The corners would bail to a deep-one-third responsibility. Initially showing a two-deep coverage discourages

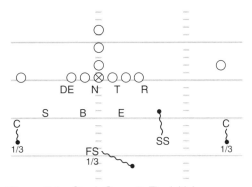

Figure 7.3 Stack Cover 3. The initial coverage shell can be a five-under, two-deep zone. The free safety spins down to a field sky alignment.

the offense from throwing quick passes in the flats (a 4-4-3 alignment is vulnerable to these passes). Spinning a safety down to linebacker depth gives the defense an eighth defender close to the football. The safety who spins down must be a good tackler and have a nose for the ball.

When implementing the 4-4-3, a coach should first teach the players the 4-4-3 alignment without using the initial two-deep disguise. This will allow each defender to learn his proper alignment and his responsibilities versus both the run and the pass. I have only used the two-deep disguise when I had players who were experienced in this system.

Position Alignments

Stack is a generic word used to describe both the 4-4-3 and the 4-3-4 defensive structures. In the Stack (like in the Eagle) structure, a placement call is used to align the defensive personnel. The Stack defense is an automatic Tight placement call. The defensive front four—the rush end, the defensive tackle, the noseguard, and the defensive end—align the same and play the same techniques in both the Stack structures. The rush end and the defensive tackle align to the tight end side of the formation. The defensive tackle is in a 3 alignment. The noseguard and the defensive end align away from the tight end. The noseguard is in a 1 alignment, and the defensive end is in a 5 alignment.

The defensive end, the noseguard, and the defensive tackle are responsible for attacking and controlling the gaps they are aligned in. Their alignment, technique, and execution are exactly the same as in the Eagle defensive structure. Each defensive lineman attacks the offensive lineman he is aligned over with the foot that is aligned over the offensive lineman. In most cases, this is the defensive lineman's inside foot. The defensive linemen should penetrate their gap versus a reach or base block, and they should squeeze an offensive lineman when he releases to the inside.

The defensive end is in a 5 alignment when no tight end is aligned to his side. When aligned to a tight end surface—that is, when the offense uses a two-tight-end formation—the defensive end is in a 7 alignment.

The rush end can be aligned in a 6, 7, or 9 technique. A 6 technique is head up on the tight end, and a 7 technique is aligned on the inside shoulder of the tight end. In both of those alignments, the rush end is responsible for controlling the 5 gap. A 6 or 7 alignment is often used in running situations because these alignments are stronger versus inside running plays.

In a 9 technique, the rush end aligns on the outside edge of the tight end and is responsible for the alley (the area outside of the tight end and inside of the contain player). A 9 alignment places the rush end in a more advantageous pass rush position versus either a tight end or an offensive tackle trying to pass protect against the rush end. It puts the rush end in a strong position to play the quarterback versus an option play, and it ensures that the defense has a contain pass rusher versus all pass actions. A rush end in a 9 alignment will also make it difficult for an offense to get the football to the perimeter of the defense on a run, a sprint-out pass, or a bootleg pass.

Different from the Eagle defense, in the Stack defense, the eagle linebacker can align to the field. When the ball is in the middle of the field, the eagle linebacker aligns to the strength of the formation. The strong safety also aligns to the field or aligns to the formation strength when the ball is in the middle of the field. The strong safety will always declare his position to avoid any possible confusion for the linebackers regarding their alignments. This is particularly important when the ball is in the middle of the field. The inside linebacker aligns to the boundary or in the middle of the formation depending on the defense called and the offensive formation. The Sam linebacker aligns to the boundary, or if the ball is in the middle of the field, he aligns away from the strong safety.

Some coaches choose to have the eagle linebacker always align to the call side (which is to the tight end) with the rush end. The Sam linebacker would then travel away from the call side with the defensive end, as he does in the Eagle defensive structure. This would simplify the run responsibilities and alignments for each linebacker. However, it makes the linebackers' coverage responsibilities more difficult.

4-4-3 Stack Defense

In the Stack 4-4-3, I prefer to have the rush end positioned in a 9 alignment, with his inside leg aligned on the outside leg of the tight end. In addition to the aforementioned benefits of a 9 alignment, it also allows the defensive coach to play an undersized player at the rush end position. A 9 alignment does not have the same physical requirements that a 6 or 7 alignment does. Holding the edge versus a tight end is very different from having to handle a base block from a head-up position or a zone scheme with the offensive tackle and the tight end double-teaming the rush end (before one of the two blockers slips off to the eagle linebacker or Sam linebacker).

I have seen the rush end position played successfully by large inside linebackers who were a step slow to play off the line of scrimmage. The position has also been played effectively by linebackers who didn't have a knack for diagnosing offensive plays but were active, tough, hard-nosed players. These were players who could attack a tight end and hold the edge versus a reach or base block, and they were active pass rushers.

Having coached both the 4-4-3 and 4-3-4 Stack defensive packages, I prefer the 4-4-3 structure primarily because of the coverage played. In the 4-4-3 defense, both corners play a deep one third, and the free safety plays the deep middle third. Playing a three-deep zone coverage gives the defense depth and vision on the football, which is critical to preventing an opponent from executing explosive plays (runs and passes over 15 yards) against the defense.

In the 4-4-3 structure, the alignment rules are the same versus a two-back, one-tight-end offensive formation and versus a two-tight-end, one-back offensive formation (see figure 7.4). I have always treated the second tight end as a fullback aligned on the line of scrimmage. As mentioned earlier, a Tight placement call is made, which aligns the four defensive linemen. Versus a two-tight-end formation, the placement call should be set to the field tight end. Versus a two-back offense or a two-tight-end offense, the strong safety

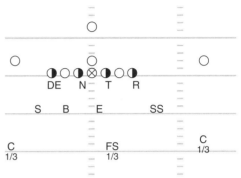

Figure 7.4 Stack Cover 3 versus a double-flanker formation.

aligns two yards outside of the widest defensive lineman to the field (this will be the rush end if the tight end is to the field or the defensive end if the tight end is to the boundary). The strong safety should be five yards off the line of scrimmage.

When the strong safety is aligned in the area across from the offensive line and close to the line of scrimmage, he makes a "box" call, notifying the eagle and inside linebackers that he is in the box. A box call instructs the eagle linebacker to align over the offensive guard to the field. This call instructs the inside linebacker to align over the offensive guard to the boundary. Both players key the offensive guard they are aligned over for their initial run-pass read.

The eagle and inside linebackers are both fast-flow, two-gap players versus the run. They should press the line of scrimmage as quickly as possible. As a general rule, they should take on any offensive lineman who attempts to block them with their inside arm. On some plays, the offensive linemen may double-team the down lineman in front of either the eagle or inside linebacker, and the fullback will be on a course to block the linebacker. In this situation, the linebacker should press the line of scrimmage and attack the fullback as deep into the backfield as possible, taking on the fullback with his inside arm.

Having the eagle and inside linebackers take on blockers with their outside arm—thus forcing the ballcarrier to the outside—may seem like an effective strategy. In theory, when the linebacker spills the ball to the outside, the strong safety to the eagle linebacker's side of the field or the Sam linebacker to the inside linebacker's side of the field should be unblocked and in position to make the play. However, that is not always the case. For example, versus a twin formation, the number two receiver can crack back on the strong safety. Versus a pro formation, the boundary receiver can crack the Sam linebacker and force the boundary corner to make the tackle. Experience has taught me that the best strategy is to have the eagle and inside linebackers take on all blockers with their inside arm, forcing the ballcarrier to cut back.

However, the inside and eagle linebackers will not be able to take on every blocker with their inside arm. For example, when aligned over the offensive guard to a tight end surface, it will be a challenge for the linebacker to get to the outside edge of the offensive tackle when the tackle first steps out to check a possible inside move by the rush end. After checking the rush end, the tackle turns back to block on either the eagle or inside linebacker. In this situation, the linebacker must press the line of scrimmage and attack the offensive tackle as quickly as possible, preventing the offensive tackle from getting his shoulders squared up into the 5 gap. By attacking the offensive tackle as quickly as possible, the linebacker can put the tackle's body into the 5 gap and close the 5 gap. This will force the ballcarrier to either cut back or bounce deep in the backfield to the outside.

If the offensive tendencies indicate that most of the offense's run game is to the tight end side of the formation, both the eagle and inside linebackers should "boss" their alignment to the tight end. This means that the eagle linebacker should align over the offensive tackle on the tight end side and the inside linebacker should align in the 1 gap to the split end side (assuming that the tight end is aligned on the eagle linebacker's side of the field). Staying low and square and pressing the line of scrimmage are the keys to being successful at the eagle and inside linebacker positions in the 4-4-3 Stack structure (or in any defensive structure).

The Sam linebacker and the strong safety have mirrored responsibilities versus the run. As the ball is snapped, both players should bounce in place as they get their initial read. The strong safety and the Sam linebacker should not be too quick to support the run. They must first clear a play-action pass and make sure of the intentions of the play. Versus a perimeter run, they are the contain or force players to their respective sides of the ball. Versus an option play, they have the pitch. Versus an inside or off-tackle running play at them, they should shuffle up to the heels of the defensive or rush end, keeping their outside arm free and maintaining outside leverage on the ballcarrier. If the ballcarrier bounces outside, the strong safety or Sam linebacker should be in position to contain and tackle the ballcarrier. Because of our use of the 9 alignment for the rush end, we have seen very few perimeter plays to the strong safety or the Sam linebacker that would necessitate fast perimeter support.

If the ballcarrier's course penetrates through the 5 or 3 gap, the hole will clearly declare itself. The strong safety or Sam linebacker should step up and tackle the ballcarrier. Both the Sam linebacker and the strong safety should not be too quick to attack the line of scrimmage in either the 3 or 5 gap. They do not want to be caught up inside if the ballcarrier bounces to the outside at the last instant.

If the play starts away, the strong safety or Sam linebacker should shuffle, staying on the back hip of the ballcarrier and in position to play the cutback. In most cases, the strong safety or the Sam linebacker will be unblocked when the play starts away from his position. Before the Sam linebacker or the strong safety pursues a play away, he must clear the possibility of a cutback, a reverse, or a bootleg. The players at these two positions must possess good football awareness.

Versus a pass, both the eagle linebacker and the inside linebacker are responsible for the hook to the curl zones. The strong safety and the Sam linebacker are responsible for the curl to flat zones.

The corners are responsible for their respective deep-one-third zones versus the passing game. They have secondary containment responsibility versus a running play to their side of the field. Versus the pass, the free safety is a deep-one-third defender in the middle of the field. Versus the run, he is an inside-out alley defender.

The only coverage adjustment is made when the offense is in a twin formation with two running backs (see figure 7.5). To maintain an eight-man front (eight defenders in the box), the coverage checks to Cover 7, which is a two-deep coverage with the strong safety being the curl defender to the field. In this alignment, the strong safety is in position to continue to support the run as he does in Cover 3. The free safety is the deep-one-half defender to the field. The field corner is the flat defender to the field, and the

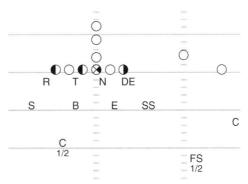

Figure 7.5 Stack Cover 3 checks to Cover 7 versus a twin formation.

boundary corner is the deep-one-half defender to the boundary. The Sam linebacker continues to be the flat defender to the boundary. The inside linebacker is a hook defender to the boundary, and the eagle linebacker is a hook defender to the field. Cover 7 should make it very difficult for an offense to throw the ball when using a twin formation with two running backs. The strong safety is still in a box alignment, so the offense should still find it difficult to run the ball because the defense should have an unblocked defender.

Versus a one-back formation with twin receivers to the field and a flanker set (a tight end and a wide receiver) to the boundary, the strong safety will be aligned on the outside edge of the number two receiver, five to seven yards off the line of scrimmage (see figure 7.6). Versus a two-by-two set with twin receivers to the field, the strong safety will make an "I'm gone" call to the linebackers.

The linebackers' alignment is now different from the box alignment used

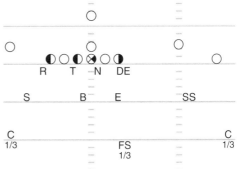

Figure 7.6 Stack Cover 3 versus a twin pro formation.

against a two-back formation. Versus a tight end surface to the field, the eagle linebacker aligns in the 5 gap to the field and is responsible for the 5 gap. Versus a two-by-two formation with the tight end into the boundary, the eagle linebacker aligns in a 3 alignment. The inside linebacker aligns in the 1 gap to the tight end side. The eagle and inside linebackers are responsible for the gaps they are aligned in versus an inside running play. They should stay in their respective gaps, and the ball should be funneled to them unless a teammate makes the tackle first. If one of the down defensive linemen loses his gap, the linebacker to that side would then replace that lineman in his gap.

The Sam linebacker always aligns to the boundary, and his alignment remains the same as when he aligns versus a two-back formation. If there is no tight end into the boundary, the Sam linebacker's inside foot should cover the outside foot of the defensive end. If a tight end is aligned into the boundary, the Sam linebacker should align with his inside foot on the outside foot of the rush end. His run responsibility is the same as when the offense uses a two-back formation. If the ball is in the middle of the field, the Sam linebacker will widen his alignment approximately three yards to help the corner with underneath coverage on the wide receiver to that side of the field.

If twin receivers are aligned into the boundary (see figure 7.7), the Sam linebacker will align on the outside shoulder of the number two receiver, five to seven yards off the line of scrimmage. The Sam linebacker will make an "over" call to the inside and eagle linebackers. This call tells them that the Sam linebacker is now aligned over the number two receiver and that they should slide their alignment toward the boundary and align in the next open gap. The inside linebacker would now be aligned in and be responsible for the boundary 3 gap. The eagle linebacker

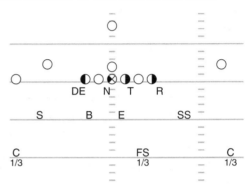

Figure 7.7 Stack Cover 3 versus a twin pro formation with the formation strength into the boundary.

would be aligned in and be responsible for the 1 gap to the tight end side. The strong safety would be responsible for the 5 gap to the field. The strong safety plays the 5 gap the same as he would versus a two-back formation with the tight end to the field. To simplify the rules for the strong safety, he would still make a "box" call, because he is in his box alignment. However, the "over" call by the Sam linebacker would command the inside and eagle linebackers to slide toward the boundary.

Versus a trips formation (see figure 7.8), the placement continues to be made to the tight end, setting the defensive front. The coverage remains Cover 3. Cover 3 allows the defense to continue to outnumber the offense in the box versus the run game. The three linebackers remain in the box, and there is a linebacker or a defensive lineman in each inside gap. Playing Cover 3 balances the coverage and the run support. Cover 3 also makes it difficult for an offense to throw and execute a bubble screen to the field or to the boundary. The downside to playing Cover 3 versus a one-back offensive formation is the threat of four vertical

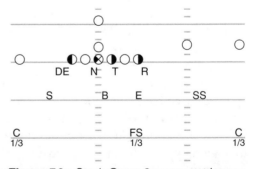

Figure 7.8 Stack Cover 3 versus a trips pro formation.

receivers going against a three-deep coverage. (See chapter 8 for information on defending four vertical pass routes when playing Cover 3 against a two-by-two or three-by-one offensive formation.)

4-3-4 Stack Defense

In a 4-3-4 defensive structure, most teams play quarters coverage (as shown in figure 7.1 on page 78), which I refer to as *Cover 44*. Cover 44 is particularly strong on run downs, putting both safeties in the box and close to the line of scrimmage. Versus the passing game, the corners and safeties divide the field into four deep quarters. Another coverage routinely played with a 4-3-4 alignment is Cover 2 (see chapter 8). In Cover 2, both safeties are responsible for a deep one half of the field, and the corners and linebackers are responsible for the five underneath zones. Cover 2 is used primarily in passing situations. It looks similar in structure to Cover 44, but it is a more conservative coverage than Cover 44.

Versus a two-back, one-tight-end offense, Cover 44 makes the Stack 4-3-4 defense a nine-man front, which is very strong against the run. Cover 44 is also an effective pass defense versus a short passing attack, four vertical pass routes, and most pass routes inside of the hashes.

When playing Cover 44 versus a two-back, one-tight-end offense, the linebackers align in the 5, 1, and 3 gaps. The inside linebacker always aligns in the 1 gap to the tight end side. The Sam linebacker or the eagle linebacker is in a 5 alignment when positioned to the tight end side of the formation. When positioned to the split end surface, the Sam or eagle linebacker aligns in a 3 alignment. The Sam linebacker aligns to the boundary. The eagle linebacker aligns to the field.

Versus a twin formation, the eagle linebacker aligns in a walk position, splitting the distance between the number two receiver to the field and the offensive tackle. His run-pass key is the offensive tackle. His run responsibility is still the 3 gap. If the eagle linebacker is walked too far from the 3 gap to be able to quickly fill the 3 gap versus a running play, he has the option of checking to a Fin stunt, which commands the defensive end to execute a rip stunt into the 3 gap. The eagle linebacker would now be a 5-gap (or alley) defender.

The Sam, inside, and eagle linebackers are fast-flow players. The free safety or the strong safety is the cutback player when the play starts away from his original alignment. The safeties are the force or contain players when the play starts to their side of the field. The safeties are responsible for the pitch versus an option play.

The free safety is aligned to the field over the number two receiver. Versus the passing game, the free safety is responsible for a deep one fourth of the field. The free safety aligns 8 to 10 yards off the line of scrimmage when aligned over a tight end. He will align 10 yards deep when aligned over a wide receiver.

Versus a pro formation with a tight end and a flanker to the field and two backs in the backfield, the free safety reads the number two receiver for his run-pass key. If the number two receiver blocks, the free safety bounces for an instant and reads whether the play is a run or a play-action pass. Versus a run to his side of the ball, the free safety is responsible for containment if the rush end is in a 6 or 7 alignment. If the rush end is in a 9 alignment, the free safety is still responsible for containment, but the ball shouldn't get outside of the rush end. If it does, the free safety should bounce, diagnose the play, and fit where needed. Versus a play away, the free safety is responsible for the cutback.

If the number two receiver releases vertically past a depth of nine yards, the free safety locks on and covers him man to man. If the number two receiver releases into the flat zone to the field at a depth of less than six yards, the free safety looks to help defend the number one receiver to the field. If the number two receiver releases across the formation, the free safety can rotate to the deep middle of the field or look to help defend the number one receiver to the field or to the boundary, depending on the game plan.

Versus a two-back, one-tight-end formation with the tight end aligned to the field, the boundary safety is aligned over the offensive tackle to the boundary. The number two receiver into the boundary is the running back aligned in the backfield. This is one of the main reasons I have placed the strong safety into the boundary when playing Cover 44. The boundary safety's read is the running back. When the running back does anything but release vertically, the strong safety is free of any responsibility for a deep pass. This puts the strong safety in position to quickly support a running play. Versus a pass play, the strong safety is free to help defend the number one receiver into the boundary. If there is a number two receiver on the line of scrimmage into the boundary, the boundary safety will play the number two receiver. In this case, the boundary safety's responsibilities in pass coverage and run support are exactly the same as the free safety aligned to the field over the number two receiver.

The advantage to playing Cover 44 is the run support provided by both safeties. However, that is also the risk involved in playing Cover 44 versus the run game. Both safeties have to be careful not to be reckless when supporting the run. I don't like seeing the safeties getting closer than five yards from the line of scrimmage as they support the run, although they will make many tackles close to the line of scrimmage in the course of a game. If the ballcarrier does penetrate through the defense, a safety who is too close to the line of scrimmage can get caught up in the traffic of offensive and defensive bodies. When this occurs, the ballcarrier can explode right by the safety. And no one is behind the safeties if the ball does get past them.

Both safeties must have good football awareness and must be sure tacklers. As mentioned earlier, the safeties are the cutback player versus a running play away from their alignment. They should be in position to make a play at a depth of five yards from the line of scrimmage when the running back cuts back. If the ballcarrier stays on a course away from the safety's alignment, the safety should rotate through the deep middle.

Because the safeties get their run read off the number two receiver, who is often the tight end to the field and a running back to the boundary, the safeties are occasionally caught flat-footed on a hard run fake. Play-action passes are another risk when playing Cover 44. If the safety gets held by an effective run fake with the number two receiver blocking, the safety must then turn and sprint to get depth in his deep one fourth of the field. Because of the risk of losing the safety on a hard play-action fake, both corners should play with inside leverage on the wide receivers and must be prepared to defend the post route without help.

Both corners are man defenders on the number one receiver to their side versus any vertical route past nine yards. This would include an out, streak, or post route. The corners should not expect help from the safety when defending the post route. If the number one receiver runs a crossing route at eight yards or less, the corner stays in his deep one fourth of the field. Because each corner is man to man versus the number one receiver to his side (without underneath help), the weakness in Cover 44 is against an out route or a tight curl route by the number one receiver. However, very few quarterbacks throw the out route well enough to consistently move the ball down the field.

Versus a trips formation, the defense usually checks to Cover 3 and floods the underneath coverage to the trips (see figure 7.9). The Sam linebacker drops past the number three receiver to the curl area inside of the number two receiver. The inside linebacker walls the number three receiver and carries the number three receiver if he pushes vertical. If either of the receivers aligned to the field releases across the formation into the boundary, the inside linebacker calls out "crosser." He then drops down

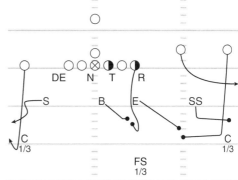

Figure 7.9 Stack Cover 44 checks to Cover 3 and checks flood versus a trips formation.

the boundary hash, expecting a square-in route from the number one receiver aligned into the boundary. When the Sam linebacker hears "crosser" from the inside linebacker, the Sam linebacker should have vision on the approaching crossing receiver and should be in position to break on him. (Refer to chapter 8 for detailed descriptions of Cover 3 and flooding the underneath zones versus a trips formation.)

Offenses rarely set a trips formation into the boundary. Over the course of our 12-game schedule at Penn State University in 2006, opposing offenses only snapped the ball with a trips formation into the boundary five times. However, defenses should prepare for the possibility. When the offense sets a trips formation into the boundary, both Cover 2 and Cover 44 check to Cover 3.

The Sam linebacker walks out and aligns over the number two receiver into the boundary. The Sam linebacker also makes an "over" call to the inside and eagle linebackers (this is the same adjustment the Sam linebacker makes versus twin receivers aligned to the boundary). An "over" call instructs the inside and eagle linebackers to adjust their alignment to the boundary and align in the first open gap. If a tight end is aligned into the boundary, the inside linebacker aligns in a 5 technique and is responsible for the 5 gap. The eagle linebacker would align in and be responsible for the 1 gap to the tight end side. If there is a split end surface into the boundary, the inside linebacker aligns head up on the number three receiver but is still responsible for the 3 gap. The eagle linebacker aligns in the 1 gap to the tight end side. Versus both trips formations, the strong safety aligns to the field, two yards outside of either the rush end or defensive end.

CHAPTER 8

Stack Coverage Calls

One of the best features of the Stack defensive structure is the flexibility of coverages that can be played behind the Stack front, including Cover 3, Cover 44, and Cover 2. This chapter presents these coverages and the adjustments I use with each. Although a defense can play all three coverages, it is difficult to be thoroughly practiced and effective at all three. I prefer to play Cover 3 in all situations, particularly in run down situations, and I use Cover 2 for a change-up coverage. However, many professional, college, and high school teams base out of Cover 44. The coverage package you select should reflect your defensive philosophy.

Stack 4-4-3 Coverage

The Stack 4-4-3 defensive structure has four underneath defenders and three deep defenders in the three deep zones. This coverage is referred to as *Cover 3.* The strong safety is aligned to the field. When the ball is on the hash and the offense is in a pro formation (see figure 8.1), which has one tight end aligned to the field and two running backs in the backfield, the strong safety's inside foot should be one to two yards outside of the widest defensive lineman to his side of the field. Versus a pass, the strong safety should take an exit angle approximately 8 to 10 yards deep at a midpoint between the tight end (the number two receiver) and the wide receiver (the number one receiver). I refer to this drop as a *V drop.*

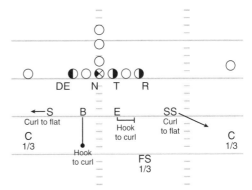

Figure 8.1 Stack Cover 3 versus a pro formation.

The strong safety, as with all underneath defenders, should have his head on a swivel. He must be able to see both the number one and number two receivers as well as the quarterback. The strong safety is a curl to flat defender to the field. He should stay in the curl zone and only expand to the flat if the flat is threatened. If the number one receiver runs an out route to the field, the strong safety's initial alignment would make it difficult for him to provide underneath help to the corner. However, if the strong safety gets a good break on the passing action, he can get in the throwing lane and make the quarterback put air under the pass. This would give the corner a chance to break on the pass and break it up. Very few quarterbacks have the arm strength and accuracy to consistently throw the out route to the field.

When the offense aligns in a one-back formation with twin receivers to the field (see figure 8.2), the strong safety aligns one yard outside of the number two receiver if that receiver is aligned on or inside of the hash. If the number two receiver is aligned outside of the hash mark, the strong safety will align head up to inside of the number two receiver. Versus twin receivers to the field, the strong safety will align five to seven yards off the line of scrimmage, depending on the style of offense and the skill level of the offensive passing game. Versus a strong running offense or an offense that throws several bubble screens during the course of a game, the strong safety will align five yards off the line of scrimmage. Versus a strong passing attack, the strong safety should align seven yards deep. If the offense runs a sprint-out pass, the strong safety would then sprint through the curl zone to the flat. If the number two receiver releases to the flat, the strong safety should take a V drop through the curl zone of the number one receiver. The strong safety should stay in the curl zone as long as possible before expanding to the flat with the number two receiver.

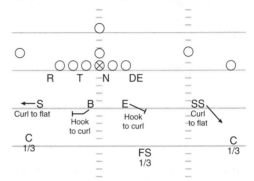

Figure 8.2 Stack 4-4-3 defense versus a one-running-back offense.

As a general rule, the strong safety should not widen past the numbers. This keeps him in position to break on a pass thrown in both the flat and curl zones. The one exception is when the number two receiver runs a wheel route, which has the number two receiver running through the flat zone and turning up the sideline. Because the corner would squeeze and run with the number one receiver on a post route, the strong safety would widen and run with the receiver on a wheel route. A wheel route would declare itself earlier and have a different look to the strong safety than a normal flat and curl route combination.

The Sam linebacker is aligned to the boundary and has the same pass responsibility as the strong safety. The Sam linebacker aligns with his inside foot on the outside foot of the widest defensive lineman to his side of the field. Because the Sam linebacker is aligned into the boundary, he can get underneath a hitch, out, or slant route when the quarterback takes a three-step drop. To do so, the Sam linebacker must take a flat pass drop at the depth he is aligned, which is 5 yards. If the Sam linebacker takes a V drop and exits at an angle of 8 to 10 yards, he will be on top of any pass thrown from a three-step drop. If the quarterback takes a five-step drop, the Sam linebacker should take his initial flat drop to defend a possible three-step pass route, and then he should backpedal on the numbers, which will put him in position to break on both an out and a curl route.

The eagle and inside linebackers both drop and defend the hook zone. If there isn't a threat to the hook zone, the linebacker on that side will expand to the curl zone. For example, versus a pro formation—which has two running backs in the backfield and a tight end and a wide receiver on one side of the football—the linebacker to the tight end side would wall the tight end if he runs an option or hook route. If the tight end releases quickly to the flat, the linebacker expands his drop to the curl zone, looking to defend the next receiver on his side of the ball.

Both corners are responsible for a deep one third of the field. Each corner aligns 8 to 10 yards off the line of scrimmage, depending on the ability of both the receiver and the corner. The corners may align either on the outside or the inside of the wide receiver to their side of the field. Playing on the inside of the wide receiver helps the corner defend the skinny post, but it creates a challenge for the corner in trying to get a good break on a receiver running an out route. Playing on the outside shoulder of the receiver improves the corner's vision of the quarterback and the pass action but makes it more challenging to play the skinny post.

When playing on the outside edge of the receiver on a skinny post route, the corner needs to stay on top of the receiver and drive through the receiver's upfield shoulder as the ball arrives. The split of the receiver will also influence whether the corner aligns to the inside or outside of the receiver. If the receiver takes an abnormally wide split—for example, outside of the numbers—the corner will align inside of the receiver. If the receiver aligns close to the field hash mark, the corner should expect a route that breaks outside and should align a yard outside of the receiver. Both corners read the ball through the receiver they are aligned over, and they should backpedal as the ball is snapped.

When the ball is on the hash and the offense is in a pro formation, the free safety aligns over the offensive tackle to the field. He is positioned 12 yards deep. If the ball is in the middle of the field, the free safety aligns over the offensive guard to the strength of the formation. When the ball is on the hash and the offense is in a twin formation to the field, the free safety aligns 1 yard outside the offensive tackle to the field. The free safety keys the ball and backpedals on the snap of the ball as he diagnoses the play.

As noted in chapter 7, the only coverage adjustment made from Stack Cover 3 is that when the offense is in a twin, two-back formation the coverage needs to check to Cover 7 (see figure 7.5 on page 83). Cover 7 makes it difficult for the offense to throw the ball because an underneath defender is positioned in each of the five underneath zones. In addition, three defenders are aligned to the twin side of the formation to defend the two receivers to the field. Cover 7 also makes running the ball difficult because the strong safety is still in a box alignment, which gives the defense one more defender than the offense has blockers.

When playing Cover 3, defending four vertical passing routes is a challenge. This situation must be constantly emphasized and worked on. The first step in defending four vertical passing routes is for the free safety to make a "verty alert" call any time the offense is aligned in a two-by-two formation (as in figure 8.2). If the number two receiver to the field pushes vertically, the strong safety sinks and carries him. The inside linebacker also sinks down the boundary hash if the number two receiver into the boundary releases vertically. The inside linebacker should not widen beyond the hash because doing so could allow the number two receiver to bend in behind him. The inside linebacker should zone turn back to the ball so he has vision to play the ball rather than the receiver. This approach also puts the inside linebacker in position to make a play on the ball when it is thrown.

Using the strong safety to the field and the inside linebacker to the boundary to carry the number two receivers to their side of the field should force a high and deep throw, allowing the free safety to give ground and play in between the two inside receivers. The free safety should be able to read the quarterback's eyes and shoulders, which will allow him to get a great break on the ball when it is thrown.

A "verty alert" call also tells the boundary corner to play inside of the number one receiver into the boundary. This puts him in position to break on a ball thrown to the number two receiver into the boundary. Because the strong safety and the inside linebacker are going to carry a vertical release by the number two receiver to their side of the field, the corners, the free safety, and the Sam linebacker need to call out any release that isn't a vertical release (such as calling out "crosser" if they see a crossing route). They need to alert the strong safety and the inside linebacker that there are not four vertical pass routes so that both defenders can settle in their pass drops and execute their Cover 3 pass responsibilities.

Versus a trips formation to the field, the underneath coverage should flood the coverage to the field (see figure 8.3). The strong safety should read the number three receiver through the number two receiver. The strong safety should continue to sink with the number two receiver if he reads both the number three receiver and the number two receiver pushing vertically. If either receiver is not pushing vertically, the strong safety should expand to the flat.

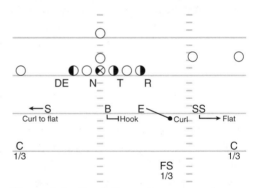

Figure 8.3 Stack Cover 3 versus a trips pro formation.

The eagle linebacker should expand past the number three receiver to the curl zone inside of the number two receiver. If the eagle linebacker reads both the number two and number three receivers releasing vertically, he should drive back to the line of scrimmage in case the running back releases across the line of scrimmage. The inside linebacker should open with width and vision to the number three receiver and should defend the hook zone. If the number three receiver releases vertically, the inside linebacker should sink straight back and defend the number three receiver vertically.

Versus a trips formation with the tight end into the boundary, the eagle linebacker aligns over the number three receiver; however, he will never align wider than five yards outside the defensive end. If the ball is run into the 3 gap, the eagle linebacker is still responsible for the 3 gap. Versus a reach block on the noseguard and the defensive end, both of these players will widen and expand the 3 gap, making it possible for the eagle linebacker to get back into the 3 gap and fill it. If the defensive end gets blocked by the reach block, then the ball will spill out to the eagle linebacker. If the eagle linebacker does have to widen to five yards outside of the defensive end, the eagle linebacker can check to a Fin stunt. A Fin stunt tells the defensive end, who is aligned as a 5 technique, to execute a rip technique inside, closing the 3 gap and forcing the ball outside to the eagle linebacker.

Stack 4-3-4 Coverage

The Stack 4-3-4 package differs from the Stack 4-4-3 package in the coverage played and in the alignment and responsibilities of the linebackers. As noted in chapter 7, Cover 44 is an effective pass defense versus four vertical pass routes, a short passing attack, and most pass routes inside of the hashes.

In Cover 44, the corners and the safeties divide the deep zones into quarters. The three linebackers play a matchup zone on the number two and number three receivers. The eagle and Sam linebackers are curl to flat defenders; however, they only expand to the flat if it is threatened by the number two or number three receiver. If the number two receiver releases vertically past a depth of 9 yards, the eagle or Sam linebacker will allow the safety to pick up and cover the vertical route. The eagle and Sam linebackers do not drop deeper than a depth of 10 yards.

Versus a two-back offense with one tight end (see figure 8.4), Stack Cover 44 aligns the linebackers in the 5, 1, and 3 gaps. The inside linebacker always aligns in the 1 gap to the tight end side. The eagle linebacker is in a 5 alignment if he is to the tight end side of the formation. He aligns in a 3 alignment

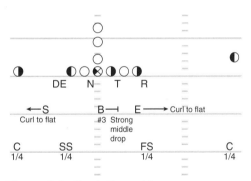

Figure 8.4 Stack Cover 44 versus a two-running-back pro formation.

if he is to the split end surface. The Sam linebacker also aligns in a 5 alignment when he is to the tight end and a 3 alignment when he is to the split end surface. The eagle linebacker aligns to the field, and the Sam linebacker aligns to the boundary.

When the offense shows pass, each of the three linebackers initially bounces in place and reads the release of the number two and number three receivers. Versus the pass, the eagle and Sam linebackers have mirrored pass responsibilities. They are curl to flat defenders. The Sam and eagle linebackers only expand to the flat if the number three receiver to the field (usually the running back) or the number two receiver into the boundary releases to their flat. The inside linebacker opens his hips to the side of the number three receiver (again, most often the running back), who usually releases to the field.

The three linebackers play a matchup zone on the three inside receivers. The linebackers should be close enough to the receivers to defend and deny a pass to the receiver in their area. As a rule, the linebackers do not cover a pass route at a depth of less than 5 yards or deeper than 10 yards. Here are several examples to help explain the zone concept. If the tight end (initially the number two receiver) runs an 8- to 10-yard hook route over the middle, he becomes the new number three receiver. In this case, the eagle linebacker matches up with and defends the tight end. If the running back (initially the number three receiver to the field) runs a flat route, then the inside linebacker matches up with and defends the tight end, and the eagle linebacker expands and defends the running back in the flat. Verses a pro, two-back formation, if the running back, who is the number two receiver to the weak side, runs a flat route, the Sam linebacker expands and covers the running back (see figure 8.5).

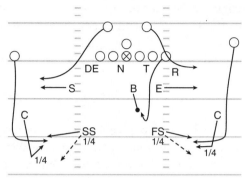

Figure 8.5 Cover 44 versus a pro, split-back formation and pass route.

If any receiver runs a crossing route, the linebacker to the side of the crosser should call out "crosser" to his teammates and that linebacker should expect a crossing route coming from the opposite side of the formation to enter into his area. The eagle and Sam linebackers accept and expand with a crosser and cover the crosser into their flat zones (see figure 8.6).

The inside linebacker continues to be the hook defender off the number three receiver. The inside linebacker defends the hook threat to whichever side the number three receiver releases. The inside linebacker does not chase a crossing receiver, but

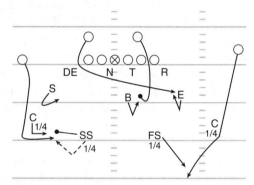

Figure 8.6 Stack Cover 44 versus a pro formation and crossing routes.

rather escorts the crosser to either the Sam or eagle linebacker and returns to the middle hook zone. If no receivers are in the middle hook zone, the inside linebacker settles at a depth no deeper than 10 yards and looks for a deep crossing route or a delay route out of the backfield. The matchup zone concept used by the three linebackers makes Cover 44 a strong pass defense against short and intermediate pass routes between the hashes.

Versus a twin formation, the eagle linebacker aligns in a walk position, splitting the distance between the number two receiver to the field and the offensive tackle. His run-pass key is the offensive tackle. His run responsibility is still the 3 gap, and his pass responsibility remains the same against both a pro and a twin formation.

Figure 8.7 shows an offensive formation with twin receivers and two running backs. In the play shown, the number one receiver to the field runs a square-in route, and the number two receiver to the field runs a flat route. The eagle linebacker expands with the number two receiver and looks to help with the number one receiver. The field corner reads the number two receiver through the number one receiver and breaks up on the number two receiver as he enters the flat zone. The free safety reads the number two receiver, and when this receiver releases flat, the free safety locates the number one receiver and plays the curl or square-in route to the post route or the post route to the curl route. The inside linebacker

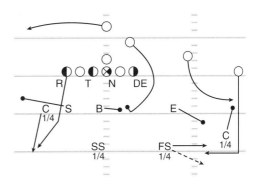

Figure 8.7 Stack Cover 44 versus a twin formation with two running backs.

matches up with and defends the running back (the number three receiver to the field). The Sam linebacker expands with the number two receiver into the boundary. The boundary corner covers the tight end, staying outside the tight end. The strong safety backs down the hash, reads the quarterback, and breaks on the ball.

Versus a twin-receiver, two-back formation with just a tight end on the boundary side of the formation, the strong safety can also make a "cloud" check to the boundary corner. This would make the corner a flat defender and a run support player. The safety becomes a deep-one-half defender to the boundary.

When playing Cover 44, the free and strong safeties align over the number two receivers on their side of the field. I usually play the free safety to the field and the strong safety to the boundary. Both are responsible for their deep one fourth of the field and must have the coverage skills to play a receiver on a deep pass route.

The free safety is aligned over the number two receiver to the field and is responsible for a deep one fourth of the field versus the passing game. The free safety aligns 8 to 10 yards deep when aligned over a tight end. He aligns 10 yards deep when aligned over a wide receiver.

When the offense uses a pro formation, which has a tight end and flanker to the field and two backs in the backfield, the following coverage rules apply. The free safety reads the number two receiver for his run-pass key. If the number two receiver releases vertically past a depth of nine yards, the free safety locks on the receiver and covers him man to man. If the number two receiver releases to the flat at a depth under six yards, the free safety opens and moves toward the number one receiver to the field to help the corner defend that receiver.

We usually play the free safety to first help defend the post route by the number one receiver and then react up if the receiver runs a curl or square-in route. I prefer this approach because it takes away the deep threat first. Big plays lead to points scored, and points scored lead to defeat. However, many teams play the free safety to rob the number one receiver—in this strategy, the safety plays to rob the curl route first and then helps with a post route from an underneath position. Playing from an underneath position forces the quarterback to throw the ball high and allows the corner to play the post route through the upfield shoulder of the receiver. Both strategies are effective. If the tight end crosses the formation, the free safety should continue to look to defend the number one receiver to the field. Your decision on how to play your safeties should depend on your defensive philosophy and the effectiveness of your corners and pass rush.

Versus a two-back formation with one tight end, the boundary safety aligns over the offensive tackle to the boundary. The safety reads the tackle for his initial run-pass read. The number two receiver into the boundary is the running back. As mentioned in chapter 7, this is one of the main reasons I have placed the strong safety into the boundary when playing Cover 44. The boundary safety's pass read is the running back, which will often free him up to provide run support or to help defend the number one receiver into the boundary. If there is a number two receiver on the line of scrimmage into the boundary, this receiver will usually be a tight end; therefore, the boundary safety plays the pass coverage and run support the same as the field safety.

Versus a twin formation to the field, the field safety and the field corner work in tandem to defend the number one and number two receivers. The corner reads the number two receiver through the number one receiver. If both receivers release vertically past a depth of 8 to 10 yards, both the safety and the corner lock on to their respective receiver and cover him man to man. If the number two receiver releases to the flat, the corner reacts up and defends the number two receiver in the flat. Because the corner is aligned 8 to 10 yards from the line of scrimmage and backpedals on the snap of the ball, his reaction to the number two receiver in the flat is delayed enough to allow the safety to work over the top to the number one receiver. However, the corner's reaction is also quick enough to hold the flat route to a minimum gain (refer to figure 8.7).

As mentioned, the corner and safety will stay with their receivers on a vertical route past a depth of 8 to 10 yards, unless the offense uses a wheel route. The wheel route is a common and difficult pass route used against Cover 44. In the wheel route play, the number one receiver runs a post route at a depth of approximately 9 to 12 yards, and the number two receiver releases vertically at a depth of 8 to 10 yards. The number two receiver breaks flat for approximately 4 yards and then turns upfield and gets vertical again down the sideline. Both the post route by the number one receiver and the wheel route by the number two receiver are in a grey area for the corner and the safety. The skinny post route by the number one receiver often provides a pick on the safety, freeing up the number two receiver on the wheel route.

The free safety and the corner can often detect a wheel route because the number one and number two receivers are aligned closer together than they would align normally. The corner and free safety should communicate the possibility of a wheel route and should call out a "quarter" alert to each other. A quarter alert indicates that the corner and safety will exchange the receivers and stay in their respective quarter of the field if a wheel route is run. When the receivers are not aligned closer than normal, the wheel route is easier to defend. Both the corner and the safety can now stay with their respective receiver and not be picked as the receivers run their pass routes.

Versus a trips formation, I have always checked to Cover 3 and flooded the underneath coverage to the trips side of the formation (see figure 8.3 on page 92). Checking to Cover 3 versus a trips formation allows the three linebackers to stay in the box, and it allows each of the front seven defenders to remain responsible for a single gap versus a running play. When the offense is in a trips formation, playing Cover 3 is the best adjustment for defending the run game, and flooding the underneath coverage to the field takes away most route combinations to the three-receiver side of the formation. Flooding the coverage to the trips side of the formation forces the offense to throw into the boundary. Very few offenses want to throw repeatedly into the boundary.

Flooding the underneath coverage to the field does have its drawbacks. For example, when the offense attacks into the boundary (such as in a trips shotgun formation with the running back offset to the boundary), the defense cannot defend a flat route by the running back and a curl route by the boundary receiver. Against this formation, the linebackers simply communicate "flood off" to each other, and they take their normal Cover 3 pass drops. However, before making a "flood off" adjustment, the defense should first make the offense prove that they are capable of and willing to repeatedly throw into the boundary.

Checking to Cover 3 can be a constant strategy for your defense versus a trips formation. By practicing against the various pass route combinations week after week, defenders will gain confidence in their assignments and move toward flawless execution.

Although I choose to check to Cover 3, many teams stay in Cover 44 versus a trips formation (see figure 8.8). The field corner and safety continue to play Cover 44 and defend the number one and number two receivers as they do when defending a twin formation. The inside linebacker continues to open to the number three receiver, who is on the line of scrimmage. The inside linebacker walls out and defends the number three receiver if the receiver enters the middle hook zone past a depth of 5 yards and under a depth of 10 yards. The boundary safety aligns on the boundary hash.

Recognizing a trips formation to the field, the boundary safety makes a "Cheat"

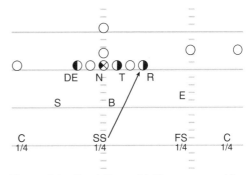

Figure 8.8 Stack Cover 44 Cheat versus a trips pro formation.

call to the boundary corner and the Sam linebacker. The boundary safety now keys the number three receiver to the field and covers him man to man if the receiver pushes vertically. When running a vertical route, the number three receiver to the field will usually bring his route to the boundary safety on the boundary hash.

The boundary corner covers the number one receiver into the boundary man to man on all routes except a shallow crossing route across the formation. The Sam linebacker covers the running back man to man if he releases into the boundary or over the middle. If the boundary safety reads the number three receiver to the field taking any release other than a vertical release, the safety is free to help defend the number one receiver into the boundary versus a post, square-in, or curl route.

Cover 2 Coverage

In both the 4-4-3 and 4-3-4 structures, Cover 2 (see figure 8.9) is an effective coverage change-up and complement to both Cover 3 and Cover 44. Cover 2 is effective for defending the flats, which can be a weakness in Cover 44 and Cover 3. In Cover 2, the corners roll into both flats. Cover 2 has five underneath defenders.

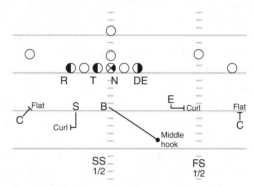

Figure 8.9 Cover 2 versus a twin pro formation.

In Cover 2, both corners align at a depth of five to seven yards from the line of scrimmage with their inside foot aligned on the outside foot of the number one receiver. I like to play the corners at a depth of seven yards. This depth is deep enough to disguise the coverage as either Cover 44 or Cover 3, and it makes reading the corner's technique and responsibility difficult for the receiver. It also gives the corner a little more time to read whether the play is a run, a play-action pass, or a five- or three-step passing action. If the play is a pass, the corner will have more time to read the pass route combinations.

The corners are the flat defenders to their respective sides of the field. They should work to funnel the number one receiver inside to the safety (the safeties are deep-one-half defenders). The corners read the number two receiver through the number one receiver. If the number two and number one receivers both release vertically, the corner should give depth and climb vertically with the number one receiver. This is another reason for the corners to play at a depth of seven yards. Cover 2 can also be adjusted to be a four-deep coverage versus an offensive two-by-two alignment and four vertical passing routes.

In Cover 2, both the eagle and Sam linebackers are the curl defenders to their respective sides of the field. If the eagle linebacker has twin receivers to the field, he widens and leaves the box. His alignment will split the difference between the offensive tackle and the number two receiver. The eagle linebacker keys the offensive tackle for his run-pass read. This alignment slightly weakens the defense against a running play; the eagle linebacker is still responsible for the 3 gap to the field. This is why Cover 2 is used as a change-up coverage when a coach suspects that an offense will try to throw a quick pass to the flat. It is also the reason why Cover 2 is used primarily in long-yardage passing situations.

The inside linebacker is the middle hook defender. Whether the ball is on the hash or in the middle of the field, the inside linebacker's drop is to the middle to the field (or in the middle of the formation if the receivers' splits are abnormally tight to the ball) at a depth of 10 to 12 yards. The inside linebacker wants to drop deep enough to defend a deep square-in route. However, he must also be careful not to drop too deep, putting himself on top of a square-in route or getting too deep to defend the running back on a check-down route over the middle.

The Sam linebacker aligns in the 5 gap to the boundary if there is a tight end surface to the boundary. He aligns in the 3 gap to the boundary if there is a split end surface to the boundary. The Sam linebacker is responsible for the boundary curl zone. He has to be careful not to widen from his original alignment because he is already aligned off the boundary hash. I teach our linebackers to always look to collide with and rub the number two receiver when he takes a vertical release, particularly when the number two receiver is the tight end (whose alignment and body type make jamming the receiver an easier task).

However, the Sam and eagle linebackers should be careful not to chase and abnormally widen their pass drops in an attempt to collide with the number two receiver. Doing so makes the defense susceptible to the number two receiver bending in behind the curl defender at a depth of 18 to 20 yards. This route is referred to as a *bender route*. When the curl defender abnormally widens his pass drop, this opens a passing lane down the hash and underneath the deep-one-half defender (the safety). Most dig and bender routes are completed on or near the hash. As a general rule, the curl defenders should not widen past the college hash marks. The only exception to this rule is when the number two receiver releases to the flat zone. In this case, the curl defender widens and plays under the number one receiver, defending the slant, curl, and square-in routes.

The keys to a linebacker's success in zone pass coverage are his awareness of his area of responsibility (also known as his *landmark)* and his ability to drop to that area (or spot dropping). A linebacker should maintain vision on the quarterback and on potential receivers in his area, and most importantly, he should break on the ball as it leaves the quarterback's hand. The five underneath defenders must communicate with each other, alerting teammates of approaching receivers and route combinations (for example, making a smash call or a crossing call). Defenders should take a direct angle to the ball, aggressively attacking the football and expecting to get the interception. These principles, in my opinion, make zone coverage a more effective coverage philosophy than man coverage.

Both safeties are aligned on their hash marks at a depth of 12 to 14 yards, depending on whether a tight end or a split end is aligned to their side of the field, how far the twin receivers are split apart to the field, and whether the safety is aligned to the field or the boundary. The speed of the receivers may also factor into the depth of the safeties. The safeties are responsible for defending their deep one half of the field.

Versus a trips formation, the defense can still play Cover 2. The eagle linebacker aligns between the number two and number three receivers. The inside linebacker aligns inside of the number three receiver and is a middle hook defender, walling the number three receiver. Four vertical pass routes from a trips formation can be defended in three ways.

The first option is to have the boundary corner funnel the number one receiver inside and disrupt his release. As long as no threat to the boundary flat exists, the corner should sink with the number one receiver. The Sam linebacker opens up with vision to the field, seeing both the running back in the backfield and the number three receiver to the field. If the number three receiver releases on a vertical course toward the middle of the field and climbs to the boundary hash, the Sam linebacker continues to sink down the hash, climbing to a depth of 18 to 20 yards. If any of the four receivers on the line of scrimmage run a route that is not vertical, the defender aligned over that receiver must communicate the situation so that all defenders know they should play normal Cover 2.

The second way to defend four vertical pass routes is to check to "2 Cheat." The boundary safety cheats his eyes to the number three receiver to the field, and the boundary corner plays man to man against the number one receiver to the boundary. If the number three receiver releases vertically, the boundary safety covers him man to man. The field safety has the number two receiver on a vertical release. The field corner continues to read the number two receiver through the number one receiver. If the number two and number one receivers release vertically, the field corner sinks and becomes a deep-one-fourth player. The disadvantage to playing "2 Cheat" against a trips formation is that the defenders cannot cover the out route to the boundary. However, the defense's Cover 2 alignment often discourages the offense from throwing the out route to the boundary.

The third option for defending a trips formation when Cover 2 is the huddle call is to check to Cover 3 and flood the underneath coverage to the trips side of the formation. As mentioned earlier, until an offense proves that they can consistently attack the defense into the boundary with the passing game, checking to Cover 3 and flooding the underneath coverage would be my first adjustment. The simple way to communicate this check is to call "Stack Cover 2 Check 3." The defense would check to Cover 3 when the offense aligns in or motions to a trips formation. The defense would check back to Cover 2 if an offensive motion puts the offense back in a two-by-two formation. If a coach wants to stay in Cover 2, he would call "Cover 2 Play It," notifying the defense to stay in Cover 2 regardless of the offensive formation.

CHAPTER 9

Stack Stunt Packages

An effective zone and man pressure package is a valuable part of all defensive systems. The Stack defense is structured well for running stunts and blitzes with either zone or man coverage. Because the placement call is always made to the tight end side of the formation, a coach can always predict the offensive surface he is stunting toward or into. The Stack package provides a balanced front to execute both zone stunts and man blitzes.

One of the positive aspects of defensive pressure is that it controls the execution of the defenders involved in the stunt or blitz. Players often need to be commanded to aggressively attack the line of scrimmage because defensive pressure can change the tempo of the game. When your defense makes a big defensive play by disrupting the offense and forcing them to make a mistake, it can ignite your team and energize your fans. However, when your team pressures the offense, you must be sure they do so with minimal risk of giving up a big play defensively. Refer to figure 5.1 on page 42 for a checklist of defensive principles and concepts that will help you develop and coach your pressure package.

Zone Coverage Stunts

When a defense pressures an offense with linebackers or one of the defensive backs while playing zone coverage behind the stunt, this is referred to as a *zone stunt*. Zone stunts are an effective way to pressure an offense while minimizing the risk of giving up a big play. Zone coverage—as opposed to man coverage—gives a defense 11 sets of eyes on the ball, putting each defender in position to break on the ballcarrier if he penetrates through the line of scrimmage. Versus a pass, defenders with vision on the quarterback are in position to break on both the quarterback's throwing action and the ball when it is in the air. Because zone stunts decrease the risk of giving up big plays and increase the chances of the defense creating a negative play by the offense, these stunts can make a defensive coach more likely to be aggressive calling defenses. An effective zone stunt package that your players know inside and out will arm you with that flexibility.

As noted in chapter 7, there are two ways to align the outside linebackers. Each type of alignment has its advantages and disadvantages. This chapter describes the outside linebackers' stunt responsibilities in general terms. You should align your outside linebackers in a way that fits your defensive philosophy and the ability and learning levels of your linebackers.

At Penn State, we currently have our eagle linebacker align to the field and our Sam linebacker align to the boundary. This alignment is helpful to our linebackers and their coverage responsibilities. The other option is to use the Eagle defense alignment rules, which will simplify the run responsibilities for each linebacker. When using these alignment rules, the eagle linebacker aligns to the call side, and the Sam linebacker aligns away from the call side. This option would apply to each stunt and blitz detailed in this chapter.

Stack Slant Go Cover 2

Stack is a defense and a placement call, setting the rush end and the defensive tackle to the tight end side of the formation. The noseguard and defensive end align away from the call side (away from the tight end). The eagle linebacker aligns to the call side and the Sam linebacker aligns away from the call side. The inside linebacker aligns in the 1 gap to the tight end side.

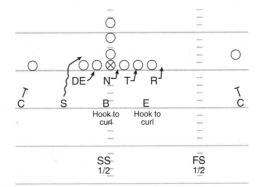

Stack Slant Go versus a pro formation.

On the snap of the ball, the defensive front four—the rush end, defensive tackle, noseguard, and defensive end—all execute a rip technique toward the tight end. The outside linebacker away from the call side stems up to the line of scrimmage and blitzes off the edge. He should "take a picture" as he crosses the line of scrimmage. He needs to instantly determine if the play is a run and whether the play is to him or away from him. Versus an option play to him, he has the quarterback. Versus an inside or off-tackle run, the blitzing linebacker should stay square and work inside and under the blocker, spilling

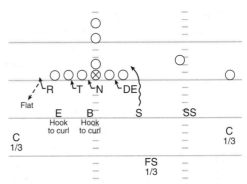

Stack Slant Go versus a twin formation.

the ballcarrier outside. This is critical to preventing the ballcarrier from hitting the inside hole and getting downfield quickly. The outside linebacker should first stun the blocker for a count before he rips inside of the blocker. Doing so will give the ballcarrier an inside path read.

If the outside linebacker rips underneath the kick-out block too quickly, the ballcarrier will quickly bounce the ball outside and get on the edge. Versus a running play away from the stunting linebacker, he should "squeeze smart" down the line of scrimmage. "Squeeze smart" is a term we use to instruct any stunting edge rusher to stay close to the line of scrimmage, keep his shoulders square, and shuffle down the line of scrimmage. Squeezing smart will put the stunting outside linebacker in position to play a possible reverse, a bootleg by the quarterback, or a cutback by the running back.

The coverage played is a four-under, two-deep zone versus a pro, two-running-back formation. Versus a twin-receiver, two-running-back formation, the coverage checks to four underneath defenders and three deep defenders. Versus a one-back alignment with twin receivers to the field and a tight end and flanker to the boundary, the coverage also checks to a four-under, three-deep coverage. Any time the rush end is aligned to the boundary, he drops into the boundary flat and adds to the coverage versus a pass. The rush end needs to make sure he first plays the run before dropping into coverage. Versus a running play away from the rush end, he can fold behind the defensive tackle and play for the possible cutback by the running back. For this stunt, the coverage will include four underneath defenders against all but one formation—versus a trips pro formation, the boundary flat is left uncovered.

Stack Gopher Go Cover 2

Stack Gopher Go is a stunt that provides the opposite movement of Stack Slant Go and is a good complement to that stunt. Stack Gopher Go is best used versus a two-running-back formation. A Stack call places the rush end and defensive tackle to the tight end side of the formation, and it places the noseguard and defensive end away from the placement call and the tight end. The defensive front four execute a Gopher stunt, which commands them to execute a rip technique away from the tight end.

The outside linebacker to the call side stems to the line of scrimmage just before the snap of the ball or just as the ball is snapped, and he stunts off the butt of the rush end. The stunting outside linebacker should stay tight off the butt of the rush end and should cross the face of all blockers, spilling the ball to an unblocked strong safety (or to the boundary corner if the tight end is aligned into the boundary). As the stunting outside linebacker stems up

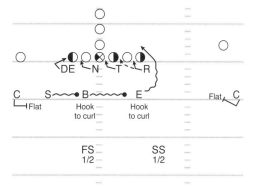

Stack Gopher Go Cover 2 versus a pro formation.

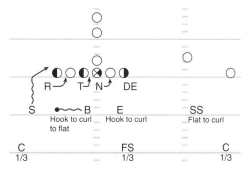

Stack Gopher Go Cover 3 versus a twin formation.

to the line of scrimmage, the remaining two linebackers should stem over the offensive guard on their side of the ball and then flow to the ball. If the ball starts away from the stunting outside linebacker, he should squeeze smart and flatten down the line of scrimmage, staying in position to play a reverse, a bootleg, or a possible cutback.

Against a pro formation, the secondary plays Cover 2. Versus any twin or trips formation, the coverage checks to Cover 3. Versus a twin formation with the tight end aligned into the boundary, the flat is left uncovered. The only eligible receiver who could quickly release for a pass would be the tight end. The boundary corner is in position to cover the tight end. As with all zone or man stunts, the edge rusher would peel with a flare release pass route by the running back. Additionally, most running backs will have to block the edge rusher to try to prevent the pressure from getting to the quarterback. Stack Gopher Go Cover 3 is primarily a run stunt, but it has also been effective versus a play-action pass.

Stack Blast Tango Cover 2 Wall

Stack Blast Tango Cover 2 is a stunt designed as a pass rush stunt. This stunt has five defenders rushing the quarterback, giving the illusion of an all-out blitz on the quarterback. A variation of Cover 2 is played in the secondary. The corners and safeties play Cover 2 just as it is described for Stack Slant Go Cover 2.

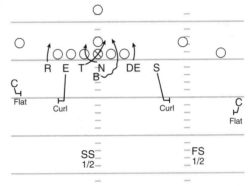

Stack Blast Tango Cover 2 Wall versus a twin formation.

The word *Wall* is an alert to the eagle and Sam linebackers. The eagle and Sam linebackers should show blitz, occupying the attention of the running back and the offensive linemen. Just before the snap of the football, the eagle and Sam linebackers should back off the line of scrimmage and get in position to defend and execute their coverage responsibilities. The eagle and Sam linebackers are curl defenders and are responsible for walling out the number two receiver to their side of the formation. This gives the defense three defenders to cover two receivers, while rushing five defenders.

Both the eagle and Sam linebackers should shuffle back and maintain inside position on the number two receivers. While doing so, the linebackers should have "their head on a swivel," going from one side of the formation to the other. This enables them to maintain vision on the number two receiver to their side of the formation, the quarterback, and a potential receiver coming from the opposite side of the formation. Maintaining vision on the quarterback is crucial to getting a good break on the ball as it leaves the quarterback's hand. When the technique is done properly, the defender should arrive at the receiver as the ball reaches the receiver.

If either number two receiver were to run a seam or dig route to the inside, the eagle or Sam linebacker would maintain inside position on the receiver, sinking vertically with a seam or vertical route or walling out a dig route. If either receiver were to quickly cross the formation at a depth of less than six yards, the eagle or

Sam linebacker should slide a couple of yards with the receiver, call out "crosser" to the other linebacker, and be prepared to accept a crosser from the other side of the formation. Typically, in most pass routes, when one receiver crosses or leaves a zone, another receiver is crossing into that zone from the other side of the formation. When both of the number two receivers run crossing routes, the eagle and Sam linebackers exchange receivers.

The Tango stunt refers to the defensive tackle and the noseguard. The *t* in *Tango* refers to the defensive tackle, and the *n* in *Tango* refers to the noseguard. When the Tango stunt is executed properly, it should take both offensive guards and the center to block the stunt.

The defensive tackle takes a lead step with his inside foot at the near hip of the center. The defensive tackle should drive his body through the center's near hip, banging the center and proceeding to cross the plane of the center's body, behind the center. The defensive tackle should work to the 1 gap on the opposite side of the football and penetrate to the quarterback. When the defensive tackle rips through the hip of the center, this should force the offensive guard (who is pass setting on the defensive tackle) to take a hard step inside. The defensive tackle's penetration at an approximate 45-degree angle should make the guard have to turn his shoulders to block the defensive tackle's inside charge.

The noseguard aligns in an inside shade on the offensive guard. The noseguard takes a jab step at the guard, freezing the guard and the center for a count. This allows the defensive tackle to penetrate through the center's hip. The noseguard should then scrape tight off the butt of the defensive tackle to the quarterback. The offensive guard should have a difficult time getting his shoulders turned back square to the line of scrimmage to block the noseguard.

The term *Blast* refers to the inside linebacker and commands the inside linebacker to stunt through the 3 gap to the split end side of the formation. Ideally, the Tango stunt should allow the inside linebacker to penetrate the line of scrimmage unblocked to the depth of the running back. If the protection has the running back responsible for blocking the inside linebacker, the inside linebacker should rip up through the running back's inside shoulder to the quarterback.

Versus a trips formation, the coverage checks to Cover 3, and the outside linebacker aligned into the boundary is the flat defender. The eagle or Sam linebacker aligned to the field is the middle hook defender off the number three receiver.

Stack Double Dagger Drop Cover 2

This stunt is also strictly a pass rush stunt designed for long-yardage situations such as third and long. Stack Double Dagger Drop is designed to look like Stack Bomb, a six-man blitz with man coverage. However, it simply exchanges the pass rush lanes and pass rush responsibilities of the Sam linebacker and defensive end, as well as those of the eagle linebacker and rush end.

Both the eagle and Sam linebackers stem up to the line of scrimmage and stunt off the edge of the offensive formation to the quarterback. The defensive end and the rush end take a quick jab step and reach their hands at the offensive lineman they are lined up over; then they spot drop to an area approximately eight yards deep. When aligned to the field, the defensive end or rush end should drop eight yards deep and split the difference between his original alignment and the alignment of the number two receiver to the field. The end aligned to the boundary should drop straight back, always staying inside of the number two receiver. Both ends should have their head on a swivel so they are able to see both the receiver in their area of responsibility and the quarterback. The inside linebacker shows blitz in the tight 1 gap. Just before the snap of the ball, he backs up and drops

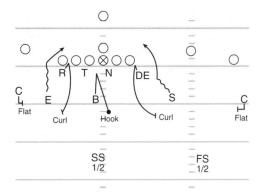

Stack Double Dagger Drop Cover 2 versus a twin formation.

into the middle hook zone. The corners and safeties play Cover 2.

Versus a trips formation, the coverage checks to Cover 3. The strong safety to the field spins down over the number two receiver to the field, and the free safety rotates to the deep middle of the field. The rush end or defensive end to the field continues to drop outside of the number three receiver and inside of the number two receiver, still at a depth of eight yards. The inside linebacker is the middle dropper off the number three receiver, and he makes a "flat" call to the defensive or rush end into the boundary, telling him to drop into the boundary flat. The quarterback will feel quick outside pressure and will usually throw the ball quickly.

Man Coverage Stunts

The two six-man stunts I like the most are run out of the Stack defense. They both involve blitzing the Sam and eagle linebackers, who can be blitzed either off the edge of the formation or inside through the run gaps they are responsible for. Both Stack Bullets and Stack Bomb are balanced blitzes, with six defenders pressuring the line of scrimmage and the four defensive backs in coverage to handle all variations of formations. Simply stated, the linebackers blitz, and the defensive backs cover.

Both blitzes can be effective versus both the run and the pass; however, I favor using Stack Bullets (with the outside linebackers blitzing inside) to stop the run and using Stack Bomb (with the outside linebackers blitzing from the outside, off the edge of the formation) to pressure the quarterback. The four defensive backs are in man coverage on the four receivers on the line of scrimmage. Versus a pro, two-running-back formation, the strong safety has the tight end, and the free safety has the first running back to the boundary side of the formation. The inside linebacker has the running back to the tight end side of the formation. Versus a twin, two-running-back formation, the inside linebacker has the running back to the tight end side of the formation, the boundary corner has the tight end, the strong safety has the running back to the field, the free safety has the number 2 receiver to the field, and the field corner has the number 1 receiver to the field. Versus running back motion or an offset running back, the safety is the adjuster and takes the running back, and the inside linebacker has the running back in the home position.

Stack Bullets Cover 0

Stack alignment rules apply. The Sam and eagle linebackers blitz the gaps they are responsible for. Versus a two-tight-end offense, the placement is made to the field or to a dominant tight end if a team has one tight end who is clearly a much better blocker than the other tight end. Versus a formation with no tight end, the placement is made to the field. The linebacker to the 3-technique side (usually to the field) makes a "G" call to the defensive tackle. A G call commands the defensive tackle to rip into the 1 gap, opening the 3 gap for the linebacker to blitz through.

The defensive front four—the rush end, the defensive tackle, the noseguard, and the defensive end—all attack and penetrate one yard across the line of scrimmage. Versus a pass, the defensive front four should continue upfield to pressure the quarterback. The defensive end and the rush end are responsible for containment. Versus an option play, they are responsible for the pitch.

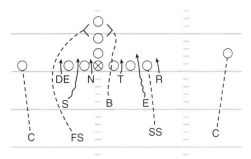

Stack Bullets versus a pro formation.

The defensive tackle and noseguard can also run a Tango stunt as part of a Bullets blitz. The Sam and eagle linebackers blitz the gap they are responsible for. I recommend that the Sam and eagle linebackers be at the line of scrimmage when the ball is snapped. They can accomplish this by exploding up to the line of scrimmage just before the snap of the ball, or by lining up in the gap they are going to blitz. To disguise the blitz, the Sam and eagle linebackers can line up at the line of scrimmage (in their gap), and just before the snap of the ball, they back up to their normal alignment.

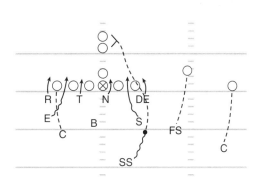

Stack Bullets versus a twin formation.

The inside linebacker aligns in the 1 gap to the tight end side. Versus a running play, he should shuffle and close in on the ballcarrier. In many cases, the ballcarrier will cut back to the tight 1 gap. The inside linebacker must realize that he and the two safeties are the erasers if the ball does penetrate the line of scrimmage. Versus a passing play with the offense in a two-back formation, the inside linebacker has the running back to the tight end side of the formation. If one of the backs is offset, the strong safety has the offset back man to man, and the inside linebacker has the running back in the dot position (behind the quarterback). Versus a one-back formation, the inside linebacker has the running back man to man in coverage.

Versus a pass, the inside linebacker should assume that the running back will be responsible for blocking one of the blitzing linebackers. The inside linebacker should quickly close up to the running back and become the seventh defender rushing. The inside linebacker is often the unblocked rusher. Closing up to the running back is also important because it helps the inside linebacker prevent a slip screen to the running back. Screens are potential big plays for an offense versus man and zone pressure.

The strong safety aligns to the boundary. Versus a two-by-two formation, the strong safety has the number two receiver to the boundary. Versus a trips formation, the strong safety has the number three receiver to the field.

The free safety has the number two receiver to the field. When either safety is covering a tight end or a running back, the safety should align at a depth of nine yards and should bounce as the ball is snapped. If the tight end or running back blocks, the safety should fit the run. Versus an option play, the safeties have the quarterback. As with the inside linebacker, the safeties have to be the erasers if the ball does get through the front line. They must be sure tacklers and put the ball on the ground.

Stack Bomb Cover 0

Stack Bomb Cover 0 is the same blitz as Stack Bullets for all defenders except the defensive ends and the outside linebackers. They exchange responsibilities. The Sam and eagle linebackers blitz off their respective edges. The rush end and the defensive end execute a rip technique inside. This blitz is used primarily in neutral or passing situations. You can also run this stunt with a double twist between the defensive tackle and the rush end, and between the noseguard and the defensive end. As with the Bullet blitz, the inside linebacker should blitz engage the running back he has in coverage, becoming the seventh rusher. He must also close up on the running back in case of a slip screen. The defensive tackle and noseguard can also run a Tango stunt as part of a Bomb blitz. Like the double-twist stunt, this will control the execution of the front four rushers and will add to the pass rush.

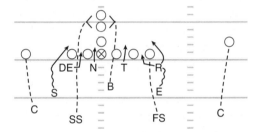

Stack Bomb Cover 0 versus a pro formation.

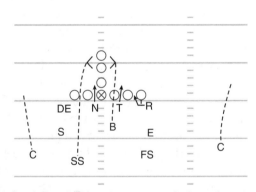

Stack Bomb Cover 0 versus a twin formation.

CHAPTER 10

Stack Versus Common Running Plays

This chapter provides details on the practical application of the Stack 4-4-3 defense versus a cross section of common running plays, including information on each defender's initial read and reaction to various blocking schemes. The plays diagrammed in this chapter will provide you with a basic understanding of how to defend the multitude of offensive plays your defense will encounter during the course of a season.

As you review the diagrammed plays, you should realize that the blocking schemes used in a particular diagram may differ from the blocking schemes you see from the teams you play. Also, the way you choose to defend a particular play—that is, each individual defender's fit within the defense—may vary from my philosophy. That is part of what makes the game of football so interesting. There is more than one way to close gaps and shut down offensive running lanes. All coaches should be strong in their beliefs but also willing to explore new ideas.

Defending the Run

This section details the responsibilities of the front eight defenders versus common running plays. The responsibilities for the corners and the free safety are not described. When playing Cover 3, the free safety and the corners are secondary run support players. The free safety initially takes two steps backward and reads the play. When he reads that the offense is running the football, he fits where needed and puts himself in position to tackle the ballcarrier if the ballcarrier penetrates through the defensive front. Each corner should always be in position to contain the football when it is run to his side. The corner should also be in position to engage in a deep pursuit course when the ball is run away from him.

■ Stack Cover 3 Versus an Isolation Play to the Tight End Side

The **strong safety** is aligned five yards off the line of scrimmage, two yards outside of the rush end. The strong safety's run-pass read is the tight end. The strong safety is responsible for containing the football. When the strong safety recognizes full flow (both running backs at him), he should bounce and stay in a stack position behind the rush end. He will now be in position to make a play in the alley if the ballcarrier bounces the ball outside.

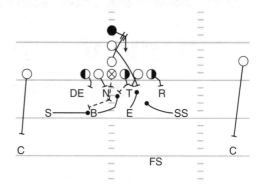

He will also be in position to fit in the 5 gap if the ballcarrier's path takes him through the 5 gap. The strong safety should always keep his outside arm free.

The **rush end** is in a 9 alignment. He is responsible for controlling the alley (the area outside of the rush end and inside of the strong safety). He reads the tight end for his initial run-pass read. The rush end should attack the tight end with his inside foot and should constrict the 5 gap.

The **defensive tackle** is in a 3 alignment, which is an outside shade on the offensive guard. He is responsible for controlling the 3 gap. As the defensive tackle attacks the offensive guard and feels a double team by the offensive guard and tackle, the defensive tackle should attack the base block of the guard, stopping his charge. He should then grab the guard and execute a seat roll into the offensive tackle's legs, creating a pile in the 3 gap.

The **eagle linebacker** is in a 3 alignment. On this play, the eagle linebacker will read the offensive guard's helmet attacking the outside shoulder of the defensive tackle, and he will feel full flow to his side of the ball. When this occurs, the eagle linebacker should quickly check the path of the backs. If both backs are on a course toward the 1 gap, the eagle linebacker should attack the 1 gap and take on the fullback with his inside leg and arm. If both backs are on a course toward the 3 gap (as shown in the diagram), the eagle linebacker should fast flow and press the first open seam tight off of the defensive tackle's butt. His fit should be as tight as possible, and he should take on the fullback with his inside leg and arm.

The **noseguard** is in a 1 alignment. He should attack the center with his inside foot. As the noseguard feels the center attempting to release to the inside linebacker on a scoop block, the noseguard should squeeze the offensive center into the frontside 1 gap for two counts, keeping him off the inside linebacker. The noseguard should then release to the football.

The **inside linebacker** is in a 3 alignment. As the inside linebacker reads the scoop release of the offensive guard and feels full flow away, the inside linebacker should fast flow to the far 1 gap.

The **defensive end** is in a 5 alignment and is responsible for the 5 gap. As he attacks the offensive tackle and reads the offensive tackle releasing inside on a cutoff block, the defensive end should squeeze the offensive tackle into the 3 gap. While doing so, the defensive end needs to stay square.

The **Sam linebacker** is in a hip alignment, four yards deep and two yards outside of the defensive end. The Sam linebacker reads the offensive guard for his run-pass key. As he reads the scoop block by the guard, the Sam linebacker should shuffle toward the ball, staying on the back hip of the ballcarrier. He should always clear the bootleg pass, the reverse, and a possible cutback. He should maintain an outside-in relationship on the ballcarrier.

■ Stack Cover 3 Versus an Isolation Play Away From the Tight End Side

The **strong safety** is aligned five yards off the line of scrimmage and two yards outside of the rush end. His run-pass read is the tight end. The strong safety is responsible for containing the football. When the strong safety recognizes that the play is starting away from his alignment, he should shuffle and be in position to tackle the ballcarrier if he cuts back. The strong safety should always clear the bootleg pass and the reverse, and he should maintain an outside-in relationship on the ballcarrier.

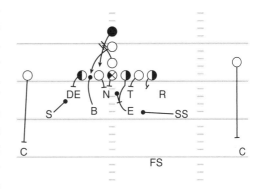

The **rush end** is in a 9 alignment, which is an outside shade on the tight end. He is responsible for controlling the alley. His run-pass read is the tight end. As the tight end releases inside on a cutoff block, the rush end should attack the tight end and squeeze him into the 5 gap, staying square and constricting the cutback lane.

The **defensive tackle** is in a 3 alignment, which is an outside shade on the offensive guard. He is responsible for controlling the 3 gap. The defensive tackle will read the guard releasing inside on a scoop course, and he will also feel the offensive tackle on a scoop course. When this occurs, the defensive tackle should squeeze the guard into the 1 gap for two counts before flattening to the ball.

The **eagle linebacker** is in a 3 alignment. He will read the offensive guard's helmet attacking the inside shoulder of the defensive tackle, and he will feel full flow away. The eagle linebacker should attack the 1 gap (with his inside arm across the face of the offensive guard) and should flow to the ball.

The **noseguard** is in a 1 alignment. He should attack the center's base block with his inside foot. As the noseguard feels a down block by the offensive guard, he should grab the center and execute a seat roll into the offensive guard, staying on the line of scrimmage and creating a pile in the 1 gap.

The **inside linebacker** is in a 3 alignment. As the inside linebacker reads the double team by the offensive guard and feels full flow into the 3 gap, he should attack the fullback and meet him on the offensive side of the ball. The inside linebacker should take on the fullback with his inside arm. He should either make the play or force the ballcarrier to deviate radically from his intended path.

The **defensive end** is in a 5 alignment and is responsible for the 5 gap. As he attacks the offensive tackle and reads the offensive tackle attacking his outside arm, the defensive end should attack the offensive tackle with his inside foot and should control the 5 gap.

The **Sam linebacker** is in a hip alignment, four yards off the line of scrimmage and two yards outside of the defensive end. As the Sam linebacker reads the offensive tackle executing a base block on the defensive end, he should step and stack behind the defensive end, maintaining an outside-in relationship on the ballcarrier. He must be in position to make the tackle in the 3 gap or in the alley (if the ballcarrier bounces to the outside).

■ Stack Cover 3 Versus a Trap Play to the Defensive Tackle

The **strong safety** aligns five yards off the line of scrimmage and two yards outside of the rush end. His run-pass read is the tight end. The strong safety is responsible for containing the football. When the strong safety recognizes full flow at him, he should bounce and stay in a stack position behind the rush end. He is now in position to make a play in the alley. He is also in position to fit in the 5 gap if the ballcarrier's path takes him through the 5 gap. The strong safety should always keep his outside arm free.

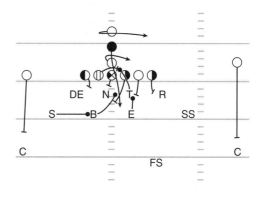

The **rush end** is in a 9 alignment. He is responsible for controlling the alley. His run-pass read is the tight end. The rush end should attack the tight end with his inside foot and should constrict the 5 gap.

The **defensive tackle** is in a 3 alignment, which is an outside shade of the offensive guard. He is responsible for controlling the 3 gap. As the defensive tackle attacks the offensive guard and feels a veer release by the offensive guard, the defensive tackle should squeeze and disrupt the release of the offensive guard. The defensive tackle should try to stay as square as possible and cross the face of the trapping guard.

The **eagle linebacker** is in a 3 alignment. As the eagle linebacker reads the offensive guard on a veer release inside and hears a "pull" call from the inside linebacker, he should fast flow tight off the butt of the defensive tackle. His fit should be as tight as possible inside of the offensive tackle.

The **noseguard** is in a 1 alignment. The noseguard should attack the center with his inside foot. As the noseguard feels the center executing a base block on him, he should squeeze the center back into the far 1 gap. The noseguard should stay square and keep his outside arm free.

The **inside linebacker** is in a 3 alignment. As the inside linebacker reads the offensive guard pulling across the formation, he should call out "pull" and should fast flow to the far 1 gap. The inside linebacker must press the 1 gap inside of the offensive guard.

The **defensive end** is in a 5 alignment and is responsible for the 5 gap. As he attacks the offensive tackle and reads the offensive tackle's inside release on a cutoff block, the defensive end should squeeze the offensive tackle into the 3 gap while staying square.

The **Sam linebacker** is in a hip alignment. The Sam linebacker reads the offensive guard for his run-pass key. As he reads the guard pulling, the Sam linebacker should shuffle to the ball, staying on the back hip of the ballcarrier. This puts him in position to play a possible cutback, reverse, or bootleg pass.

■ Stack Cover 3 Versus a Sweep Play to the Tight End Side

The **strong safety** aligns five yards off the line of scrimmage and two yards outside of the rush end. His initial run-pass read is the tight end. The strong safety is responsible for containing the football. When the strong safety recognizes both running backs on a wide course at him, he should bounce for an instant, staying in a stack position behind the rush end. If the rush end beats the tight end's reach block and contains the ballcarrier, the strong safety will be in position to make a play in the 5 gap. If the rush end gets blocked or is not upfield far enough to contain the ballcarrier, the strong safety should attack 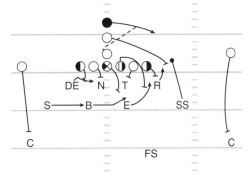 the fullback (as shown in the diagram). In doing so, the strong safety should stay square to the line of scrimmage and should move no more than two yards across the line of scrimmage. He should contain the running back, forcing him on a course inside of the strong safety. The strong safety should keep his outside arm free. He should be in position to flatten to the outside to make a play on the ballcarrier if the ballcarrier bounces to the outside.

The **rush end** is in a 9 alignment. His read is the tight end. As the tight end tries to execute a reach block on the rush end, the rush end should attack the tight end with his inside foot and press the tight end's body two yards across the line of scrimmage. Doing so will turn the tight end's shoulders perpendicular to the line of scrimmage, allowing the rush end to defeat his block. This will force the ballcarrier inside of the 5 gap or force him deep and wide to the outside, which will allow the defensive pursuit to run the ballcarrier down.

The **defensive tackle** is in a 3 alignment and is responsible for controlling the 3 gap. As the defensive tackle attacks the offensive guard and reads him pulling to the outside, he will know immediately that the offensive tackle is blocking down on him. The defensive tackle should beat the offensive tackle's down block across the line of scrimmage and flatten to the ballcarrier. Another option is for the defensive tackle to club across the face of the offensive tackle and flatten to the ball. If the defensive tackle crosses the face of the offensive tackle, the defensive tackle should be careful not to get displaced off the line of scrimmage, which would interfere with the linebacker's pursuit course.

The **eagle linebacker** is in a 3 alignment. As the eagle linebacker reads the offensive guard pulling to the outside, he should yell "out" and immediately press the first open seam to the ballcarrier. He should take on all blockers with his inside arm.

The **noseguard** is in a 1 alignment. The noseguard should attack the center with his inside foot. As the noseguard feels the center on a wide scoop path, he should try to disrupt the center's path and flatten down the line of scrimmage in pursuit of the ballcarrier.

The **inside linebacker** is in a 3 alignment. As the inside linebacker reads the offensive guard on a flat scoop course, feels full flow away, and hears an "out" call, he should fast flow across the face of the center and pursue inside out to the ballcarrier.

The **defensive end** is in a 5 alignment. As he attacks the offensive tackle and reads the offensive tackle's inside release on a cutoff block, the defensive end should squeeze the offensive tackle into the 3 gap. The defensive end should stay square and should cross the offensive tackle's face in pursuit of the ballcarrier.

The **Sam linebacker** is in a hip alignment. The Sam linebacker reads the offensive guard for his run-pass key. As he reads the guard on a scoop course and hears an "out" call, the Sam linebacker should begin to shuffle in pursuit of the ballcarrier. He should always clear a possible reverse or bootleg pass—as well as a potential throw back to the quarterback—before taking a deep pursuit course to the ball.

■ Stack Cover 3 Versus a Power Play to the Tight End Side

The **strong safety** is aligned five yards off the line of scrimmage and two yards outside of the rush end. His run-pass read is the tight end. The strong safety is responsible for containing the football. When the strong safety recognizes full flow at him and a wide path by the fullback, he should shuffle quickly to a stack position behind the rush end. He should take on the full-back with his inside arm. The strong safety should stay square and keep his outside arm free. This puts him in position to tackle the ballcarrier if the ballcarrier runs

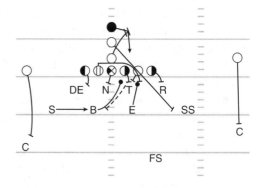

through the 5 gap or to contain the football if the ballcarrier bounces outside.

The **rush end** is in a 9 alignment. His read is the tight end. As he reads the tight end trying to execute a base block on him, the rush end should attack the tight end, constrict the 5 gap, and keep his outside arm free.

The **defensive tackle** is in a 3 alignment. On this play, the defensive tackle will read the offensive guard attacking his outside shoulder, and he will feel the double team from the offensive tackle. When this occurs, the defensive tackle should attack the offensive guard's base block and stop his charge. The defensive tackle should grab the offensive guard and perform a seat roll into the offensive tackle, creating a three-man pile at the line of scrimmage.

The **eagle linebacker** is in a 3 alignment. As the eagle linebacker reads the double team and hears a "pull" call, he should press tight off of the butt of the defensive tackle, beating the guard into the hole. He should take on the offensive guard with his inside arm.

The **noseguard** is in a 1 alignment. The noseguard should attack the center with his inside foot. As the noseguard feels the center attempting to execute a base block on him, he should squeeze the center into the far 1 gap. He should stay square and stay in position to make the tackle if the ballcarrier cuts back into the 1 gap.

The **inside linebacker** is in a 3 alignment. As the inside linebacker reads the offensive guard pulling across the formation, he should call out "pull" and should fast flow into the far 1 gap.

The **defensive end** is in a 5 alignment and is responsible for the 5 gap. As he attacks the offensive tackle and reads the offensive tackle's inside release on a cutoff block, the defensive end should squeeze the offensive tackle into the 3 gap while staying square.

The **Sam linebacker** is in a hip alignment. He reads the offensive guard for his run-pass key. As he reads the guard pulling, the Sam linebacker should shuffle to the ball, staying on the back hip of the ballcarrier. He should always clear a possible reverse or bootleg pass before pursuing the ballcarrier.

■ Stack Cover 3 Versus an Inside Zone Play to the Tight End Side

The **strong safety** aligns five yards off the line of scrimmage and two yards outside of the rush end. The strong safety's initial run-pass read is the tight end. On this play, the strong safety will read the tight end executing a base block on the rush end, and he will feel the split flow of the running backs in the backfield. The strong safety should stack behind the rush end and fit where needed.

The **rush end** is in a 9 alignment. His read is the tight end. As he reads the tight end trying to execute a base block on him, he should attack the tight end, staying square and constricting the 5 gap.

The **defensive tackle** is in a 3 alignment. As the defensive tackle reads the offensive guard attacking his outside shoulder, he should attack the guard and control the 3 gap.

The **eagle linebacker** is in a 3 alignment. The eagle linebacker will read the offensive guard attacking the defensive tackle, and he will feel the split flow of the running backs in the backfield. When this occurs, the eagle linebacker should stack behind the defensive tackle and be ready to shuffle back into the 1 gap, anticipating a cutback.

The **noseguard** is in a 1 alignment. The noseguard should attack the center with his inside foot. As he reads the center releasing upfield on a scoop course, the noseguard should squeeze the center into the far 1 gap for two counts. He should then penetrate into the backfield and pursue the ballcarrier.

The **inside linebacker** is in a 3 alignment. As the inside linebacker reads the offensive guard flatten on a scoop block, he should step and stack behind the noseguard. As he feels the split flow of the running backs in the backfield, the inside linebacker should be prepared to react to the ballcarrier on a potential cutback.

The **defensive end** is in a 5 alignment. As the defensive end attacks the offensive tackle and reads the tackle's veer release, he should squeeze and disrupt the offensive tackle's release. As he squeezes the release, he will close the 3 gap. As the defensive end reads the fullback on a course to kick him out, he should attack the fullback's inside shoulder and cross the face of the fullback.

The **Sam linebacker** is in a hip alignment. He reads the offensive guard for his run-pass key. As he reads the guard on a scoop course and feels the split flow of the running backs in the backfield, the Sam linebacker should shuffle to the ball. He should stay on the back hip of the ballcarrier and keep his outside arm free. If the ballcarrier cuts all the way back behind the defensive end, the Sam linebacker is responsible for containing and tackling the ballcarrier.

■ Stack Cover 3 Versus an Inside Zone Play Away From the Tight End Side (From a Twin Pro One-Back Formation)

The **strong safety** is aligned five yards off the line of scrimmage and one yard outside of the number two receiver. He is responsible for containment versus a running play.

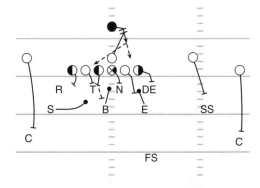

The **rush end** is in a 9 alignment. When the tight end releases inside to execute a cutoff block, the rush end should attack and squeeze the tight end into the 5 gap.

The **defensive tackle** is in a 3 alignment. As the defensive tackle reads the offensive guard releasing inside on a scoop block, the defensive tackle should squeeze the offensive guard into the 1 gap. Doing so will close the 1 gap and will prevent the guard from having a free release to the inside linebacker.

The **eagle linebacker** is in a 3 alignment. As the eagle linebacker reads the offensive guard attempting to execute a reach block, he should shuffle, stun the guard, and control the 3 gap, keeping his outside arm free.

The **noseguard** is in a 1 alignment. The noseguard should attack the center with his inside foot. As he reads the center attempting to execute a reach block on him, the noseguard should maintain control of the 1 gap and press upfield to the ballcarrier.

The **inside linebacker** is in a 1 alignment. As the inside linebacker reads the offensive guard stepping inside on a scoop course and feels the running back flow away on a tight path, the inside linebacker should press the 1 gap and take on the guard with his inside arm.

The **defensive end** is in a 5 alignment. He should attack and control the 5 gap.

The **Sam linebacker** is in a hip alignment. He reads the offensive tackle for his run-pass key. As he reads the tackle on a scoop course, the Sam linebacker should shuffle to the ball, staying on the back hip of the ballcarrier. If the offensive tackle were to release up to him, the Sam linebacker should squeeze the offensive tackle into the 5 or 3 gap, keeping his outside arm free.

PART IV

Eagle-Stack Combos

CHAPTER 11

Eagle With Stack Modifications

The Eagle and Stack defensive structures can effectively stand alone, and many college and high school programs use the Eagle or the Stack defense exclusively. The value in adhering to one defensive package is that the coaching staff gets to know the defense thoroughly. That familiarity should enable them to make all the adjustments needed versus various formations, personnel groupings, and offenses. In addition, when a coach knows his system inside and out, this allows him to teach and communicate it effectively to his players. The result is better execution. And a defense's first and foremost concern should be its own execution.

Sticking to a single defensive package can also reduce the amount of time required to practice against the opponent's offense. Each defensive package has adjustments to various formations that are unique, and each package has problem areas that need to be practiced so your team can make additional adjustments to handle these areas. Thus, when a defense stays primarily in one defensive structure and the team knows that structure well, the defensive unit can focus more on the opponent's tendencies and any offensive irregularities that an opponent might use. And perhaps most important, when a team technically and tactically masters a defensive package, this gives each player great confidence in his alignment, assignments, and execution. When players are confident that they can man their areas of responsibility—and when they keep a low pad level and have a strong desire to get to the ball—they can afford to be less concerned about being outfoxed by the offense.

On the other hand, blending elements of two defensive packages does have its advantages. In the case of the Eagle and Stack defenses, the proper combination can make a defense more versatile and better able to deal with the many varieties of offenses it will see in the course of a season. In this chapter, I describe how adding elements of the Stack to what is primarily an Eagle attack can be very effective. Then, in chapter 12, I'll explain how mixing in aspects of the Eagle can make a Stack defense even stronger.

Strengthening the Eagle With the Stack

For most of my years at Colorado, our primary defensive package was the Eagle defense, which was particularly successful at stopping the strong running attacks we faced in the then Big Eight Conference. At the time, Oklahoma, Nebraska, and Oklahoma State were among the nation's best offenses, each a potentially explosive combination of both power and speed.

In 1992, I joined Gary Barnett's Northwestern staff as the defensive coordinator and installed the same Eagle defensive package used at Colorado. By the time I arrived at this new post, I knew the Eagle thoroughly and was able to teach it effectively to our players. Soon their knowledge of and confidence in the system grew.

In our first three seasons at Northwestern, we made considerable improvement in stopping our Big Ten opponents' ground attack, which is the first and most important step in defending against any offense. And, as explained previously, the Eagle defensive package was designed to stop the running game.

The problem was that we were seeing an increasingly higher percentage of "spread" offensive formations in both conference and nonconference competition. The *spread* refers to offensive sets featuring one running back in the backfield and four receivers on the line of scrimmage (one of the receivers may or may not be a tight end). Versus spread formations, we were limited in our Eagle defensive options.

So, just before the 1995 season, our defensive staff made the decision to blend the Stack 4-3-4 defensive structure with our Eagle defensive structure. Why? Adding elements of the Stack defense to an Eagle defensive structure provided our defensive scheme with more versatility in defending the passing game in general, and more specifically, spread formations.

However, because of our progress in stopping the run, I was reluctant to make too drastic a change three years into our rebuilding effort at Northwestern. So, against a two-back offense of any kind, we stayed in the Eagle. One reason for this strategy is that in the Eagle each defender is responsible for only one gap. Another is that in the Eagle, although the placement of all 11 defenders on the field can be altered radically by changing the placement call, their alignment, assignment, reads, and technique remain the same in most cases. Also, there are 8, and often 9, defenders in the box against two-back formations, which improves the odds for the defense at the point of attack. Yet, the Eagle also includes a deep safety, which is important in defending an opponent's running attack and is critical in preventing big plays.

The switch to a Stack 4-3-4 structure against spread offenses and in third-down passing situations allowed us to expand our coverages. Passing situations are better suited to playing Cover 2 (see chapter 8). The Stack defensive structure also balances the defensive front versus spread formations. The rush end is always in a 9 alignment to the tight end, and the defensive tackle is always in a 3 alignment to the tight end side. The noseguard is always in a 1 alignment away from the tight end side, and the defensive end is always in a 5 alignment away from the tight end.

Another appealing aspect of blending the Stack defensive structure into the Eagle package was the new blitz possibilities it presented. Because of the balanced defensive alignment in the Stack structure, both the eagle and Sam linebackers are in a position to blitz from the inside or from the outside, off the edge of the offensive formation. Blitzing just the two outside linebackers leaves the inside linebacker, who is aligned in the middle of the formation, to cover the running back and leaves the four defensive backs to match up man to man with the four eligible receivers on the line of scrimmage. The Stack structure also gives a defense the opportunity to develop a pressure package with zone coverage played behind it, which is described later in this chapter.

Specific Coverages in the Stack

Cover 2 is frequently used in passing situations. Cover 2 sets up best against a balanced two-by-two formation with two receivers on each side of the ball. Playing Cover 2 allows the defense to have three defenders in position to defend two receivers—two of these defenders are in the curl and flat underneath zones, and the other is a deep-one-half defender. Cover 2 also includes a middle hook defender to add to the coverage. This gives the defense a numeric advantage. And, although the Sam linebacker is in a walk alignment—which means he splits the difference between the offensive tackle and the number two receiver to the split end side—he is still close enough to the 3 gap to quickly fill it versus the run (although that is a challenge versus a running play when playing Cover 2).

Versus a trips formation, Cover 2 places three defenders covering one receiver into the boundary and three defenders over three receivers to the field. The inside linebacker is a potential fourth defender to the field depending on the passing route and formation. To balance the coverage versus a trips formation—and to help ensure that the defense is strong and effective against both the run and the pass—we usually check to Cover 3.

When playing Cover 2 versus a trips pro formation, two linebackers are responsible for defending three gaps between the split-side offensive tackle and the tight end (this is because the eagle linebacker would have to align in a walk position, which splits the distance between the number two and number three receivers). When a tight end is aligned as the number three receiver to the trips side of the formation, this presents a stronger run threat than a split end surface does.

Walking the eagle linebacker in Cover 2 versus a trips pro formation would give the offense the advantage in the run game. On the other hand, Cover 3 keeps all three linebackers in the "box," which means there is a defender close to and assigned to every offensive gap. (Figure 7.8 on page 84 illustrates Stack Cover 3 versus a trips pro formation.) This defensive call would be Stack Cover 2-3. As mentioned, we would play Cover 2 versus a two-by-two formation, and we would check to Cover 3 versus a three-by-one, or trips, formation.

When the defense checks to Cover 3, versus a pass, the underneath coverage floods to the trips side of the formation, which puts a defender in each of the underneath zones. This takes away all possible route combinations by the offense to the three-receiver side. (Refer to figure 7.9 on page 87 for the underneath defenders' pass drop zones when flooding the underneath zones.) If the number three receiver releases vertically, the inside linebacker sinks and carries him, allowing the free safety to play in between the number two and number three receivers if the offense runs four vertical pass routes.

Versus a trips formation with the quarterback in a shotgun formation and the running back offset to the one-receiver side, we no longer flood the underneath coverage to the trips side of the formation. This is because of the possibility of the offense being able to get two quick receivers out to the single-receiver side of the formation. In this situation, the linebackers would say, "flood off." The inside linebacker would now drop straight back and down the boundary hash. The inside linebacker needs to have vision on the running back to the single receiver into the boundary and on the number three receiver to the field. In third-and-long situations when there is a very low percentage that the offense will attempt a running play, we will mix in "Cover 2 Play It" calls, which mean we will stay in Cover 2 regardless of the offensive formation. This helps prevent our defense from becoming predictable.

Versus a trips pro formation, the eagle linebacker will drop to the curl zone inside of the number two receiver. The inside linebacker will drop into the middle hook zone off of the number three receiver, and the Sam linebacker will drop down the boundary hash. Both corners remain flat defenders.

As mentioned, the Eagle defensive structure was designed to stop a two-running-back offense. In the Eagle defense, each of the front four defensive linemen, as well as the eagle and inside linebackers, are single-gap players, and the strong and free safeties are in position to quickly support the run.

Versus any one-back formation, the Eagle defense checks to Cover 3. When playing Field Eagle Cover 3 versus a trips pro formation, there is not a defender responsible for supporting the alley. The free safety's alignment and his deep-one-third pass responsibilities in Cover 3 make it unrealistic to expect him to make the tackle consistently on a ballcarrier in the alley for less than a five- to seven-yard gain.

Another feature of blending the Stack defense with the Eagle defense is that it provides an effective solution to this problem. When playing Field Eagle Cover 5, if the offense aligns in a trips pro formation, the defense automatically checks to Stack Cover 3. In Stack Cover 3, the rush end stems out to a 9 alignment and is in position to become the alley defender to the field. The defensive tackle, the noseguard, and the defensive end remain in their 3, 1, and 5 alignments, responsible for the gap they are aligned in. The eagle linebacker is now aligned in and responsible for the 5 gap. The inside linebacker is aligned in and responsible for the 1 gap. The Sam linebacker is aligned in the 3 gap and is responsible for the 3 gap.

Defender Alignment Changes

Because of the similarities in the Eagle and Stack defensive structures, adjusting the Eagle defensive personnel into the Stack defensive structure can be a smooth transition. In both defensive structures, a placement call is made to align the front seven defenders. In the Stack defense, the placement is always to the tight end. The word *Stack* is both the front and the placement call to the front seven defenders, just as the words *Field, Short, Split, Strong,* and *Weak* are placement calls in the Eagle defensive structure.

When Stack is called, the rush end and the defensive tackle align to the "call side," which in the Stack defense is always to the tight end. The noseguard and the defensive end align away from the call side, which is to the split end side of the formation. The defensive linemen's responsibilities and reads remain the same as they are in the Eagle defense with the exception of the rush end.

In the Eagle defense, when the rush end is aligned to a tight end, he is in a 7 alignment, which is an inside shade on the tight end. This alignment is stronger inside against a run. However, in passing situations, a 7 alignment puts the rush end close to the offensive tackle, who doesn't have to get as much depth in his pass drop to get his hands on the rush end. A 7 alignment also makes the rush end vulnerable to the tight end slamming down on him (before releasing into a pass route).

In the Stack, the rush end aligns outside of the tight end in a 9 alignment. This alignment puts the rush end on a wide outside path to the quarterback and makes it very challenging for an offensive tackle to kick back and pass protect against a hard-charging rush end. If the tight end is assigned to pass block the rush end in a 9 alignment, the tight end will have to pass set like an offensive tackle. Most tight ends do not devote the time in practice—nor do they have the desire—to become a quality pass protector. In most cases, the rush end will have the advantage when matched up against a tight end in pass protection.

In the Stack defense, the rush end now has the advantage over the tight end or the offensive tackle in passing situations. Versus the running game, a 9 alignment puts the rush end in a position that makes it difficult for the tight end to execute a reach block on a play designed to get on the perimeter. In a 9 alignment, the rush end is now the alley defender (the area just outside of the tight end).

Against a spread offensive formation, playing the rush end in a 9 alignment with Cover 3 clearly defines each defender's run gap and run responsibilities. For example, versus a twin pro formation (with twin receivers to the field, a tight end and flanker into the boundary, and one running back in the backfield), the Sam linebacker is responsible for the 3 gap, the inside linebacker has the 1 gap, and the eagle linebacker has the 5 gap. The rush end is responsible for the alley, the defensive tackle has the 3 gap, the noseguard has the 1 gap, and the defensive end has the 5 gap. The rush end aligned in a 9 technique should ensure that the ball will not get on the perimeter to the tight end side, which is where most big plays in the run game occur.

When playing Cover 2, the Sam linebacker is walked out of the box, which is why Cover 2 is a better pass defense than a run defense; however, the Sam linebacker still reads the offensive guard for his run-pass key. Against a running play, it is surprising how quickly the Sam linebacker can support the run in the 3 gap. When playing Cover 2, the eagle and inside linebackers are still responsible for the 5 and tight 1 gaps.

The alignment rules for the three linebackers are simple, but their reads and run responsibilities are different from the Eagle defense. In the Stack modification, just as in the Eagle defense, the eagle linebacker aligns to the call side. He travels with the rush end, and his alignment is always a 5. The Sam linebacker aligns away from the call side, which will align him to the split end side of the formation.

When playing Cover 2 versus a two-by-two formation, the Sam linebacker is in a walk alignment splitting the difference between the number two receiver and the offensive tackle. Versus a three-by-one formation with the tight end aligned to the trips side of the formation, the Sam linebacker (who aligns away from the call side, putting him to aligns in and is responsible for the 3 gap. Versus a three-by-one formation where the tight end is aligned into the boundary and the three wide receivers are aligned to the field, the Sam linebacker aligns over the number three receiver. He now becomes the alley defender and is responsible for the area between the defensive end and the strong safety. The inside linebacker aligns to the call side in the tight 1 gap.

Generally, all three linebackers align 4 yards from the line of scrimmage. In a third-and-long situation, they will line up 5 yards from the line of scrimmage. On a third down with more than 15 yards needed for a first down, the linebackers should move to a position 7 yards from the line of scrimmage. To simplify the linebackers' reads, I have coached the linebackers to continue to key the offensive lineman they are aligned over for their initial run-pass reads (the same as they do in the Eagle defense).

The corners align the same as they do in the Eagle defense—left and right or field and boundary, depending on your philosophy. The alignment of the safeties is also consistent with the Eagle defense alignment rules, and this works well against most formations. The strong safety aligns to the call side, which puts him to the tight end side of the formation. He aligns on the hash and 12 yards deep when playing Cover 2. The free safety aligns away from the tight end, also on the hash. Versus a twin pro formation, which is a two-by-two offensive alignment, the strong safety would be aligned to the tight end side and would play a deep one half of the field.

In the Eagle defensive structure, the strong safety is always in a primary support position; in most cases, he is not as athletic as the free safety. Aligning on the tight end side of the formation puts less stress on the strong safety in pass coverage. When in man coverage, the strong safety would always match up against the tight end. The free safety—who is more athletic and has better coverage skills than the strong safety—is the deep-one-half defender away from the tight end. In man-to-man coverage, the free safety has the number two receiver away from the tight end.

Versus a trips pro formation, which is a three-by-one offensive alignment with the tight end aligned to the trips side of the formation, I have most often checked to Cover 3. This is the same adjustment check as in the Eagle defensive structure. Because the tight end is on the trips side of the formation, the strong safety would align to the trips side of the formation. The strong safety should recognize the trips formation, hear the check to Cover 3, and then align in a sky alignment five yards off the line of scrimmage and one yard outside of the number two receiver to the trips side of the formation. This alignment is also the strong safety's primary alignment in the Eagle defense. In Cover 3, the free safety plays the deep middle third of the field, which is his base alignment and responsibility in the Eagle defense versus a trips formation.

The trips twin formation is an exception to the rules for the alignment of the safeties. The trips twin formation is a three-by-one offensive alignment in which the tight end is the single receiver on the weak side of the formation and the three wide receivers are on the same side of the ball. Against this formation, the free safety would align in the sky alignment, one yard outside of the number two receiver and five yards from the line of scrimmage. The strong safety would now be the player responsible for the deep middle third. In the past, I've encountered far more trips pro than trips twin formations. However, if you encounter a team that uses a lot of trips twin formations, you could simply tell the strong safety to align to the field whenever a zone coverage is called. He would then be in position to "sky down" over the number two receiver versus any type of a trips formation.

Blitz Additions

Another benefit of adding elements of the Stack defensive package to the Eagle defense is the addition of two Stack blitzes: Stack Bullets and Stack Bomb. Both blitzes are played with Cover 0, which is straight man-to-man coverage, and are described in detail in chapter 9. When running Stack Bullets, the eagle and Sam linebackers blitz the gaps they are aligned in. The eagle linebacker blitzes the 5 gap, and the Sam linebacker blitzes the 3 gap. In Stack Bomb, the eagle and Sam linebackers blitz from the outside, off the edge of the formation. In both blitzes, the inside linebacker and the two safeties, who are not involved in the blitz, are close to the line of scrimmage. I refer to these three defenders as *the erasers*. They are in position to make a play on the ball if the ball does get through the line of scrimmage.

In general, Stack Bullets is the better of the two blitzes to stop the run. Versus any formation with one tight end, every gap is being attacked and penetrated. In a neutral or pass situation, I favor running Stack Bomb, where both the eagle and Sam linebackers blitz from the outside. This puts them in a better position to rush the quarterback. One of the two linebackers should be matched up on his blitz against the running back. The linebacker should frequently win that matchup. Blitzing a linebacker off the edge also forces an offensive lineman to take a deep pass set and to block a fast edge rusher on a wide path. On the snap of the ball, the inside linebacker should immediately go to the running back and snug him up.

When running Stack Bomb, which is a pass blitz first, you can also have your nose-guard be the spy who covers the running back versus a pass. Using the noseguard as the spy frees up the inside linebacker to add to the rush and protects the defense against a slip screen play. If the running back were to flare out of the backfield, the edge rusher would peel with the flare release and cover the running back. The rule of peeling with a running back's flare release carries over to all man and zone stunts for the edge rusher.

Since the safeties are not involved in the blitz, the four defensive backs can match up with the four receivers on the line of scrimmage. For example, versus a two-by-two formation, the corners would have the number one receiver (the widest receiver) to their side, and the safeties would have the number two receiver (the second receiver from the outside). If one of the number two receivers were to motion or shift from one side of the formation to the other, the safety would not run with that receiver. The safety would simply bump the shifting receiver to the safety already aligned on the trips side of the formation. The first safety would then rotate over and cover the number three receiver to the trips side. This protects the safeties from being outleveraged to the side of the motion. It also helps disguise the blitz and the fact that the secondary is playing man coverage. However, for matchup purposes, the corners would run with the number one receiver if the number one receiver motioned across the formation, which rarely happens in a spread formation.

When running Stack Bullets or Stack Bomb, the inside linebacker is responsible for covering the remaining back in the backfield (unless you have the noseguard spy on the running back while the inside linebacker adds to the blitz). In all Stack defenses, the inside linebacker aligns in the tight 1 gap versus a one-back offensive formation. This alignment puts him in the middle of the formation. From there, he is in position to be able to cover the running back in man coverage (his assignment in both Stack Bullets and Stack Bomb) or to blitz in the direction the running back pass sets to.

Whether the inside linebacker is covering the running back man to man or blitzing, the inside linebacker should quickly close up on the running back when the ball is snapped. Versus a blitz, the pass protection scheme for most offenses will have the running back responsible for blocking one of the blitzing outside linebackers, which will prevent the running back from getting out of the backfield and running a pass route. However, a screen pass to the running back is always a concern. That's why either the inside linebacker or the noseguard must spy and close up on the running back versus a pass.

Zone Stunt Concepts

As mentioned, one of the main reasons for blending the Stack defensive structure with the Eagle defensive structure is the ability to play a balanced front. In the Stack structure, the front is balanced against all spread offensive formations, with Cover 2 in the secondary. The Stack structure allows a coach to design a stunt package that can attack an offense with any one of the three linebackers or a combination of two linebackers rushing at the same time (with one of the front four defensive linemen dropping into coverage).

The Stack structure with Cover 2 complements the Eagle zone stunt package. Opposing offenses know that one of the weaknesses in the various Eagle zone stunts with Cover 3 is that the field or boundary flat is initially uncovered. Incorporating the Stack structure allows a defense to develop a zone stunt package with a Cover 2 concept played behind it.

In the Stack defensive system, as explained in chapter 8, the corners are flat defenders. They align at a depth of five to seven yards off the line of scrimmage and read the number one receiver through the number two receiver. If the number two and number one receivers release vertically, the corner would funnel and jam the number one receiver, slowing down the number one receiver's release. The corner would then sink, giving ground with the number one receiver and staying even or in a trail relationship with the number one receiver. If the number two receiver releases to the flat, the corner would now immediately come off the number one receiver and defend the number two receiver releasing into the flat.

Because of the added pressure on the quarterback, the ball will be thrown sooner than normal, and the quarterback will be looking in the direction he will be throwing, allowing defenders to react and break quickly on the ball as it leaves the quarterback's hand. When a defense mixes in a variation of Cover 2 with both corners rolled up in the flat, this makes it difficult for a quarterback to predict with any degree of certainty—while under the pressure of a stunt coming at him—where the defense is vulnerable and where to throw the football.

During my first three seasons as the defensive coordinator at Northwestern, we stayed predominantly in the Eagle defensive structure. Versus an opponent's passing attack, we rushed the four defensive linemen and dropped seven defenders into coverage. When we did blitz, it was with six-man pressure and straight man-to-man coverage behind the blitz. Occasionally, we would rush five and play "man free" coverage, which is man coverage on all of the eligible receivers with the free safety in the deep middle and not assigned to a receiver. The free safety reads the quarterback and is free to break on the ball and help with deep routes.

In the 1992 through 1995 seasons, our opening games were against Coach Lou Holtz's Notre Dame team. In the 1993 matchup, we played Notre Dame on even terms and held the lead in the third quarter. Then, Notre Dame converted a couple of key third downs and moved the ball across our 40-yard line. In an effort to stop their drive, on the next third-and-long situation, I called Field Eagle Lightning, a six-man blitz with man-to-man coverage. Notre Dame kept seven players in to protect the quarterback. They blocked our blitz and provided time for their talented receivers to get deep and open against our defensive backs. Consequently, we gave up a big play, and Notre Dame eventually scored, regained the momentum, and went on to win the game. This game typified many of our Big Ten Conference games as well as our 1994 season opener against Notre Dame.

With our Eagle package at Northwestern, we could overload the offense at the line of scrimmage on first and second down and could compete with most teams with our run defense. Stopping the opposing offense on third down was our challenge. If we played zone coverage and rushed our four defensive linemen, the quarterback often had ample time to eventually find an open receiver. When we blitzed and played man-to-man coverage, we were still challenged to get immediate pressure on the quarterback. Playing man-to-man coverage in the secondary also made us vulnerable to giving up a big play. Our challenge was to be able to get pressure on the quarterback without exposing our secondary to man-to-man coverage.

As I studied Notre Dame in the summer before the 1995 season, I soon realized that the teams that had been successful defending Notre Dame were able to contain their running game and put consistent pressure on the quarterback in the passing game. This was easier said than done. Notre Dame's quarterback at the time was Ron Powlus, who had thrown for 298 yards and four touchdowns against our Wildcat defense in 1994, and both of the Notre Dame receivers had double-digit yards per reception. In studying Notre Dame during the summer, I observed that they had not thrown to their tight end much. In fact, I discovered that their tight end averaged only one catch per game in the three previous seasons.

Going into the 1995 season opener against Notre Dame, I had doubts that our four-man rush would be effective, and I knew that all-out pressure with man coverage behind it would put us at risk of again giving up big explosion plays in the passing game. This is when it became apparent that adding aspects of the Stack 4-3-4 structure to our Eagle defense would provide a way to develop a zone stunt package with a variation of Cover 2 in the secondary.

In the first half of the game, our defense forced a Notre Dame turnover deep in their territory. Our offense quickly converted the turnover into a touchdown that put us in the lead. Experience told me that Coach Holtz would start the next series with a passing play, throwing the ball downfield in an attempt to make a big play and regain momentum. I took a calculated risk and called Stack Slant Go Cover 2 (see chapter 9). Sure enough, the Notre Dame quarterback dropped back to pass, and the stunt surprised the Notre Dame offense. Our Sam linebacker ran right by the offensive tackle assigned to fan out and block him and sacked the Notre Dame quarterback. We went on to win the game 17 to 15, and the zone pressure package out of the Stack defense became an instrumental part of our defense.

Chapter 9 has a complete description of all of the stunts used in the Stack defensive package as well as each stunt's application. Of those stunts, Stack Slant Go is the one I have used most frequently in the Stack defense. It provides a good illustration of how the Stack 4-3-4 zone stunt package has added to our Eagle defensive package. The Slant Go stunt originated in the Eagle package and has been one of my most used stunts throughout my years in coaching. In the Eagle package, this stunt was one of the few times a Tight placement call was used, which placed the rush end and defensive tackle to the tight end side. The noseguard and defensive end aligned away from the tight end. All four down defensive linemen executed a rip stunt toward the tight end. Since most offenses run the majority of their running plays toward the tight end side of the formation, and because the Sam linebacker blitzes off the split side of the formation, Slant Go has always been an effective stunt.

Executing the Slant Go stunt out of the Stack defensive structure made the stunt better for two reasons. First, the rush end in the Stack structure is already aligned in a 9 technique, so he doesn't have to rip outside to get to the edge. Second, the Stack structure is set up to play Cover 2, which allows the defense to have both corners disrupting and double-covering the wide receivers versus a pro, two-back formation. The Stack Slant Go stunt commands the defensive line to execute a rip technique to the tight end. The Sam linebacker stems up to the line of scrimmage just before the ball is snapped and blitzes off the edge to the split end side of the formation.

The most common running play an offense will use in a neutral to long-yardage situation is the draw play. Stack Slant Go will disrupt the inside running lanes against a draw and most other running plays that start to the tight end side of the ball. Versus a pro two-back formation, you can play an aggressive Cover 2 behind the stunt, with both corners aligning five to seven yards off the line of scrimmage on the outside edge of the receiver. The corners are responsible for jamming and disrupting the receiver's release. They should also funnel the receiver in to the safety to their side of the field. The safety is a deep-one-half defender. Unless the corner has a threat to his flat, he should sink and provide underneath help on the receiver, and the safety should provide deep coverage over the top of the receiver. Essentially, the corner and safety double-team the wide receiver to their side.

The eagle linebacker is aligned in the 5 gap over the inside shoulder of the tight end. He covers the tight end man to man if the tight end releases on a vertical pass route, or if the tight end runs a hook route over the middle. If the tight end crosses the formation, the eagle linebacker calls out "crosser" to the inside linebacker, who will escort the tight end (with depth) to the corner. The eagle linebacker would then drop to the hash mark on his side of the field, staying inside out on any receiver who might come into his area. If the tight end releases to the flat, the eagle linebacker widens with the tight end to the hash, then releases the tight end to the corner; the eagle linebacker then looks to provide underneath coverage on the number one receiver to his side of the field. The corner comes off the wide receiver late if the ball is thrown to the tight end in the flat.

Against a twin-receiver formation, the defense checks to Cover 3. In Cover 3, the eagle linebacker is aligned into the boundary in the 5 gap to the tight end side of the ball. The eagle linebacker is a hook to curl to flat defender, which means he will wall out the tight end inside out, expanding to the curl or flat zones only if they are threatened. The inside linebacker is responsible for the hook to curl zones on the twin side of the formation.

CHAPTER 12

Stack With Eagle Modifications

Throughout most of my career, I have coached on staffs that preferred the Eagle as the base defensive structure. However, in 2004 at Penn State, our base defense changed to the Stack 4-4-3 with aspects of the Eagle mixed into our defensive package.

The main reason we converted to the Stack as our base structure is that it allowed us to better defend against the spread formations that are so popular today. With our opponents lining up in spread formations 58 percent of the time and throwing the ball more, the move to a Stack base only made sense. The move to Stack also gave our defense greater flexibility in its coverage package. The Stack simply positions players more effectively versus one-back, three- or four-receiver sets than the Eagle defense does. Cover 2, Cover 3, man, and "man free" coverages all function better out of the Stack defensive package.

Yet, we also saw great value in retaining several features of the Eagle and incorporating them into the Stack structure. The zone and man stunt packages within the Eagle are specifically suited to stop two-back and two-tight-end offensive attacks. The Eagle also has a superior goal line package since most goal line offenses use a two-tight-end, two-running-back attack. The Eagle goal line package (discussed in detail in chapter 16) is essentially a Split Eagle defensive front on both sides of the ball.

The Eagle defensive structure also sets up the best to defend an offensive formation with two tight ends, two running backs, and one wide receiver (which we refer to as a personnel grouping of 22). When both running backs are in the backfield and the wide receiver is on the line of scrimmage, this is referred to as a *flanker formation*. Versus a flanker formation, my base defensive call would be Field Eagle with Cover 5 in the secondary. A detailed explanation of Field Eagle Cover 5 versus a flanker formation is provided later in this chapter.

To sum up our rationale, we adopted the Stack structure because it is a superior alignment against spread formations. The flexibility of its pass coverage packages allows the defense to present many possible looks for the opponent to prepare for before a game and respond to during the contest. By incorporating elements of the Eagle into the Stack, we strengthened the defense against the two-tight-end, two-back formation and running attack, and we enhanced the defense's zone stunt and goal line packages.

When used in this way, the Stack and Eagle combination provides a defensive coach with tremendous versatility when putting together a game plan (see chapter 17). Of course, the choice of defense in any particular situation must also take into account the personnel in the game. The Stack with Eagle modifications allows the defensive coach to effectively counter each particular offensive personnel grouping. Just how to do this and how to make other tactical adjustments using the Stack structure and Eagle features will be explained throughout the rest of this chapter.

Strengthening the Stack With the Eagle

Let's look more specifically at the Stack's structural strengths and weaknesses as well as how the proper and timely use of Eagle features can make the Stack more versatile and effective. When in Stack Cover 3, the defense has the offense outnumbered in the running game if the offense has a personnel grouping of 21 or 11 in the game. A personnel grouping of 22, however, presents challenges for a Stack defensive system.

Handling the 21 or 11 Set

Versus a 21 personnel formation—which is a two-back, one-tight-end personnel grouping—the Stack structure is a 4-4-3 with the strong safety in the box (the area close to the football) and in position to quickly support the run. The Stack 4-4-3 defense puts eight defenders close to the football and is a strong defense versus both the run and the pass. The offense has seven blockers in the box—the five offensive linemen, the tight end, and the fullback. The defense has eight defenders—the four defensive linemen, the three linebackers, and the strong safety—in the box to defend a 21 personnel formation, giving the defense an unblocked defender. Cover 3 also aligns the free safety in the middle of the field and in position to front the ballcarrier up if the ballcarrier penetrates through the interior of the defense. This is commonly referred to as an "eight-man front."

When the offense has a personnel grouping of 11—which is one running back, one tight end, and three receivers—the offense will have six blockers in the box. If the offense uses a personnel grouping of 11 and aligns in a twin pro formation (which has twin receivers to the field and a tight end and wide receiver aligned into the boundary), the strong safety aligns out of the box and over the number two receiver to the field. The defense now has seven defenders in the box. This gives the defense an advantage against a running play because one of the defenders will be unblocked. For this reason, we try to stay in Cover 3 in run situations, regardless of the offensive personnel in the game.

However, Cover 3 only has four defenders to defend the five underneath zones (the middle hook zone, both curl zones, and both flat zones). One of the features of the Stack structure is that it sets up well to play Cover 2, which in passing situations gives the defense the advantage against an offense's short to intermediate passing game. So, in obvious or neutral passing situations, we play Cover 2 to put a defender in each of the five underneath passing zones. Both corners are flat defenders, and the Sam and eagle linebackers are the curl defenders. The inside linebacker is the middle hook defender. Cover 2 should force the offense to have to throw a deeper and lower-percentage pass. In Cover 2, the Sam linebacker leaves the box, splitting the distance between the number two receiver to the field and the offensive tackle. When the Sam linebacker leaves the box, the number of defenders and blockers will be the same, and the defense will no longer have the advantage against the run (which is why we use Cover 3 against the run).

Handling the 22 Set

Although Stack Cover 3 gives the defense the advantage versus the run when the offense uses a personnel grouping of 11 or 21, it does not match up well against a personnel grouping of 22. The most common formation in this personnel grouping is a flanker formation. When the offense exchanges a wide receiver (who aligns outside the box and who is not a physical blocker) for a tight end (who aligns in the box), the offense now has a blocker for each defender close to the line of scrimmage.

At Penn State, our opponents used a personnel grouping of 22 against us 79 times during the 2005 and 2006 seasons. Although that is a small percentage of the total plays for those two seasons, we usually see this personnel grouping in critical situations, in short yardage, and on the goal line. Additionally, every season a couple of teams will use a 22 personnel grouping frequently in the course of a game to attack the Stack defense in the run game. Versus a personnel grouping of 22, I prefer to use the Eagle defensive structure.

A 22 personnel grouping versus the Stack defensive structure not only provides a blocker for each defender away from the placement call, but it also gives the offense a leverage advantage on the defense. Figure 12.1 shows the Stack defense aligned to a flanker formation. When teams that exclusively play the Stack defense face a two-tight-end offense, they make the placement call to the field, placing the rush end and the 3-technique defensive tackle to the field. Playing the rush end in a 7 alignment will make the defense stronger against the inside running game. However, the rush end must be physical enough to dominate and control the line of scrimmage and the 5 gap against the tight end he would be lined up over.

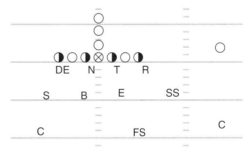

Figure 12.1 Stack 4-4-3 versus a flanker formation.

Away from the call side, the noseguard aligns in a 2 alignment, which is an inside shade on the offensive guard. The defensive end widens to a 7 alignment, which is an inside shade on the tight end. The defensive end rarely aligns in an inside shade on the tight end. Therefore, the fundamentals needed by the defensive end to play the various blocking schemes in a 7 alignment would be seldom practiced. Because the offense knows that a defense using the Stack structure will respond to a flanker formation with this adjustment, the offense can take advantage of the defense by checking their running plays to take advantage of the alignments of the noseguard and the defensive end.

A defense in the Stack structure is also vulnerable in the alley outside of the tight end and inside of the Sam linebacker. The defense is numerically balanced into the boundary, meaning the offense has five and a half offensive players to the boundary and the defense has five and a half defenders into the boundary. For the offense, when the running backs are in the I formation, each back counts as one player to both the field and the boundary. The center and quarterback together count as one player to the field and one player to the boundary. When the eagle linebacker is aligned in the 1 gap, he counts as both one-half player to the field and one-half player to the boundary. When the ball is on the hash mark, the limited space between the hash mark and the boundary can count as one-half defender into the boundary.

Although the defense is balanced numerically, when the noseguard is aligned in a 2 and the defensive end is aligned in a 7, both players have poor leverage on their potential blockers. As a result, they are both vulnerable to several blocking schemes that can open up both inside and outside running lanes. The first block-ing scheme and play that could pose a problem is the outside zone or a toss sweep. The tight end blocks down on the defensive end and the offensive guard blocks down on the noseguard (see figure 12.2). Both blockers have great leverage to execute these blocks. The offensive tackle and the center pull to the outside. The offensive tackle pulls to block the Sam linebacker, and the center pulls to block the inside linebacker. The fullback can lead through and block the boundary corner. The running back starts on a wide path and cuts up in the first hole he sees.

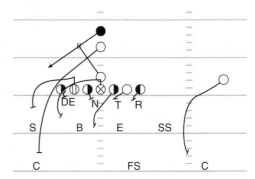

Figure 12.2   Outside zone or toss sweep versus the stack 4-4-3 defense.

The second blocking scheme and play that can create a problem for defenders in this alignment is the zone. The offense double-teams the three defensive line-men closest to the play. The blockers stay on those double-team blocks, getting movement on the down linemen, before slipping off to the second-level defend-ers—the inside and eagle linebackers and the strong safety (see figure 12.3). The fullback leads to the outside and blocks the Sam linebacker. As noted earlier, the

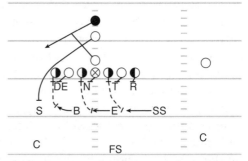

Figure 12.3   Zone play and blocking scheme versus the 4-4-3 defense.

alignment and relationship between the defensive end and the Sam linebacker versus this blocking scheme are seldom practiced. The defenders will need to work on this in order to play this blocking scheme correctly.

Another play that is a concern is an isolation play in the 3 gap (see figure 12.4). The offensive guard blocks down on the noseguard. The offensive tackle blocks out on the defensive end. The tight end blocks out on the Sam linebacker, creating a large running lane for the inside linebacker to fill in the 3 gap. The fullback leads through the 3 gap and blocks the inside linebacker. A potential cutback is a concern for the defense any time a running play starts away from the noseguard and defensive end. Because the noseguard is aligned in a 2, he can be flattened down the line of scrimmage or cut off by the offensive guard. Either way, he is susceptible to opening a large cutback lane for the ballcarrier.

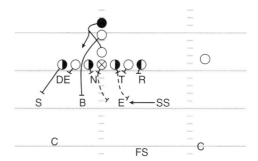

Figure 12.4 Isolation play versus the 4-4-3 defense.

The defensive end in a 7 alignment has the same issues and concerns as the noseguard in a 2 alignment. If the defensive end gets cut off by the tight end, this will also open a cutback lane for the ballcarrier. The Eagle defensive structure

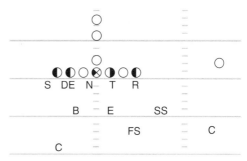

Figure 12.5 Field Eagle Cover 5 versus a flanker formation.

addresses these problems and puts the Sam linebacker on the line of scrimmage in a 9 alignment versus a tight end surface. The Eagle structure tightens the alignment of the defensive end to a tight 5, and it moves the noseguard to a 1 alignment, which is his normal alignment (see figure 12.5). The Eagle defensive structure also provides a surface that is conducive to executing defensive line stunts and second-level stunts to knock out inside running lanes.

One main difference between the Stack and Eagle structures will require a small degree of learning for your players—in the Eagle defense, the strong safety now travels with the call, and the Sam linebacker travels away from the call. Everyone else in the defense aligns either to or away from the call as they do in the Stack structure.

At Penn State, versus a flanker formation, our base defensive call would be Field Eagle Cover 5. If the ball is in the middle of the field, we would call Strong Eagle Cover 5, setting the call side to the strength of the formation. The rush end aligns in a 7 to the call side and is responsible for the 5 gap. The strong safety is aligned five yards outside of the tight end and five yards from the line of scrimmage. He is responsible for containing the football and for the curl to flat zones versus a pass.

The free safety is a prime run support player in Cover 5. He is aligned eight to nine yards off the line of scrimmage, over the tight end. The free safety keys the tight end for his run-pass read. If the tight end blocks, the free safety fills the alley between the tight end and the strong safety. If the tight end releases vertically, the free safety covers him man to man. If the tight end releases to either flat, the free safety rotates back to the deep middle third.

The field corner is a deep-one-fourth defender over the number one receiver. The boundary corner is a deep-one-half defender. Because the boundary corner is aligned to the closed side (a tight end surface) of the formation, he can align nine yards deep, over the inside shoulder of the boundary tight end. This will put him in position to support the run and fit where needed at a distance of five to seven yards from the line of scrimmage if the ball penetrates the line of scrimmage. The closeness of the strong and free safeties and the boundary corner makes Field Eagle Cover 5 a 10-man front to defend the opponent's running game.

The defensive tackle aligns in a 3 to the call side, and he is responsible for the 3 gap. The eagle linebacker aligns to the call side in a 1 alignment, and he is responsible for the 1 gap. The eagle linebacker's nickname is "Mr. Inside." Versus any running play that threatens the 1 gap, the eagle linebacker should attack in the 1 gap. Versus any perimeter or off-tackle play, the eagle linebacker should press the first open seam to the football. Because the strong safety is the contain player to the field and the free safety is the alley player to the field, the eagle linebacker is an inside-out player and has the freedom to press the first open seam to the ballcarrier.

As mentioned, the noseguard is in a 1 alignment away from the call and is responsible for the 1 gap. The defensive end is aligned in a tight 5 away from the call, and he is responsible for the 5 gap. The inside linebacker is aligned in a 3 and is responsible for the 3 gap. The Sam linebacker's alignment is different from any alignment he has in the Stack defensive structure. Versus a tight end surface, the Sam linebacker is in a 9 alignment on the line of scrimmage. His inside foot is aligned on the outside foot of the tight end. His key is the tight end's helmet, which will tell the Sam linebacker if the play is a run or a pass, or if the tight end is trying to execute a reach block, a base block, or a cutoff block. Field Eagle Cover 5 allows each defender to be responsible only for the gap he is aligned in.

Blitz Additions

Within the Eagle defensive structure, there are two stunts that are particularly effective for attacking a flanker formation. Both stunts involve bringing one of the two safeties off the edge of the offensive formation. Zone or man coverage is played behind each particular stunt. In addition, the Eagle zone stunt package includes many other stunts that can be used to attack all formations.

Stunts for Attacking a Flanker Formation

The Eagle defensive structure has the versatility of being able to use a Field, Short, Strong, or Weak placement call versus a 22 personnel grouping. Being able to use any of these placement calls gives the defensive coordinator flexibility in where he wants to place the call side against a flanker formation. This flexibility is particularly useful when using your stunt and blitz package.

At Penn State, one of our more frequently called defenses against a flanker formation is Short Eagle Lightning Cover 3. During the 2005 and 2006 season, 30 percent of our total defensive calls were either Short or Field Eagle Lightning Cover 0. The strong safety, rush end, eagle linebacker, and defensive tackle follow their Eagle defense alignment rules—with a Short placement call, this aligns them into the boundary. The Lightning stunt commands the rush end and defensive tackle to execute a Gopher stunt, where they execute a rip technique inside, canceling the 3 and 1 gaps. The strong safety blitzes off the boundary edge.

Because the strong safety is a bigger and more physical player, and the corners are typically smaller and not as physical, we favor blitzing the strong safety instead of the corner. The placement call allows a coach to align his players in position to use their strengths. In Short Eagle Lightning, the strong safety aligns into the boundary and is the player who does the blitzing.

The defensive risk in this stunt is voiding the boundary flat versus a pass. Bringing the stunt from the boundary minimizes that risk. If the ball is in the middle of the field and you want to bring the stunt from the closed side of the formation, you can make a Weak placement call, which will set the reduction away from the strength of the formation. This will also minimize the risk of a pass in the exposed flat. Bringing the strong safety now gives the defense nine defenders aggressively attacking the line of scrimmage.

In Short Eagle Lightning Cover 3, the eagle linebacker is responsible for expanding into the boundary flat if the flat is threatened in the passing game. Although the eagle linebacker may occasionally get caught up in a play-action fake, and a running back may slip by him into the boundary flat, this is a minimal risk because it would be into the boundary flat. The advantage to playing Cover 3 is having three deep defenders, all with vision on the ball, which will help prevent big plays from occurring.

If Field Eagle Lightning Cover 0 is called, the strong safety aligns to the field, as do the rush end, eagle linebacker, and defensive tackle. The rush end and defensive tackle run a Gopher stunt and execute a rip technique inside. The strong safety blitzes off the edge from the field. The only difference between Short Eagle Lightning Cover 3 and Field Eagle Lightning Cover 0 is the coverage played behind the stunt. Cover 0 is man-to-man coverage.

When Field Eagle Lightning is called, the risk of vacating the flat to the field is far greater than into the boundary. Therefore, I prefer to play man-to-man coverage. The eagle linebacker now keys the running back to the field and is locked on him from the snap of the ball until the play is over. If the running back were to release to the field flat, the eagle linebacker would cover him man to man.

Short Eagle Flame (see figures on page 48) has been our complement stunt to Short Eagle Lightning and our second most used stunt versus a flanker formation. The placement call for both stunts is the same. A Short placement call aligns the defensive reduction into the boundary. Short Eagle Lightning has the rush end and defensive tackle executing a rip technique toward the field, with the strong safety blitzing off the boundary edge. Short Eagle Flame has the Sam linebacker, defensive end, noseguard, defensive tackle, and rush end all executing a rip technique toward the boundary, and the free safety blitzes off the edge from the field.

As mentioned, the front four defenders execute a rip technique toward the boundary. The rush end is the contain player to the boundary versus the run. Versus an option play, he is responsible for the pitch. Versus a running play away, the rush end should fold and play the cutback. Versus a pass, he is responsible for the boundary flat.

The defensive tackle will rip across the face of a down block. He is responsible for containment versus a pass. He must clear a naked bootleg by the quarterback before pursuing a running play away. The noseguard rips across the face of the center. The defensive end executes a long rip technique, which will take him all the way to the 1 gap.

When aligned to a split end surface, the eagle linebacker aligns in the 1 gap. When aligned to a tight end surface, he is in a 5 alignment. Versus a run away, the eagle linebacker should flow to the ball. In most cases, he will be unblocked. Versus a pass, he is responsible for the middle hook. The Sam linebacker executes a rip technique inside. Versus a run to him, he should cross the face of all blockers and spill the ball outside. Versus a run away, he should flatten and look for the cutback. Versus a pass, he must rush inside of all blockers. The inside linebacker scrapes tight off the butt of the Sam linebacker versus a run to him. Versus an inside run away, the inside linebacker shuffles slowly, expecting the ball to cut back. Versus a pass, he is a curl defender, building a wall on the number two receiver.

The free safety aligns as if in Cover 2. He rotates to linebacker depth just before the snap of the ball and then blitzes off the edge to the field. As the free safety blitzes off the edge, he should "take a picture" as he crosses the line of scrimmage. He must instantly determine if the play is a run and whether the play is to him or away from him. Versus an option play to him, he is responsible for the alley, meaning if the quarterback gets to the free safety, the free safety takes the quarterback. If the Sam or inside linebacker takes the quarterback, the free safety would then fill the alley inside of the field corner, who is responsible for containment and the pitchback. Versus an inside or off-tackle run, the free safety should settle his hips, stay square, and squeeze and constrict the play. The free safety is the contain player and should hold the edge. Versus a run away, the free safety should "squeeze smart," staying square and shuffling down the line of scrimmage for a possible reverse, naked bootleg, or cutback.

The strong safety aligns into the boundary in a Cover 4 alignment—12 yards from the line of scrimmage, over the boundary hash mark. Just before the snap of the football, he rotates his alignment to the field hash and is responsible for the deep one half to the field.

The boundary corner aligns in a Cover 4 alignment, and just before the snap of the ball, he backpedals to a depth of 12 yards, 2 yards outside of the hash. He is responsible for the deep one half of the field into the boundary.

The field corner aligns at a depth of 7 yards and 1 yard outside of the receiver. On the snap of the ball, the field corner squats and plays a cloud technique in which he is responsible for the flat. Having the field corner play a cloud technique takes away a three-step passing game to the field.

Stunts for Attacking All Formations

In addition to the stunts used for attacking a flanker formation, the Eagle defense provides an effective structure for running zone stunts against any personnel grouping or formation. The placement calls within the Eagle structure allow the defense to predetermine the defensive alignment regardless of the offensive formation. In a Stack structure, the placement call and the defensive alignment are determined by where the tight end aligns. Short Eagle Lightning Cover 3 is one example of the defense placing the strong safety, rush end, eagle linebacker, and defensive tackle into the boundary to execute a stunt from. Each defender should know exactly what to do versus every possible formation.

Short Eagle Blast Cross Cover 3 and Short Eagle Brave Cover 3 are other examples of using placement calls to organize zone stunts to attack an offense in any personnel grouping—and to stop both the run and pass game. The Short placement call commands the strong safety, rush end, eagle linebacker, and defensive tackle to align into the boundary. The strong safety aligns on the boundary hash, 12 yards deep, showing a two-deep coverage shell.

When executing Short Eagle Blast Cross (see figures on page 45), on the snap of the ball, the strong safety spins down to a depth of 7 yards directly over the ball. He then mirrors the ball and tackles the ballcarrier if he penetrates the line of scrimmage. Versus the pass, the strong safety is the middle hook defender. The free safety rotates to the deep middle third of the field.

In both stunts, the noseguard, the defensive tackle, and the rush end all execute a rip technique toward the boundary. The rush end is the contain player versus a running play, and he has the pitch versus an option. Versus a pass, he drops into coverage and is responsible for the curl and flat zones. The defensive tackle is responsible for containment versus a pass. The noseguard rips across the face of the center. The defensive end plays a wide 5 technique and is responsible for the 5 gap. He has the quarterback versus an option play.

On the snap of the ball, the inside linebacker blitzes the near 1 gap, and the eagle linebacker blitzes tight off the butt of the inside linebacker. The Sam linebacker is in a 9 alignment on the line of scrimmage, and he is the contain player to the field. He has the pitch versus an option, and his pass responsibility is the curl and flat zones.

In Short Eagle Brave Cover 3 (see figures on page 46) the defensive front four all have the same responsibilities as they do in Short Eagle Blast Cross, except for the defensive end who rips to the 1 gap. The Sam linebacker blitzes off the edge of the formation (from the field side). Versus an option, he has the pitch. Versus the run, he is responsible for support and containing the ballcarrier. Versus a pass, he rushes the quarterback and is responsible for containment. The inside linebacker blitzes tight off the butt of the defensive end. The eagle linebacker flows to the ball and is usually unblocked versus the run. Versus the pass, he is the middle hook defender. The free safety spins down over the number two receiver and fits where needed versus the run. He is the curl to flat defender versus the pass. The strong safety rotates to the deep middle third. In both stunts, the corners play Cover 3.

My purpose in describing each defender's alignment, assignment, and responsibilities here is to illustrate the similar organization of many of the Eagle zone stunts and to demonstrate how they can supplement the Stack defensive structure. You will find both Short Eagle Blast Cross Cover 3 and Short Eagle Brave Cover 3 described in more detail in chapter 5.

During our August preseason training camp, we install our base Stack defense, the coverage adjustments, and the defensive line movements during the first two days of practice. On the third day of practice, we install our Stack blitz package: Stack

Bullets, Stack Bomb, and Stack Slant Go Cover 2-3. On the fourth day of practice, we introduce the Eagle defensive structure, and then we begin teaching our zone stunt package. We normally teach two stunts per day that are similar, such as Short Eagle Blast Cross and Short Eagle Brave, both with Cover 3. The following day we teach two more zone stunts from the Eagle defensive structure. By the sixth day of practice, we install Field Eagle Cover 5 and our goal line package.

Goal Line Package Addition

Adding elements of the Eagle to the Stack allows us to add a goal line scheme based on the Eagle defensive structure. The scheme I use most often is a 6-5 alignment, and for teaching purposes it is nothing more than an Eagle defense aligned away from the call on both sides of the ball. The goal line defense is called *60,* and there is no placement call. (Refer to chapter 16 for more information on the 60 and other goal line schemes.)

The goal line defense is used primarily inside the five-yard line against flanker formations and other types of 22 personnel groupings. One of the two corners is replaced by a fourth linebacker. Both sides of the football have mirrored responsibilities. The noseguard and defensive tackle are in 2 alignments. The defensive end and rush end are in tight 5 alignments, which is the same alignment and responsibility that the defensive end has in both the Stack and Eagle defensive packages. Both the eagle and inside linebackers are in 3 alignments, and they are responsible for the 3 gap. Versus a pass, they are responsible for the hook to curl zones.

The Sam linebackers have the same alignment, technique, and responsibilities that they do in the Eagle defensive structure. Both Sam linebackers are in 9 alignments, and they are responsible for containing all running plays. Versus a pass, they are flat defenders.

Both safeties are aligned over the tight end to their side of the ball, six yards off the line of scrimmage. The safeties key their tight end for their run-pass read, just as they both do in Cover 44 (or as the free safety does in Cover 5 and Cover 4). Versus a run, both safeties would fit where needed. Most often, they fit in the 5 gap, but they also need to be prepared to support the perimeter if the ballcarrier bounces outside. Versus a pass, the safeties cover the tight end man to man on all routes except shallow crossing routes, in which case they would pass the crossing route to the other safety and look for a crossing route coming to them. They would also not cover the tight end if he were to release in the near flat; instead, they would stay in their one fourth of the field. The corner has the single receiver man to man, and he runs with all motions.

The Eagle defensive structure has greatly enhanced our ability to develop a game plan each week to defend what our opponent does best. For our game plan, we are able to take the best aspects of what both the Stack and Eagle defensive structures have to offer. We are careful not to install more defense than our players can execute with confidence and precision. You can see that the Eagle package is well organized, and once our players understand the concepts behind the Eagle defense, this package has blended well with our Stack defensive structure.

PART V

Reads, Stances, and Techniques

CHAPTER 13

Defensive Linemen

I coached the defensive line for nine seasons at the University of Colorado and greatly enjoyed everything about coaching the position. Defensive linemen combine many of the qualities that make football the great game that it is. Typically, defensive linemen are very aggressive players, and they enjoy physical contact. They usually have the attitude that they are superior to the player they are aligned across from. What separates a defensive lineman from an offensive lineman is a more aggressive nature as well as the ability and quickness to disengage from blockers and get to the ballcarrier.

In addition to developing fundamentally proficient players, the challenge in coaching defensive linemen is to get them to pursue the ballcarrier with great effort on every play. All-out pursuit of the ballcarrier can be difficult for defensive linemen because they are bigger than other defenders and because they have to physically battle an offensive lineman on every play.

Two players have made a lasting impression on me as great examples of defensive effort and desire to get to every ballcarrier. Those players are Matt Rice and Tamba Hali. Matt played noseguard at Northwestern University on the 1995 and 1996 Big Ten championship teams. I remember watching a game tape during the 1995 season, the morning after a key win in a very close football game. I was using the remote control to freeze a play just before a tackle that Matt made 20 yards from his original alignment. As I stopped the play with the remote, I realized that Matt would not have made the play if he had not taken the proper angle to the ball and sprinted relentlessly to get to the point where he could intercept the ballcarrier.

If Matt hadn't given great effort to make that particular play, the ballcarrier would have probably scored a touchdown. Everyone else—including the defensive backs to that side of the field—was either blocked or out of position. That one play may well have determined the outcome of the game, and consequently, our season. Whenever possible, you should show these types of plays to your entire defense to constantly reinforce the importance of unbridled effort on every play.

Tamba Hali was a rush end at Penn State University who played on the 2005 Big Ten championship team. Tamba was a player who knew only one speed—full speed.

It didn't matter to him what day of the week it was or whether we were in shorts or full gear. He gave 100 percent effort on every play, and he demanded the same from his teammates in an encouraging way. It was only fitting that Tamba made the key sack—causing a fumble from Ohio State quarterback Troy Smith to stop their last drive—that secured a Penn State victory and propelled the Nittany Lions to a share of the Big Ten championship in 2005.

Keys

Being able to master the mental aspects of their position is what often separates a good player from a great player at any position. A defensive lineman should always be aware of the down and distance and the game circumstances. This will help him to anticipate the next play.

Successful defensive linemen, such as Northwestern noseguard Matt Rice, must be aggressive and demonstrate unbridled pursuit of the ballcarrier.

He should also study the stance of the offensive lineman for run and pass keys. For example, on first and 10 with the game tied, the defensive tackle may see that the offensive lineman aligned across from him has most of his weight forward in his stance. If this is the case, the defensive tackle should anticipate a running play and a run block from that offensive lineman. In the same situation, if an offensive guard has very little weight forward, with his heels flat on the ground and his butt low, the defensive tackle should anticipate either a pass set by the guard or that the guard may be pulling. If the guard is aligned off the line of scrimmage and deeper than the other offensive linemen—and if the offensive tackle is aligned on the line of scrimmage with his weight forward—chances are the guard is pulling.

At Colorado, our defensive linemen and linebackers often made calls based on the stances of the offensive linemen. A "Red" call was made when the offensive linemen had their weight forward in anticipation of a running play. *Red* meant run. If the linemen had their weight back, we called out "Green," which symbolized a traffic light turning green—this told the defensive linemen that it's time to hit the gas and get upfield. If an offensive lineman had his weight back while the others around him had their weight forward, this indicated he was going to pull. In this situation, we would make a "Purple" call.

Communicating across the defensive front helps reinforce what each player is seeing. For example, a defense will often know when a counter misdirection play is going to be run because one side of the defensive front will make a "Green" or "Purple" call and the other side of the line will see "Red" stances. This tells both sides of the ball that the "green" linemen are most likely pulling to the other side of the ball.

Clear communication is also particularly helpful when the defensive line anticipates a pass play. When a pass of any type is called, the offensive linemen usually adjust their weight back so that they can set quickly in pass protection. Any time defensive linemen anticipate a pass, they should visualize the move they are going to use to beat the blocker across from them. When the ball is snapped, they should accelerate upfield, executing their pass rush technique. They can't wait for the ball to be snapped to react to a pass set by the offensive line.

Also, when a defensive lineman anticipates a pass, he should key the ball. The ball will always move a fraction of a second before the offensive lineman does, so keying the ball helps the defensive lineman get the jump on the offensive lineman. On game day, the defensive linemen often find it easy to read the offensive line's stances, particularly as the game goes on and the offensive line starts to fatigue. When defensive linemen are tuned in to game situations and stances, this will give them a tremendous advantage.

Stance

The proper stance is necessary for any physical activity. This principle holds true for all athletic functions. If the stance is flawed, the athlete is less likely to be successful, whether it's a baseball player in his stance in the batter's box, a golfer preparing to tee off, or a basketball player at the free throw line preparing to shoot. The same is true for all football players at every position. Because linemen are making contact within their first two steps, being in a stance that gives a lineman the best opportunity for success is critical. The following descriptions of position-specific stances will help ensure that your linemen achieve quick reactions and efficient movement:

■ **Stance for a noseguard in a 1 alignment.** The noseguard should usually be in a three-point stance, similar to the one used by the defensive tackle. The difference is that the noseguard's body is slightly tilted in toward the center (figure 13.1). He should be as close to the football as possible without encroaching into the neutral zone. The noseguard's inside foot should be back and staggered behind his outside foot in a heel–toe relationship. His inside hand should be on the ground, and his outside hand should be up and open with the palm facing toward the center. The noseguard's inside foot should be aligned on the outside foot of the center.

As the ball is snapped, the noseguard should attack the V of the center's neck by taking a 6- to 10-inch jab step with his inside foot. This step must be in a straight

Figure 13.1 Tilted noseguard stance.

line at the V of the center's neck. When a noseguard is learning the tilted technique, he will often step underneath himself or step across the face of the center. In both cases, the step will prevent him from defeating both the reach and the scoop block. Practice and repetition will eliminate these false steps. When the noseguard attacks the V of the center's neck, he will be in great position to defeat the various blocking schemes he will see.

■ **Stance for the 3-technique defensive tackle and the 5-technique defensive end.** This stance should start with the inside foot (the foot closest to the ball) staggered behind the outside foot in a heel–toe relationship. The defensive lineman's inside foot should split the crotch of the offensive lineman he is aligned over. His feet should be shoulder-width apart or slightly wider. However, if his feet are too wide, this may cause the defensive lineman to take a false step underneath himself. If this occurs, the defensive lineman will lose his base, and it will likely cause him to rise up and lose his leverage.

As the defensive tackle or defensive end eases into his stance, he should bend at the knees and sit back as if in a chair. Then he should reach out and put his inside hand on the ground. His outside hand should be up and open with the palm facing toward the lineman he is across from. The defensive lineman's back should be flat, with his butt slightly elevated. His head should be up. The majority of the defensive lineman's weight should be on his legs. His weight should be balanced in his stance, and he should be able to easily move right, left, or straight ahead. All players on the defensive front four must be careful not to get themselves in an overextended position that would limit their ability to react laterally as the ball changes direction.

The defensive lineman's eyes should be locked on the headgear of his primary key—the offensive lineman he is aligned over. His peripheral vision should enable him to see the ball, which is his initial key for when to attack the line of scrimmage. As mentioned, the ball will move a fraction of a second before the offensive line does.

When the offensive center's hand touches the ball, all four defensive linemen should be in their stances, ready to attack the offensive player across from them. They should align tight to the line of scrimmage. As the ball is snapped, the four defensive linemen should step with their inside foot, attacking the line of scrimmage with a 6- to 10-inch step straight ahead. Stepping with the inside foot helps defensive linemen keep their shoulders square to the line of scrimmage. Conversely, stepping with the outside foot first versus a base block would allow the defender's shoulders to be turned more easily, which would open a vertical seam in the defense. Stepping with the outside foot also hinders a defensive lineman's ability to squeeze an inside release by an offensive lineman.

After the initial inside step, the defensive lineman should quickly follow up and step with his outside foot, squaring up his body. The goal is for the defensive lineman to take two steps across the line of scrimmage before making contact with the offensive lineman. This is challenging to do, but it reinforces beating the offensive lineman off the line of scrimmage and getting both feet moving forward. It also reinforces that the defensive linemen should keep their bodies square to the line of scrimmage. Of course, they must continue to keep their pads low.

As the defensive lineman attacks the line of scrimmage, his initial read is the head-gear of the offensive lineman he is aligned over. The offensive lineman's headgear will give the defensive lineman his key for recognizing the blocking scheme and diagnosing the play.

■ **Stance for a defensive tackle or defensive end in a 4 eye alignment.** In this alignment, the defensive lineman uses the same stance as when aligning in a 3 or 5 technique, except the 4 eye defender now aligns with his outside foot over the offensive tackle's midpoint. On the snap of the ball, the defensive lineman should attack with his outside leg. His gap responsibility is the 3 gap.

■ **Stance for rush end.** If he is in a three-point stance, the same principles described for the defensive end's and tackle's stances apply to the rush end. If the rush end is in a two-point stance, he uses a linebacker stance. In a two-point stance, the rush end does not step forward on the snap of the ball, regardless of his alignment. He mirrors the movement of the offensive lineman or the tight end he is aligned over. However, he reacts to all of the blocks exactly as he would if he were in a three-point stance.

Position-Specific Fundamentals

Each defender has a set of fundamentals he needs to master if he is to be success-ful at his position. The defensive line is no exception. A well-drilled player who is grounded in the fundamentals for his position will successfully execute his role in each defense called. When all eleven defenders execute the fundamentals at each of their positions, the defense will be successful.

Noseguard

The noseguard must be successful in his stance, his alignment, and his first step. Because the center is aligned over the football, the noseguard has the advantage of being able to crowd the football and the center. He can attack the center with his inside foot, making contact with the center's body before the center has the opportunity to gain any forward momentum with his attempted block. The noseguard must be prepared to take on all of the following blocks:

■ **Base block.** Versus a base block by the center (which involves the center putting his helmet in the middle of the noseguard and trying to drive him off of the line of scrimmage), the noseguard should attack the center with his inside foot. He must maintain leverage on the center by keeping his pad level low and his back flat. As the noseguard is making contact with the center, he should thrust his hands inside the center's breastplate and grab the center (figure 13.2).

Figure 13.2 Noseguard taking on a center's base block.

He should then drive the center one yard into the backfield (or at least maintain the line of scrimmage). The noseguard should then lock his arms out, gaining separation from the center and putting himself in position to disengage to the football. To execute this technique, the key fundamentals for the noseguard are stepping with his inside foot—straight ahead—and maintaining a flat back as he delivers a hand shiver up through the armpits of the center. The noseguard should keep his outside arm free and his shoulders square in order to control the 1 gap. If the ball starts away, the noseguard should squeeze the center through the front-side 1 gap and disengage to the ball after he has cleared any threat of a cutback to his 1 gap.

■ **Scoop block.** The noseguard's tilted alignment is a huge advantage in defeating the scoop block. When the noseguard steps with his inside foot at the V of the center's neck, he is anticipating and taking away the scoop block. By definition, a scoop block is when the center releases away from the noseguard and moves upfield to block the inside linebacker. Working with the center, the offensive guard drives his helmet flat and into the far hip of the noseguard to cut off and prevent his pursuit to the ballcarrier. The noseguard's tilted alignment enables him to take the best possible step to defeat the scoop block. By attacking the center at an angle and thrusting his hands into the breastplate of the center, the noseguard is in perfect position to flatten the center down the line of scrimmage. This makes it very difficult for the center to get to the inside linebacker. I have always instructed the noseguard to grab cloth and squeeze the center through the front-side 1 gap for two steps, which will disrupt the center's path to the inside linebacker. It will also make it challenging for the offensive guard to get in position to block the noseguard.

■ **Reach block.** The noseguard's tilted alignment also offers an advantage in defeating the reach block. In addition, being able to defeat a reach block by the center is the reason the noseguard aligns with his inside foot on the outside foot of the center. Because the noseguard can align an inch from the center's helmet, the center must take a flat step in his attempt to reach the outside shoulder of the noseguard. As the noseguard takes his initial step at the V of the center's neck, he will press the center's helmet into the backfield. As the noseguard reads the helmet of the center and recognizes the attempted reach block, he should step for width with his outside foot and jam the center's helmet with his outside hand, keeping the center's helmet from getting to the noseguard's body. This will also cause the center to turn his body parallel to the line of scrimmage. The noseguard should then lock his arms out, disengage from the center, and flatten to the football.

■ **Double-team block.** When taking on a double-team block, the noseguard must first defeat the center's base block and maintain the line of scrimmage. His pad level must be under the center's pad level. This is the key to defeating the center's block. As the noseguard feels the offensive guard on a down block—creating a double-team block—the noseguard should grab the center and execute a seat roll into the guard's legs. To execute a seat roll, the noseguard drops his outside knee and drives his outside shoulder into the ground. This will prevent the guard from bouncing up to the linebacker and will create a three-man pile in the hole. The noseguard should then fight back upfield through the seam between the center and guard, grabbing legs and looking to make a play. If the guard's intention is to slam the noseguard and then bounce off the noseguard to the linebacker, the noseguard needs to stay low and stay on his feet. He should fight to keep his body square to the line of scrimmage. As mentioned, the noseguard needs to defeat the center's block first. He should fight the guard's pressure, and when the guard slips off to block the inside linebacker, the noseguard should throw his body into the 1 gap.

When the center blocks back on the 3-technique defensive tackle, the center's flat course will tell the noseguard that he is blocking back. In this situation, the noseguard should attempt to jam and disrupt the center's path to the defensive tackle. As the noseguard feels the down block from the guard, he should react upfield and penetrate through the backfield to the ball. The noseguard should stay as close to the line of scrimmage as possible. Getting too far upfield will open a vertical cutback seam. The noseguard now becomes a cutback player.

The noseguard can align inches from the center's helmet. I believe that playing the noseguard in a shaded 1 technique gives the defense an advantage. The only time I have played the noseguard in a 2 technique (which is an inside shade on the offensive guard) is versus a one-back formation with two tight ends or in our goal line defense. When playing the noseguard in a 2 technique, or when sliding the defensive tackle from a 3 alignment to a 2 alignment, the player in a 2 alignment should now stagger his stance with his outside foot back and in the crotch of the offensive guard. He should attack the offensive guard with his outside foot. A 2-technique player is responsible for the 1 gap. He will play the block combinations the same as if he were aligned as the defensive tackle in a 3 technique.

Defensive Tackle

The defensive tackle is in a 3 alignment and is referred to as a 3 technique. He is responsible for the 3 gap. As mentioned in the description of his stance, the defensive tackle aligns with his inside leg splitting the crotch of the offensive guard. He should crowd the line of scrimmage. The defensive tackle's primary key is the headgear of the offensive guard. On the snap of the ball, the defensive tackle should attack and read the guard's helmet.

- **Base block.** Against a base block, the guard's helmet will come straight at the defensive tackle. The defensive tackle should attack the guard by stepping first with his inside foot, which should be staggered back. The tackle should maintain a low pad level and explode under the pads of the guard, delivering a hand shiver up through the breastplate of the guard. He should grab cloth and lock his arms out, creating separation and keeping his head and outside arm in the 3 gap. The tackle should then disengage from the guard and pursue the football through the 3 gap. If the ball goes away from the defensive tackle, he should squeeze the guard through the front-side 1 gap. He

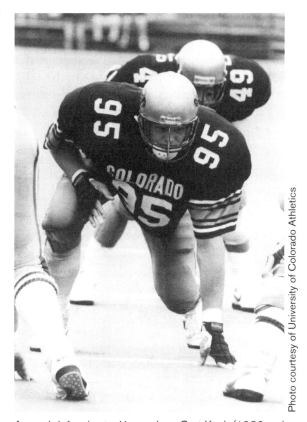

Photo courtesy of University of Colorado Athletics

A good defensive tackle, such as Curt Koch (1986 and 1987 All-American Honorable Mention), must crowd the line of scrimmage and read the guard's helmet.

should then disengage either through the 3 gap or across the face of the guard to pursue the ballcarrier.

■ **Reach block.** Versus a reach block, as the defensive tackle attacks with his inside foot, he will read the helmet of the guard moving to reach his outside shoulder. The guard is attempting to seal the defensive tackle to the inside. When this occurs, the tackle should widen with his outside foot and press the line of scrimmage with his inside foot. Pressing with his inside foot will keep his shoulders square. Pressing the line of scrimmage will also turn the guard's body perpendicular to the line of scrimmage. If the guard does get his helmet to the tackle's outside shoulder, the tackle must press the guard's body into the 3 gap. This will close the 3 gap with the guard's body and is equally effective in controlling the 3 gap. When the defensive tackle knocks the guard backward, this will flatten the guard's body and force the ballcarrier deep and wide or force him to cut back deep in the backfield. The tackle should then lock his arms out, creating separation, and disengage to pursue the ballcarrier.

■ **Scoop block.** Against a scoop block, the defensive tackle uses the same initial fundamentals as when he is taking on a base block. As the tackle attacks and reads the guard taking an inside release to the eagle linebacker, the tackle should adjust his course inside to put him in position to jam and squeeze the guard into the 1 gap. The tackle's goal is to keep the guard on the line of scrimmage for two steps, closing the 1 gap with the guard's body. After two steps, the tackle should disengage and pursue the ballcarrier. At the very least, the tackle should maintain the line of scrimmage and disrupt the guard's path to the eagle linebacker. Squeezing the guard will also keep the tackle's body away from the offensive tackle, who will be attempting to drive his helmet flat and into the far hip of the defensive tackle to cut off his pursuit to the ballcarrier.

■ **Double-team block.** When facing a double-team block, the defensive tackle must first defeat the guard's base block and maintain the line of scrimmage. To defeat the base block, the defensive tackle must keep his pad level lower than the guard's pad level (figure 13.3). As the defensive tackle feels the offensive tackle on a down block—creating a double-team block—the defensive tackle should grab the guard and execute a seat roll into the offensive tackle's legs. To execute the seat roll, the defensive tackle drops his outside knee and drives his outside shoulder into the ground. This will prevent the offensive tackle from bouncing up to the eagle linebacker and will create a three-man pile in the hole. The defensive tackle must be sure to grab and hold the offensive guard. He should then fight back upfield through the seam between the guard and offensive tackle, grabbing legs and looking to make a play.

If the offensive tackle's intent is to slam the defensive tackle and bounce up to block a linebacker (as opposed to just staying on the double team), the defensive tackle should fight to stay on his feet and should stay low so that he doesn't get knocked off the line of scrimmage. He needs to fight to keep his body square to the line of scrimmage. As mentioned, the defensive tackle must defeat the guard's block first. He should fight the offensive tackle's pressure. When the offensive tackle slips off to block the linebacker, the defensive tackle should throw his body into the 3 gap.

Figure 13.3   Defensive tackle taking on a double-team block.

■ **Down block.** When the offensive guard pulls to the outside, the offensive tackle will likely attempt a down block on the defensive tackle. The defensive tackle should be able to get a presnap read off the stances of the offensive line that will help him anticipate a pulling guard and a down or back block.

The defensive tackle can play the down block in two different ways. First, as the tackle reads the guard taking a bucket step back and beginning to pull to the outside, the defensive tackle should expect a down block from the offensive tackle. After his initial step forward, the defensive tackle should reach with his outside arm to club and grab the offensive tackle's outside shoulder pad. He should then work across the offensive tackle's face and pursue the football.

The defensive tackle wants to be sure not to give up ground as he works over the top of the down block. If he does start to get displaced off the line of scrimmage, the defensive tackle should accelerate back to the line of scrimmage and work inside out to the football. When a defensive lineman gets displaced off of the line of scrimmage, he interferes with the linebacker's path to press downhill toward the ballcarrier.

The second way to play this scheme is for the defensive lineman to accelerate across the line of scrimmage as quickly as possible on the snap of the ball. He should attempt to get in the pulling guard's hip pocket and flatten to the football. The defensive lineman must beat the down block with his quickness across the line of scrimmage. A defensive tackle should use both techniques during the course of a game and season. Playing a down block over the top one time makes playing it underneath another time effective. This creates a challenge for the offensive tackle who must anticipate how a defensive tackle will react to his down block.

■ **Back block.** When the offensive guard pulls across the formation, the center usually blocks back on the defensive tackle. As the defensive tackle reads the guard taking a bucket step back to begin his pull across the ball, the tackle should expect a back block from the center. After his initial step forward, the defensive tackle should reach with his inside arm to club and grab the center's far shoulder pad. He should then work across the center's face, maintaining an inside-out relationship to the ballcarrier.

The defensive tackle must avoid giving up ground as he works over the top of the back block. Trying to penetrate into the backfield on a back block seldom puts the defensive tackle in position to make a play; it does just the opposite, creating a cutback lane over the center's original alignment. As mentioned earlier, versus a back block, the noseguard will get a piece of the center and will then penetrate and become the cutback player. This allows the defensive tackle to work over the top of the center's face—often untouched by the center—and pursue the ballcarrier inside out.

This combination works so well that I have had opposing coaches ask me how we guessed right so often and stunted into their play each time they pulled the guard across the formation. The defensive tackle worked so cleanly over the top that it looked like a stunt. Again, when the defensive tackle can get a presnap read indicating that the guard is pulling, this allows the tackle to anticipate and play the blocking scheme successfully.

Defensive End and Rush End

The defensive end aligns as a 5 technique, with his inside leg splitting the crotch of the offensive tackle. If the defensive end is aligned to the field, he may widen his alignment by putting his inside leg on the outside leg of the offensive tackle. A wider alignment helps ensure that the defensive end doesn't get caught in a reach block or lose containment. Down and distance will also influence the alignment of the defensive end. On third and long, both the defensive end and the rush end (who is aligned in a contain position on the opposite side of the ball) will widen in order to focus on containment and gain a pass rush advantage over the offensive tackle.

The defensive end and the rush end are responsible for containing all pass actions, controlling the 5 gap versus all running plays. As mentioned, the defensive end is always in a 5 alignment. The rush end can be in a 5 alignment, a 6 alignment (which is head up on the tight end), or a 7 alignment (which is an inside shade on the tight end). In a 5, 6, or 7 alignment, the rush end is responsible for the 5 gap.

■ **Base block.** On a base block, the offensive tackle will attack the defensive end with his helmet straight across the line of scrimmage. The tight end will attack the rush end in the same way. In this situation, a defensive end should attack the offensive tackle by stepping first with his inside foot, which should be staggered back. A rush end who is in a three-point stance will step with a foot over the offensive player he is aligned over. For example, when the rush end is aligned in a 7 technique (an inside shade on the tight end), the rush end will step with his outside foot. When in a two-point stance, a rush end will snap into the base block after he reads the blocker's intent.

Both the defensive end and the rush end should maintain a low pad level and explode under the pads of the offensive blocker. As they make contact with the blocker, they should deliver a hand shiver up through the blocker's breastplates. The end should grab cloth and lock his arms out, creating separation and keeping his head in the 5 gap. He should then disengage and pursue the football. If the ball goes away from the end, he should squeeze the blocker, clear a reverse or bootleg, and then disengage from the blocker to pursue the ballcarrier.

If the rush end is aligned in a 7 technique versus a base block by the tight end, the rush end will use a different technique when the ball is heading to the perimeter. In this situation, the rush end should widen the tight end into the alley, maintaining control of the 5 gap. The rush end should only disengage to pursue the ballcarrier after there is no threat of the ballcarrier cutting back into the 5 gap.

- **Reach block.** A reach block occurs when the offensive tackle is attempting to attack and reach the defensive or rush end's outside shoulder, trying to seal the end inside. After attacking with his inside foot and reading the offensive tackle's helmet, the defensive or rush end should widen with his outside foot and press the line of scrimmage with his inside foot. Pressing with his inside foot will keep his shoulders square. Pressing the line of scrimmage will also turn the offensive tackle's body perpendicular to the line of scrimmage.

If the offensive tackle does get his helmet to the end's outside shoulder, the end must press the tackle's body into the 5 gap. This will close the 5 gap with the tackle's body. When the end knocks the offensive tackle backward, this will flatten the tackle's body and force the ballcarrier deep and wide or force him to cut back deep in the backfield. It will also give the linebackers an open lane to press the line of scrimmage in pursuit of the ballcarrier. The end should then lock his arms out, creating separation, and disengage to pursue the ballcarrier.

When the ball is on the hash and the defensive end is into the boundary, the defensive end should align more head up, because there is less real estate to defend into the boundary. Versus a reach block, a defensive end should not widen more than four yards. The goal is to push the ball deep and wide or force the ballcarrier to cut back.

- **Double-team block.** When taking on a double-team block, the defensive end must first defeat the offensive tackle's base block and maintain the line of scrimmage. The end must keep his pad level under the tackle's pad level; this is the key to defeating the tackle's base block. As the defensive end feels the tight end on a down block, the defensive end should realize that the tight end's intent is to execute a combo block, rather than staying on the double team. In a combo block, the tight end slams the defensive end and then blocks up to the inside linebacker.

The defensive end should fight to stay on his feet. He should stay low and stay on the line of scrimmage. The defensive end needs to fight the tight end's pressure and keep his body square to the line of scrimmage. When the tight end slips off the defensive end to block the linebacker, the defensive end should throw his body into the 5 gap.

- **Veer release.** When a defensive end recognizes a veer release (inside release) by the offensive tackle, the defensive end should squeeze the offensive tackle, disrupting his path to the inside linebacker. He should then continue to squeeze and close the 3 gap. The inside linebacker will replace the defensive end in the 5 gap.

As the defensive end closes inside, his eyes should immediately go to the first threat to block him (a near back), then to his second threat (the front-side guard). The defensive end's third and most likely blocking threat is the back-side guard, who will pull and execute a trap block on the defensive end. Whichever blocker comes for the defensive end, the end should continue to flatten inside and cross arm the blocker. In coaching terms, he should "trap the trapper," which means to turn his shoulders and attack the inside two thirds of the blocker. This will force the ballcarrier to spill to the outside, where the inside linebacker should be in the 5 gap.

Because the rush end aligns next to a 3-technique defensive tackle (the 3 gap is the next gap inside from the rush end), the rush end does not squeeze and close hard inside versus a veer block by the offensive tackle. The rush end does close and constrict the 3 gap, but he does so with his shoulders staying square to the line of scrimmage. He does not turn his shoulders, which keeps him in position to react to the bootleg or reverse and to take the quarterback versus an option play.

- **Trap option play.** A trap option and a waggle pass are two plays that involve a bootleg with a guard pulling to block and secure the edge. Both plays have the back-side guard pulling on a flat course (down the line of scrimmage) or on a course behind the line of scrimmage to block the defensive end. When the end reads the flat course of the pulling guard, he should adjust his course to play through the guard's outside shoulder and contain the quarterback. This adjustment is challenging, but with practice an alert defensive end can make a big play for the defense.

When the offensive tackle executes a veer release inside, the defensive end is not responsible for the quarterback (the inside linebacker is responsible for the quarterback). However, if the defensive end is able to react and force the quarterback, or react with containment versus a waggle, he will greatly disrupt the play. When this occurs, the linebacker becomes a bonus player.

- **Cross block.** When executing a cross block, the tight end blocks down on the defensive end, and the offensive tackle pulls to the outside in an attempt to hook the Sam linebacker or stretch him outside. The goal of the offense in using a cross block is opening a hole outside of the Sam linebacker (if the Sam gets hooked) or in the 5 gap (if the Sam widens).

Versus a cross block, the defensive end will read the offensive tackle taking a bucket step and pulling to the outside, and he will feel the down block by the tight end. The defensive end has two ways to play this blocking scheme. The first way is to club and grab the tight end's outside shoulder pad, working across the tight end's face in pursuit of the football. The defensive end does not want to get displaced as he works over the top of the tight end. If the defensive end starts to get displaced off the line of scrimmage, he should accelerate back to the line of scrimmage and work inside out to the football.

The second way the defensive end can play the down block by the tight end is to accelerate across the line of scrimmage as quickly as possible on the snap of the ball. He should get in the pulling tackle's hip pocket and flatten to the football. The defensive end must beat the down block with his quickness across the line of scrimmage.

When the backfield flow starts on the other side of the football, the defensive end or rush end should squeeze the blocker's cutoff block. The end should initially keep his shoulders square to the line of scrimmage as he scans what is ahead of the ballcarrier, being alert for a possible reverse coming from the field. The defensive end and rush end should always be aware of a possible bootleg by the quarterback and a potential cutback by the running back. If the ball continues on its path inside of the defensive end or rush end, the end should squeeze the blocker inside, gain separation, lock his arms out, and disengage in pursuit of the ballcarrier.

Stunt Techniques

Several stunt combinations may be used, and each stunt has its own name. The term *rip technique* is used to describe the fundamentals that a defensive lineman uses when he stunts into a gap. When executing a rip technique, the defensive lineman involved in a stunt should key the ball for his initial movement. His primary and visual key is the offensive lineman he is ripping toward. The defensive lineman's secondary key, or pressure key, is the offensive lineman he is aligned over. The defensive lineman's visual key will tell him the intent of the ballcarrier. His eyes should go to his visual key as the ball is snapped.

The defensive lineman's first step is parallel to the line of scrimmage and approximately 8 to 12 inches wide, with his toes pointed upfield. On that first step, the defensive lineman will get his initial read from the offensive lineman he is stunting toward. Before moving (while in his stance), the defensive lineman should put his weight on the foot he is pushing off of. He should have very little weight on the foot he is stepping with.

If the offensive lineman's helmet starts flat and down the line of scrimmage toward the defensive lineman, this indicates that the offensive lineman is attempting to scoop the defensive lineman. This also tells the defensive lineman that the ball is going away from the direction he is stunting. After taking his initial step, the defensive lineman should immediately redirect and flatten down the line of scrimmage in the direction the ball is going. While doing so, he should use his hands to keep the offensive blocker off of him and stay as square to the line of scrimmage as possible.

If the offensive lineman's helmet drives at a 45-degree angle at the defensive lineman, the blocker is attempting to kick the defensive lineman out. In this case, the defensive lineman should cross the offensive lineman's face and square up in the hole. If the offensive lineman releases away—either on an angle up to a linebacker or on a flat course to perform a scoop block on the next down defensive lineman—the play is going in the direction the defensive lineman is stunting.

When the play is going away, the defensive lineman's pressure key (the player the defensive lineman is aligned over) will be attempting to execute a cutoff block on the defensive lineman, trying to prevent him from pursuing the ballcarrier. Versus a cutoff block, the defensive lineman's technique will be the key to his success in beating the blocker. As the defensive lineman takes his initial step in the direction he is ripping to, he will read his primary key—the lineman he is ripping toward—moving on a path away from him. The defensive lineman should bring his trail leg through while simultaneously ripping his trail forearm through, which will turn the helmet of the offensive blocker trying to cut off the defensive lineman.

The defensive lineman must stay low when executing a rip technique. A coaching point I use when teaching a defensive lineman to beat a cutoff block with a rip technique is that the defender should "grab grass" as he rips through the offensive lineman's headgear, protecting his trail leg. When drilling the rip and redirection technique, I make the defensive linemen show me grass in their fist after the play concludes. As with all defensive line fundamentals, a defensive lineman should always be in a bent-knee position, with his hips low and his shoulders square to the line of scrimmage. This puts him in position to take on blockers and pursue the football.

As mentioned, the defensive lineman's initial step should be an 8- to 12-inch parallel step moving flat down the line of scrimmage (instead of a step at a 45-degree angle into the line of scrimmage, which many coaches teach). The parallel step is used for two reasons. The first reason was explained in the description of the defensive lineman reacting to a scoop block. A parallel step makes redirecting and beating the scoop block easier.

The second reason is to effectively react to a cutoff block. In a cutoff block, the defensive lineman's pressure key (the offensive lineman he is aligned over) tries to get his head in front of the defensive lineman and cut off his pursuit to the ballcarrier. If the defensive lineman were to take a 45-degree step into the line of scrimmage, there would be no place for his trail leg to get through as he attempts to bring his trail leg and arm through. In effect, he blocks himself. When the defensive lineman takes a parallel step, his trail leg can easily clear and remove the defensive lineman's body from the offensive lineman's cutoff block.

Pass Rush Strategy

When the game situation changes from a running situation to a passing situation, the defensive front four should get excited. Rushing the passer is a great opportunity to make a big play! The defensive line should be aware of the down as well as the distance needed by the offense to obtain a first down. They should know the opponent and when the opponent is likely to throw the football.

As the defensive coach, you are the signal caller on the sideline, and you can help alert the defensive players on the field by making a "Rush" call to the defensive front. When a rush call is made, the defensive front four should crowd the line of scrimmage, get in their fastest pass rush stance, and study the stances of the offensive linemen for further indications that the offense is going to pass the ball.

Communication between the front four defensive linemen and the linebackers will reinforce the belief that the offense is going to pass the football. Before the snap of the ball, each defensive lineman should visualize the moves he is going to execute to beat the offensive lineman across from him. When the ball is snapped, the defensive lineman should accelerate across the line of scrimmage with leverage. He should keep his feet moving and get upfield as quickly as he can, closing the distance to the quarterback as quickly as possible!

Getting *home* (to the quarterback) is only one aspect of a successful pass rush. A defensive lineman can do everything right, defeat the blocker, and still not get home. For example, the quarterback may use a three-step or five-step drop and throw the ball immediately on setting up, which means the ball could be thrown in 1.7 to 2.3 seconds. The defensive linemen still play a major role in defending that pass play. Closing the pocket disrupts the quarterback's timing and pressures him into throwing the ball to his first look. This limits his ability to locate secondary receivers if the primary receiver is covered.

By staying in the correct rushing lane, a defensive lineman can limit the quarterback's vision, not giving him a window to throw through or an area to step up into to avoid a hard outside rush. Defensive linemen or blitzing linebackers should always get their hands up just before the quarterback's release of the football. Doing so limits the quarterback's vision and alters a percentage of his throws. Deflecting passes is also an effective way to stop the passing attack.

For an effective pass rush, your defensive linemen must have the attitude that enables them to give a tremendous effort on every down. The defensive linemen can never predict when the secondary will have the offense's primary receiver covered. That is when pressure on the quarterback will create an incomplete pass, cause an interception, or force a quarterback sack. You can use the following key reminders with your defensive linemen:

- Be aware of the offensive down and distance and the offensive lineman's stance.
- Be aware of a rush down by communicating "Green" calls.
- On a rush down, crowd the line of scrimmage, getting into a sprinter's stance.
- Key the ball to get off quickly and accelerate across the line of scrimmage.
- Always stay in your rush lane, get your hands up when the quarterback is in his throwing action, and pursue the ball relentlessly on the throw.

Pass rush techniques and moves fall into two categories: power and speed rushes. A player can use both techniques on the same play. One move also helps set up the other. Both are important tools for the defensive lineman to incorporate into his pass rush. With every pass rush, it is critical that the rusher turn his inside foot in and point it toward the quarterback as he attempts to clear the blocker. Doing so will turn the rusher's body onto a direct path to the quarterback. Additionally, defensive linemen should be aware of the potential pitfalls in their pass rush strategy. When rushing the passer, the defensive front four must always be aware of the possibility of a screen pass or a draw play. Both plays are designed to take advantage of aggressive pass rushers.

Power Rush Techniques

Power rushes are used primarily by the noseguard and the defensive tackle. A power rush is also used by a defensive end when converting a speed rush into a bull rush. The bull rush is designed to drive the blocker into the quarterback. When executing a bull rush, the defensive lineman should accelerate across the line of scrimmage with leverage and should charge into one half of the surface of the blocker. He should drive his hands up through the blocker's breastplates, maintaining inside hand control. He should keep his feet moving and be relentless in his charge. The defensive lineman should always maintain a position of leverage on the blocker, which will allow the defensive lineman to continue to drive the pass blocker back and into the quarterback.

The swim technique can be used after initially starting a bull rush. The blocker must be convinced that the pass rusher is on a bull rush charge, which will force the blocker to lunge and overextend forward to stop the bull rush. Once the blocker has overextended forward, the rusher should quickly pull the blocker forward, then drive his inside arm tightly over the surface of the blocker and replace the blocker's body with his own. He should then push off and accelerate to the quarterback.

The arm-under technique can also be used off of a bull rush start. The same coaching points described for the swim technique apply to the start of an arm-under rush. However, when the blocker lunges forward to stop the pass rusher's charge, instead of driving his arm tightly over the surface of the blocker, the rusher should dip and rip his arm tightly under the surface of the blocker. As soon as the rusher clears the blocker, the rusher should replace the blocker's body with his own and should accelerate to the quarterback. The rusher may reload and execute the arm-under technique again if necessary to come free. He could also convert his arm-under technique to a quick swim move. This is often a successful way to throw the blocker off balance and for the rusher to free himself up.

Speed Rush Techniques

The quickest way to get to the quarterback is a speed rush. On a speed rush, the pass rusher wants to have as little contact as necessary with the blocker as he works to get to the quarterback. An effective speed rush will often involve a head fake by the pass rusher. To execute a head fake, the defender takes an aggressive step at the blocker or to the inside or outside of the blocker. This step should get the blocker to freeze momentarily in place or get him to react in the opposite direction from where the speed rush is actually coming. The momentary pause by the blocker can give the rusher the advantage.

Another technique that can be used on a speed rush is the quick swim move, which may also involve a head fake. The rusher should accelerate across the line of scrimmage, reaching for the blocker's outside shoulder, forearm, or wrist. The rusher should grab the blocker and pull aggressively in and down. He should then drive his inside arm tightly over the surface of the blocker. After the rusher gets past the blocker, the rusher should replace the blocker's body with his own, push off the blocker, and accelerate to the quarterback.

A quick arm-under move can also be used in conjunction with a head fake. The defensive lineman accelerates across the line of scrimmage, reaching for the blocker's outside shoulder, forearm, or wrist. He should grab the first surface he encounters and pull aggressively, trying to lift the blocker's arm if possible. The rusher should then dip his shoulder and drive his arm under the arm surface of the blocker (figure 13.4).

Figure 13.4 Defensive lineman executing a speed pass rush arm-under technique.

As the rusher clears the blocker, he should replace the blocker's body with his own, push off, and accelerate to the quarterback.

Another speed rush technique is the shoulder turn. The defensive lineman should accelerate across the line of scrimmage, jamming the blocker's shoulder pad back toward the quarterback. The defensive lineman should continue to push until he turns the offensive lineman's shoulders. From that position, the defensive lineman can maneuver both the blocker's and his own body position so that they are perpendicular to the quarterback. He should then execute an arm-under move to get beyond the blocker and get to the quarterback.

For every pass rush technique, a defensive lineman needs a countermove to use off his initial move. The countermove can be a reaction to the offensive lineman taking away the rusher's initial move upfield. It can also be a preconceived plan by the defensive rusher. For example, if a defensive lineman has been having success with his speed rush to the outside, he may anticipate that the offensive lineman will be setting up very quickly and with more width than he should. The defensive lineman can use a countermove to take advantage of the offensive lineman's efforts to stop the speed rush to the outside.

When executing a countermove off an outside rush, the defensive lineman should accelerate across the line of scrimmage, jamming or reaching for the offensive blocker's outside shoulder pad. The defensive rusher must convince the blocker that his intention is to go around the blocker to the quarterback. As the blocker accelerates his shuffle to prevent the defensive lineman from beating him to the outside, he will often lose his shuffle and cross his inside foot over his outside foot. Once that happens, the offensive lineman cannot recover and react to the defensive lineman's inside countermove. The defensive lineman's speed off the ball is critical to making this happen. When the blocker does cross his feet over, his head will pop beyond the rusher's head. This is the key for when to execute the countermove. The defender should club with his inside arm and throw the blocker beyond the rusher's body position. He should then execute an arm-under move and counter under the blocker's surface to the inside and to the quarterback. The same countermove can be executed off an initial quick swim or arm-under move.

When an inside pass rusher—the defensive tackle or the noseguard—starts on a speed rush, he should try to beat his man by the third step. If the pass rusher has not beaten his man by his third step, he must execute a spin or countermove back to the quarterback. This is important in maintaining the integrity of the inside rush lanes. If the pass rusher does not execute the countermove, he may create an open window for the quarterback to throw through or escape into.

Pass Rush Pitfalls

Defensive linemen must be alert for indications that the offense will be running a screen pass or a draw play. On a screen pass, the offensive tackle will drop abnormally deep, and the quarterback will start to drift backward after his initial five-step drop. The defensive linemen may also observe or feel the running back hanging out near the line of scrimmage but not blocking. These are clues that the defensive line should be aware that a slip screen to a running back is being set up. When a defensive lineman reads that a screen play is developing, he should communicate this to his teammates, then locate and go to the running back.

If the offensive tackle turns his shoulders perpendicular to the line of scrimmage and opens a path to the quarterback, a defensive lineman should anticipate the possibility of a draw play. As with screen plays, the first step in stopping a draw play or a reverse is communication—yelling it out to teammates. When a defensive lineman hears a "draw" call or recognizes a draw play, he should retrace his steps back to the line of scrimmage. Doing so will force the ballcarrier to radically change his path and go toward another defensive lineman. A defensive lineman never wants to run around the offensive lineman in an attempt to get to the ballcarrier.

Versus a sprint-out pass, a full-flow pass, or a play-action pass that starts to the rush end or defensive end, the end should react to the reach block from the offensive tackle. As he recognizes that the play is a pass, the end should disengage from the offensive tackle as quickly as possible and take the proper angle to force the quarterback to pull up. The rush end and defensive end are responsible for containment, but they should have late contain help coming from an inside linebacker.

If a sprint-out pass, full-flow pass, or play-action pass moves away from the rush end or defensive end, the end should react to the various blocks he may encounter depending on the pass action. The end should work to get into a contain position as quickly as possible. He should always be aware of the possibility that the quarterback may reverse his course. The end should make sure he maintains a contain position with his head on the upfield shoulder of the quarterback.

CHAPTER 14

Linebackers

Linebackers are the heart of the defense. The defensive tempo is set by the enthusiasm and intensity of the linebacker play. The linebackers are also the "glue" that holds the defense together in adverse situations. The linebackers' attitude is crucial to the attitude of the defense. Many qualities are necessary to be a successful linebacker:

- Competitiveness
- Intelligence
- Physical toughness
- Leadership
- Willingness to be coached
- Quickness
- Agility
- Strength

However, the one quality that sets a great linebacker apart from the rest is his attitude. A linebacker with the right attitude has a positive, powerful presence. The ability to defeat blockers, get to the ball, and make tackles is an "attitude." Seizing the opportunity and making the big play is an "attitude." Champions play with an attitude. Attitude in a linebacker is powerful and productive on and off the field. A linebacker with the right attitude is always positive, lifting up those around him. The right attitude makes average players good and makes good players great. Desire and determination constitute the attitude that a linebacker should possess. His attitude should come from the heart. Great players have great hearts!

Penn State players Paul Posluszny, Tim Shaw, and Dan Connor exemplified all the qualities of great linebackers. Paul and Tim both finished their careers after the 2006 season. Both players earned academic All-American honors and both players were drafted into the NFL. Paul was also a two-time Chuck Bednarik Award winner as the college football defensive player of the year and the winner of the 2005 Butkus Award, which is given to college football's best linebacker. Dan Connor finished his playing career at Penn State after the 2007 season. He broke Paul's career all-time tackle record, and he won the Chuck Bednarik Award.

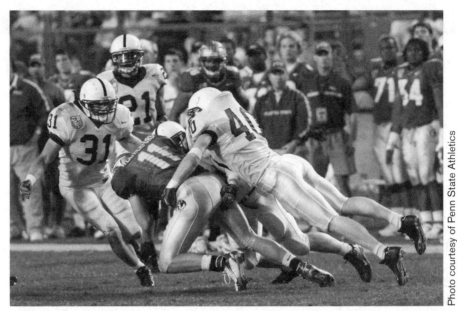

All-Americans and Bednarick winners, Dan Connor (#40) and Paul Posluszny (#31) epitomized the competitive attitude needed by all great linebackers.

What made Paul, Tim, and Dan so special was the way they led by example. From the day they arrived for their first workout, they competed to be the best at everything they did. They won every conditioning drill by a wide margin, both during the season and in the off-season. If they weren't perfect in practice, they would stay until they were. In addition, they were 20 minutes early to every meeting. All three players were encouraging and positive to their teammates. They would not hesitate to talk with a teammate who was out of line, and because of the tremendous respect and affection they each had earned, their input was always well received.

Linebacker Fundamentals

After more than 30 seasons of coaching, I can tell you with great assurance that being drilled in the proper fundamentals and being able to carry those fundamentals over to game performance are critical to any defensive player's success. The linebacker position is no exception. The essential fundamentals for a linebacker include proper stance, the stun and separate technique, pursuit, tackling, and the ability to diagnose offensive plays.

Stance

A perfect stance gives a linebacker the best possible opportunity for success. It puts the linebacker in a position to take on blockers, tackle effectively, and defend the pass. As shown in figure 14.1, the linebacker's knees should be bent and positioned over his feet. His shoulders should be over his knees. His head and eyes should be up. His arms should be relaxed and off his knees. This body position should be maintained until the linebacker meets and tackles the ballcarrier.

For the base of his stance, the linebacker's feet should be slightly wider than shoulder width. This width will allow the linebacker to take an 8- to 12-inch lateral or directional step with the foot to the side of the play. His toes should be pointed upfield. The linebacker must be careful not to widen his base too far. An extremely wide base may feel comfortable, but it will often cause the linebacker's first step to be a balance step inside. This step is referred to as a *false step*. A false step not only slows a linebacker in his effort to get to the ball, but it also leads to a crossover step on his second step. The crossover step brings both feet together, narrowing the linebacker's base. Bringing the feet together will cause the linebacker to straighten up and lose his leverage. When a linebacker loses his base and his leverage, this greatly diminishes his ability to take on blockers, change his direction, and make a tackle.

Figure 14.1 Proper linebacker stance.

Stun and Separate

Versus the run game, the linebacker's purpose is to get to the ballcarrier and put him on the ground. A linebacker will often have to defeat a blocker in his pursuit to the ballcarrier. The first step in being able to get to the ball is diagnosing the blocking scheme and the play being run. Once the linebacker has identified the blocker who is responsible for blocking him, he must attack, stun, and neutralize that blocker. The linebacker must then get separation from the blocker in order to disengage and pursue the ballcarrier.

To consistently defeat blockers, a linebacker needs to have a grasp of the stun and separate technique. Size and strength do not have a great bearing on a linebacker's ability to defeat a blocker. The stun and separate technique allows a linebacker to use two assets that he already possesses: leverage and hands.

The player with leverage—the lowest pad level—has the best opportunity of defeating his opponent. Gaining inside hand control enables a linebacker to gain control of the blocker and then get separation from the blocker. The best weapon a defensive player has is the use of his hands. A linebacker's hand thrust should attack the breastplates of the blocker. His elbows should be in, and his thumbs should be up. A lot of practice time should be spent on these important aspects of linebacker play.

To successfully attack the blocker, a linebacker also needs to have proper head placement and hip explosion. Head placement is determined by the linebacker's area of responsibility and will usually be on the outside two thirds of the blocker. Hip explosion is essential because power during contact comes from the hips. A linebacker should thrust his hips on contact in order to "shock" and neutralize the blocker.

Several essential coaching points must be stressed in practice. First, in order to neutralize or stun a blocker, the linebacker must first attack the blocker successfully. The linebacker should keep his shoulders square, maintain a proper base, and keep his pad level low. On contact, the linebacker must maintain inside-out leverage on the blocker by attacking with his inside foot up and his outside foot back (figure 14.2). The linebacker's base is stronger when his inside foot is up. Attacking the blocker with the inside foot up will keep a linebacker from getting his shoulders turned. When a linebacker's shoulders get turned, a vertical seam is created in the defense. The linebacker must stay square, with the inside foot up, to help keep the defense strong inside out. If the linebacker is bouncing the ball outside, he should thrust his outside foot up as he makes contact with a blocker.

Figure 14.2   A linebacker with proper leverage and hand position on a blocker.

Pursuit

On each play from scrimmage, the ultimate goal for a linebacker is to aggressively tackle the ballcarrier. The most demanding phase of that process is stunning the blocker and gaining separation from the blocker. This fundamental will enable a linebacker to shed blockers. Once free, the linebacker must get to the ball. This movement to the ball is known as *pursuit* and is another fundamental that linebackers must master.

For successful pursuit, linebackers need more than speed, effort, and an insatiable desire to run to the ball. They must also develop discipline and the proper technique, especially the technique to use when regaining leverage on the ballcarrier after a pursuit course. Linebackers employ the four types of pursuit—shuffle, alley, press, and angle of pursuit—described in chapter 1.

Linebackers primarily use the shuffle technique from tackle to tackle when the ball is in the "box" (the area between the split tackle and the tight end). The shuffle technique allows the linebacker to easily change direction as he reacts to the ballcarrier. The shuffle technique is known as *controlled pursuit* and is used when a linebacker has leverage on the ballcarrier. As noted in chapter 1, the coaching points for the shuffle technique are staying square and regaining the shuffle (see page 4). For linebackers, two additional coaching points should be stressed when teaching the shuffle:

1. **Vision.** The third area of emphasis when teaching linebackers to shuffle is their peripheral vision. The linebacker must focus on the ball. At the same time, he must be aware of the movement around him. He must "feel" fallen bodies and blockers in his path to the ball.

2. **Leverage and base.** I often tell my linebackers that if they have a low pad level and a proper base, they will be able to defeat most blockers regardless of size. They will also be in position to tackle effectively. A linebacker should start each play in the proper stance position and should maintain that position for the duration of the play. The start of the play is important, but the finish of the play—when the tackler meets the ballcarrier—is more critical.

As with all defenders, alley pursuit begins whenever the shuffle does not allow the linebacker to keep pace with the ballcarrier. The linebacker must turn his hips and run inside out to the ball while keeping his shoulders as square as possible and maintaining a low pad level. When the linebacker regains his leverage on the ballcarrier, he should regain his shuffle and fit inside out on the ballcarrier.

The press technique is used by a linebacker when he has an opening to the ball. The linebacker should press the ball, attacking the line of scrimmage in an attempt to make a minus-yardage play. If the ballcarrier quickly outflanks the linebacker and crosses the line of scrimmage, the linebacker needs to adjust his course to get in position to intercept the ballcarrier. As the linebacker regains leverage on the ballcarrier, the linebacker should regain his shuffle and expect the ballcarrier to attempt to cut back.

Each individual defensive player is given a grade on pursuit each play from scrimmage. The goal as a team should be to pursue effectively 90 percent of the time. Grading pursuit will help the coaching staff reinforce and illustrate the importance of great effort on every play. Pursuit should become the trademark of your defense and a source of great pride.

Tackling

Tackling is a combination of technique, toughness, and a relentless desire to get to the ball and put the ball on the ground, with or without the ballcarrier. A large part of making a tackle is simply having a "want to" attitude. A linebacker must possess a natural desire and toughness to seek out and tackle the ballcarrier. To be an effective tackler and to minimize missed tackles, a linebacker must understand and execute certain basic skills.

First, when the linebacker meets the ballcarrier, the linebacker's body should be in the same position as when the play began—his stance position. As the linebacker approaches the ballcarrier, he should bend at the knees, not at the waist, as shown in figure 14.3. Bending at the waist will cause the linebacker to overextend and lose his power. Bending at the waist will almost always lead to the initial contact being made by the tackler's head.

Second, on contact, the linebacker should get his head across the body of the ballcarrier. Doing so allows the linebacker to get the full force of his entire body into

Figure 14.3 A linebacker performing the tackle fundamental of fitting up on the ballcarrier.

the tackle, not just his arms. The linebacker should club his arms up and through the ballcarrier, which will naturally cause the linebacker's hips to thrust up and through the ballcarrier. On contact, the linebacker should also accelerate his feet and drive the ballcarrier backward. Finally, the linebacker should always maintain inside leverage on the ballcarrier, never allowing the ballcarrier to cut back across his face. As he approaches the ballcarrier, he should regain his shuffle, preventing the ballcarrier from cutting back.

The quality of the tackle is determined by a defender's ability to accomplish the following:

1. Focus on the ballcarrier's numbers.
2. Maintain his base just before contact, settling his hips and regaining his shuffle.
3. Make his placement across the ballcarrier's body with his head and eyes up and with his knees bent.
4. Stay inside out on the ball.
5. "Hit on the rise," holding an uncoiled body position until striking the ballcarrier on contact.
6. Wrap the ballcarrier up.
7. Drive his feet on contact.

Gaps and Keys

One of the most important skills that linebackers must possess is the ability to diagnose a play. In his first few steps, a linebacker must determine the blocking scheme and the play being run by the offense. The ability to do this can be developed through practice, concentration, and the study of game tape. A linebacker's ability to concentrate on his initial key—along with having an awareness of the running backs—will help him diagnose what is happening and what is going to happen.

In the Eagle and the Stack 4-4-3 defenses, the initial key for the inside linebacker is the offensive guard he is aligned over. Keying the guard has many advantages, particularly in helping the linebacker diagnose misdirection plays and plays that call for the guards to pull. The guard is a true key and will take the linebacker to the ball. Initially, it may take more discipline and slightly more training for a linebacker to get used to reading the guard. However, once they get comfortable reading the guard, most linebackers never want to deviate from it.

If a linebacker's initial read is the guard, the linebacker has a tremendous advantage when the guard pulls. When the guard pulls across the formation, the linebacker should call out "pull." He should then shuffle with the pulling guard, tracking the ballcarrier inside out to defend the trap, power, or counter play. On a power or counter play, the ballcarrier often takes a downhill path. The back-side linebacker will be in great position to make a play on the ballcarrier. I often refer to this technique as "working through the 1 to the 3 to the 5 gap" as the linebacker pursues the ball.

The linebacker opposite the pull call should accelerate immediately to the first open seam (the 5 gap or wider when the linebacker is aligned away from the call side, or the 3 gap or wider when the linebacker is aligned to the call side). Having the inside linebackers read the guard is especially effective in defending the trap, power, and counter plays. When the linebacker sees the guard pull and calls out "pull," the opposite linebacker will be in the 3 or 5 gap before the ballcarrier, and most important, before the pulling guard. The counter play gives the play-side linebacker a false key. The misdirection by the running backs continues to take the linebacker in the wrong direction. When reading the guard and communicating "pull," the linebacker gives the defense an advantage.

Reading the guard also gives the linebacker an advantage against a drop-back, play-action, or bootleg pass. Reading the guard's helmet as it pops up will provide a linebacker with an early pass read. When running a bootleg pass, an offense will often pull the guard to protect the quarterback on the perimeter. Keying the pulling guard against a bootleg pass keeps a linebacker from going with the backfield fake. It also starts the linebackers in the same direction as the receiver crossing the formation, which puts them in good position to cover the crossing receiver and to provide secondary containment on the quarterback.

In some defenses, the linebackers may key the fullback or the tailback for their initial read. I have found that linebackers who have been trained to read guards can successfully adjust to sometimes read a running back. On the other hand, linebackers who primarily read the running back often have a difficult time successfully keying the guard as an alternative read.

Eagle Defense Linebacker Techniques

The following sections detail the alignment, reads, and assignments of the eagle, inside, and Sam linebacker in the Eagle defensive structure.

Eagle Linebacker Alignment, Reads, and Assignments

The eagle linebacker should align stacked behind the defensive tackle, four yards off the line of scrimmage. This is referred to as a 3 alignment. The offensive guard is the primary key for the eagle linebacker's initial movement and his run-pass read. After the eagle linebacker gets his initial movement key, he should then pick up the flow of the running backs.

The eagle linebacker's technique is described as a 12. The first number describes the gap that the linebacker is responsible for if the play starts to his side of the ball. The second number tells the linebacker his gap responsibility on the other side of the ball if the play starts to that side. A 12 responsibility tells the eagle linebacker that he has the 1 gap versus an inside run to him. Versus an outside run to the eagle linebacker, he should press the first open seam to the ball. Of course, there is no 2 gap. In this case, the 2 tells the eagle linebacker that he is not responsible for a gap on the other side of the ball. Versus a play away, the eagle linebacker should shuffle to the ball, staying on the back hip of the ballcarrier and being prepared to play the cutback. Versus a pass, the eagle linebacker is responsible for the hook zone to the curl zone.

The eagle linebacker's reads, reactions, and responsibilities when the running play is at him are described next. Four common offensive running plays are described to show how the eagle linebacker should read and react.

■ **Fullback isolation play.** On a fullback isolation play, the fullback leads the tailback into the 1 gap and is responsible for blocking the eagle linebacker (refer to the figure on page 62). The offensive guard and tackle execute a double team on the 3-technique defensive tackle. On this play, the eagle linebacker will read the offensive guard's helmet attacking the defensive tackle's outside arm or his midpoint, and he will read the fullback on a downhill path toward the 1 gap. When this occurs, the eagle linebacker should attack the fullback in the 1 gap. His aiming point is one yard across the line of scrimmage. When attacking the fullback, the eagle linebacker should have his inside foot up, which will keep his shoulders square. He should keep his outside arm free. The eagle linebacker should attack the outside two thirds of the fullback. His goal is to either make the play himself or force the ballcarrier to radically change his path in the backfield.

When facing a large, aggressive fullback, the eagle linebacker (as well as the inside and Sam linebackers) should attack the outside two thirds of the fullback as before. However, at the last second, the eagle linebacker should drive his helmet through the fullback's inside knee pad. This technique accomplishes two goals. It will cut the fullback in the hole and slow down his charge on future isolation plays. It also gives the tailback an initial 1 gap or cutback read, then takes that path away at the last moment, forcing the tailback to change his path radically.

■ **Sweep play.** On a sweep play (refer to the figure on page 65), the offensive guard will be pulling to the outside. The eagle linebacker should make an "out" call and accelerate his alley pursuit, pressing the first open seam (5 gap or wider) and working inside out to the ball. The eagle linebacker should play over the top of all cut blocks.

- **Power or counter plays.** On a power or counter play, the offensive guard and the offensive tackle double-team the 3-technique defensive tackle (refer to the figure on page 67). The eagle linebacker will read the offensive guard's helmet attacking the defensive tackle's outside arm or his midpoint, and he will hear a "pull" call from the inside linebacker. In this situation, the eagle linebacker should accelerate and press the first open seam (3 gap or wider), taking on the pulling guard with his inside arm and staying square in the hole. If the eagle linebacker is pressing the line of scrimmage outside of the rush end, he should stay tight off the rush end's butt.

The eagle linebacker's reads, reactions, and responsibilities change when the play is on the opposite side of the center. On a scoop block, the offensive guard steps inside of the defensive tackle to release up to the eagle linebacker, and the offensive tackle to that side steps flat to cut off the defensive tackle. This is the most frequent blocking scheme that an eagle linebacker will see when the play is being run on the other side of the center. As the guard's helmet releases inside, the eagle linebacker should step first with his inside foot and pick up the flow of the backs. If there is a cutback threat in his 1 gap and the 1 gap is open, the eagle linebacker should step up and stun the guard in the 1 gap with his outside arm, keeping his inside arm free. Versus an outside threat, the eagle linebacker should pursue quickly over the guard's scoop block.

In the Eagle defense, the defensive tackle is responsible for disrupting the guard's inside release, keeping the eagle linebacker free to flow to the ball. With that said, the defensive tackle does not always get a piece of the guard, and the eagle linebacker needs to be prepared to execute his stun technique on the guard.

Versus a power, counter, or trap play away from the eagle linebacker—with the guard pulling away—the eagle linebacker must first call out "pull." He should then work through the 1 to the 3 to the 5 gap as he pursues the ball inside out. The eagle linebacker is responsible for any downhill path by the back.

Inside Linebacker Alignment, Reads, and Assignments

The inside linebacker aligns with his inside foot on the outside foot of the offensive guard. He should be four yards off the line of scrimmage. His key is the offensive guard he is aligned over. The guard's helmet placement on his first step will dictate the inside linebacker's initial movement and his run-pass read. After the inside linebacker gets his initial movement key, he should then pick up the backfield flow.

The inside linebacker's technique is described as 32. He is responsible for the 3 gap versus an inside run at him. Versus an outside run, he should quickly shuffle to a stack position behind the defensive end. This puts him in position to press the first open seam outside of the defensive end if the ball continues to the perimeter. He is also in position to shuffle back inside if the ball cuts back. When stacked behind the defensive end, the inside linebacker should expect the noseguard to beat the center's reach block and be able to make a play in the 1 to 3 gaps. If the defensive end gets blocked by a reach block, the inside linebacker should press tightly off his butt. The 2 in 32 tells the inside linebacker that he is a cutback player versus a play away. He should shuffle and stack over the noseguard, staying on the back hip of the ballcarrier. Versus a pass, the inside linebacker defends the hook and curl zones.

Descriptions of four common running plays at the inside linebacker follow. They show the reads and reactions the inside linebacker should use to respond to each play and blocking scheme.

■ **Fullback isolation play.** On this play, the fullback leads the tailback into the 3 gap, and the guard blocks down on the noseguard (refer to the figure on page 71). The guard's helmet will be high and upfield on the noseguard, and the 3 gap will remain open. The inside linebacker should immediately feel the flow of the running backs. If both backs are attacking downhill toward the open 3 gap, the inside linebacker should attack the outside two thirds of the fullback. His aiming point is one yard across the line of scrimmage. The inside linebacker should attack the fullback with his inside foot up, which will keep his shoulders square. He should keep his outside arm free. The inside linebacker's goal is to make the play himself or force the ballcarrier to radically change his path in the backfield.

■ **Sweep play.** Versus a sweep play (see the figure on page 72) with the offensive guard pulling to the outside, the inside linebacker should make an "out" call and should fast flow, pressing the first open seam (5 gap or wider).

■ **Power or counter play.** The power and counter plays have the same blocking scheme: the offensive guard will block down on the noseguard (see the figure on page 73). The 3 gap will be open initially, giving the inside linebacker the illusion that an isolation play is being run. If the inside linebacker steps up in the 3 gap, he will be blocked by the offensive tackle. This is another example of how a "pull" call by the eagle linebacker will help the inside linebacker defend a play. When the inside linebacker hears "pull," he should fast flow to the 5 gap and press the line of scrimmage as tight off the butt of the defensive end as possible. The inside linebacker should take on the pulling guard with his inside arm, staying low and square.

■ **Trap play.** Versus a trap play (figure 14.4), the inside linebacker will read the offensive guard blocking down on the noseguard. He will also hear a "pull" call and feel the defensive end closing the 3 gap in front of him. This will send the inside linebacker to the 5 gap, tight off the butt of the defensive end. Being in the 5 gap will put the inside linebacker in position to play the quarterback versus a trap option play. It will also put him in position to tackle the fullback if the fullback bounces outside of the defensive end.

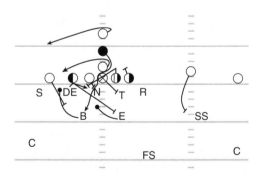

Figure 14.4 Trap play being run at the inside linebacker.

The inside linebacker's reads, reactions, and responsibilities change when the play is run to the opposite side of the center and away from the inside linebacker,. The most common blocking scheme the inside linebacker will see when the play is away is a scoop block by the guard. Different from a down block, where the guard's helmet would be high and upfield, the guard will now take a flat step toward the noseguard. The guard will keep his helmet low, with the intent to block the noseguard by cutting him off and stopping his pursuit of the ball on the other side of the center. The center will be attempting to release through and block the inside linebacker. The inside linebacker will also feel the flow of the backs away.

When the backs take an inside path, the inside linebacker should step and stack behind the noseguard, getting in position to play the cutback and maintaining inside-out leverage on the ball. The noseguard is responsible for squeezing the center into the front-side 1 gap and slowing the center's progress in trying to get to the inside linebacker. However, if the center does release up to the inside linebacker, the inside linebacker should shuffle to him and stun the center. The inside linebacker will then have to make a quick decision about whether the ball is going to cut back or stay front side. If there is any threat of the ballcarrier cutting back to the inside linebacker, the inside linebacker must keep his outside arm free. If there is no threat of the ballcarrier cutting back, the inside linebacker should work over the top of the center, only making contact with the center if he has to in order to get by him.

Versus a power, counter, or trap play on the other side of the center, the inside linebacker will read the guard pulling across the formation. The inside linebacker must first call out "pull." He should then work through the 1 to the 3 to the 5 gap as he pursues the ball inside out. The inside linebacker is responsible for any downhill path by the back.

Sam Linebacker Alignment, Reads, and Assignments

When aligned on a tight end, the Sam linebacker is in a 9 technique. His inside foot will be aligned on the outside foot of the tight end. When aligned to the boundary with no tight end on his side of the field, the Sam should align in a walk alignment, four yards deep and two yards wider than the defensive end's widest foot. When aligned to the field with no tight end, the Sam is in a walk position. Against a single receiver formation to the field, the Sam is four yards off the line of scrimmage and five yards wider than the defensive end's widest foot. Versus a twin-receiver set to the boundary or the field, the Sam should align five yards deep and on the outside edge of the number two receiver (never wider than the hash).

The Sam linebacker is the contain player to his side of the field. When he is aligned on a tight end, he is responsible for the quarterback versus an option play. When aligned in a walk position, the Sam is responsible for the pitch versus an option play. Versus a pass, the Sam's responsibility is the curl and flat area.

When aligned in a 9 technique, the Sam's first key is the helmet of the tight end. If the tight end releases outside or blocks down, the Sam's second key is the near running back. His third key is a pulling guard. The tight end will tell the Sam linebacker whether the play is a run or pass, and whether the run is to or away from him. The Sam should first be concerned with defeating the tight end's base or reach block. Because of his width, the Sam will have time to defeat and shed the block of the tight end before the ball gets to him. A common error made by the Sam linebacker is to look into the backfield, allowing the tight end to get into his body.

When aligned in a walk alignment, the Sam should key the offensive tackle for his initial run-pass read. Versus a kick-out block by the fullback, the Sam should shuffle toward the line of scrimmage and constrict the running lane to the inside. Versus a run away, the Sam linebacker should fold to the ball, keeping the ballcarrier on his inside arm, and always be aware of a possible reverse, bootleg, and cutback.

The Sam linebacker has specific techniques and responsibilities when he is aligned to the tight end. The Sam linebacker should be prepared to defend each of the following plays run to his side of the field:

- **Sweep play or outside zone play.** On this play, the tight end will attempt to execute a reach block on the Sam linebacker. As the Sam linebacker reads the tight end's helmet attacking his outside shoulder, he should step with his outside foot approximately six to eight inches wide. The Sam's second step is with his inside foot across the line of scrimmage and into the tight end. As the Sam takes his second and third steps, he should press the tight end's body across the line of scrimmage, and the Sam linebacker should drive his inside foot up to help keep his shoulders square to the line of scrimmage.

The Sam's helmet will often fit in the V of the neck of the tight end. Pressing the line of scrimmage will turn the tight end's body perpendicular to the line of scrimmage. The Sam linebacker should try to drive the tight end one to two yards into the backfield. He should keep his outside arm free and keep his head outside. Once the Sam linebacker has taken control of the tight end, he should lock his arms out and disengage to the football.

- **Inside play.** Versus any inside play when the tight end is attempting to execute a base block on the Sam linebacker, the Sam should attack the tight end with leverage and a wide base. After stopping the tight end's initial charge, the Sam should lock his arms out, creating separation from the tight end and maintaining outside leverage on the ballcarrier. He needs to be in position to make the tackle if the ballcarrier bounces outside.

- **Power or counter play.** On a power or counter play, the tight end will block down on the defensive end. As the Sam linebacker reads this block, he should shuffle quickly to the tight end's original position one yard across the line of scrimmage. If the Sam penetrates too far upfield, he will create a vertical seam between himself and the defensive end. The Sam linebacker should then locate his first threat.

If the fullback or back-side guard is coming on a kick-out course, the Sam linebacker should continue to squeeze and constrict the 5 gap, staying low and keeping his shoulders square. The Sam should avoid turning his shoulders and "wrong arming" the kick-out block. "Wrong arming" a kick-out block trades one blocker for one defender. The Sam can accomplish the same goal of closing the 5 gap by staying square and being in position to flatten down the line of scrimmage and pursue the ball when it bounces to the outside (refer to the figure on page 73).

- **Option play.** On the option, the Sam linebacker should stay square so he is in position to slow play the quarterback. Usually, the player who slow plays the quarterback is the one to make the play on a pitchback. The Sam will flatten down the line of scrimmage when the quarterback pitches the ball to the tailback. Versus an option play in which the tight end executes a reach block, the Sam linebacker should defeat the reach block, then tackle the quarterback as soon as he is in position to do so. If the quarterback ducks inside of the Sam linebacker, the defensive end or the inside linebacker should take the quarterback. Versus an inside release by the tight end up through the defensive end to the inside linebacker, the Sam linebacker should sit in his bent-knee stance position, be patient, and wait for the quarterback to get to him. By slow playing the quarterback, the Sam will force him to pitch the football.

When the offense is running a Belly G option play, the front-side guard will pull on a course to log the Sam linebacker to the inside. In this situation, the Sam linebacker must keep his shoulders square and recognize the deeper path by the offensive guard. The Sam linebacker should take on the guard with his inside arm. The Sam linebacker wants to force the quarterback to duck underneath in the 5 gap, eliminating the threat of the option and allowing the pursuit to catch up to the quarterback. Versus a running play on the other side of the center, the Sam linebacker should fold to the ball, keeping it on his inside arm, and always be aware of a possible reverse, bootleg, and cutback.

Variation Techniques

When stunts or blitzes are called, the techniques used by the eagle and inside linebackers will vary from those usually played in the Eagle defense. When a stunt is called and the linebackers are responsible for two gaps, I will sometimes have both linebackers use a tailback or fullback read so they can fast flow to their gaps. The following stunts involve variations to the linebackers' gap responsibilities:

■ **Field Eagle Fin.** A Fin stunt tells the 5-technique defensive end to execute a rip technique inside, into the 3 gap (refer to the figure on page 59). The inside linebacker is now a 52 technique. When the flow is to the inside linebacker, the inside linebacker should press tight off the butt of the defensive end. He is now responsible for the 5 gap. The inside linebacker should take on a lead blocker with his inside arm. When the flow is away, the inside linebacker should shuffle and stay on the back hip of the ballcarrier, and he should be prepared for a possible cutback behind the defensive end. The eagle linebacker remains a 12 technique.

I cannot overstate the importance of the linebaker staying tight and not allowing any seam that the ballcarrier could get through on a downhill path between the defensive lineman and the linebacker. The linebacker needs to realize that the defensive lineman will continue to work inside, which means that the linebacker must continue to work inside to stay tight off of the lineman's butt.

■ **Field Eagle Slant.** The word *slant* tells all four defensive linemen—the rush end, the defensive tackle, the noseguard, and the defensive end—to execute a rip technique to the call side, which is to the field on a Field placement call. I have most often tagged a Slant stunt with a Tight placement call, for example, Tight Eagle Slant Cover 3 or Stack Slant, which is an automatic tight placement call (refer to the figures on page 102).

The inside linebacker is a 50 technique. He is responsible for the 5 gap when the ball is run to him, and he is responsible for the near 1 gap when the ball is run away from him. When the ball is run to the inside linebacker, he should press tight off the butt of the defensive end. The inside linebacker should take on a lead blocker with his inside arm.

The eagle linebacker should align in the 5 gap. He is a 51 technique. The eagle linebacker has the 5 gap when the flow is to him. He should take on all blocks with his inside arm. Versus a reach blocking scheme, the eagle linebacker should "sit." In most cases, the rush end and the defensive tackle ripping outside will force the ball back inside to the eagle linebacker. The reason the eagle linebacker aligns in the 5 gap is to be in position to defeat a blocking scheme in which the offensive tackle executes a down block on the defensive tackle and the guard executes a fold block on the eagle linebacker. In this situation, the eagle linebacker can get pushed outside, allowing the 5 gap to widen. With the eagle linebacker aligned in the 5 gap, he now has outside-in leverage on the offensive guard and is able to constrict the 5 gap.

When the play starts to the eagle linebacker, the inside linebacker is responsible for the near 1 gap. If the guard works up to the inside linebacker, the inside linebacker should take on the guard with his outside arm, spilling the ball to the defensive end. The eagle linebacker has the far 1 gap when the play goes away from him.

■ **Eagle Gopher.** This stunt can be used with several placement calls (refer to the top figure on page 57). On this stunt, the rush end, defensive tackle, and noseguard all rip away from the call. The inside linebacker is a 32 technique. Because the noseguard is ripping to him, the inside linebacker should align stacked over the defensive end. The noseguard ripping out will widen the 3 gap. The eagle linebacker is a 52 technique. When the play is at him, he presses tight off of the butt of the rush end. The eagle linebacker should take on all blockers with his outside arm and push the ball to the strong safety. When the play is away from him, the eagle linebacker stays behind the ballcarrier and expects the ballcarrier to cut back.

Stack 4-4-3 Linebacker Techniques

The Stack defense has different alignment rules than the Eagle defense. The Eagle defense has very clear alignment rules and reads for the Sam, inside, and eagle linebackers, which is one of the reasons I recommend the Eagle defensive structure. However, there are many similarities in gap and coverage responsibilities between the Eagle and Stack defenses. In fact, the Stack 4-4-3 defense incorporates many of the fundamentals previously discussed for the Eagle defense, including the fundamental reads, the proper leverage and body positions, the techniques for taking on blockers, and the variations in responsibilities when using the defensive line stunts. This section covers the alignments, keys, and responsibilities of the Sam, inside, and eagle linebackers in the Stack 4-4-3 structure.

In the 4-4-3 defense, the Sam linebacker aligns into the boundary when the ball is on the hash. When the ball is in the middle of the field, the Sam linebacker aligns away from the strength of the formation. His inside foot should be on the outside foot of the widest defensive lineman (the defensive or rush end). He reads the offensive tackle or the tight end for his initial run-pass key.

When the ball is on the hash, the eagle linebacker aligns to the field in a 3 alignment. When the ball is in the middle of the field, he aligns to the strength of the formation. The strong safety should declare the formation strength when the ball is in the middle of the field by calling out "Safety right" or "Safety left." The inside linebacker aligns to the boundary in a 3 alignment when the ball is on the hash. When the ball is in the middle of the field, the inside linebacker aligns away from the strength of the formation (or away from the strong safety). Both the eagle linebacker and the inside linebacker key the guard they are aligned over for their initial movement. As a general rule, the eagle and inside linebackers are fast-flow players. They should take on all offensive linemen and the fullback with their inside arm.

Because the eagle and inside linebackers align to the field and boundary, respectively, they will each be aligned to a tight end or split end surface. When aligned to a tight end surface, the eagle or inside linebacker is a 12 technique, meaning he is responsible for the 1 gap when the flow is to his side of the ball. If the guard's helmet attacks the defensive tackle, the linebacker should immediately pick up the backfield flow. If there is a threat to the 1 gap, the linebacker should attack the 1 gap. If there is full flow to the tight end side and both backs are on a wide path, the linebacker should fast flow through the 5 gap, pressing the first open seam (inside out) to the ballcarrier.

When full flow is to the other side of the center, the linebacker aligned to a tight end surface should quickly determine if there is an inside or outside threat. Versus an inside threat, the linebacker should fast flow and stack behind the noseguard. If the offensive guard is attempting a scoop block on the defensive tackle, the linebacker's stacked position will force the guard to quickly leave the defensive tackle and chase the linebacker. This will allow the defensive tackle to close the back-side 1 gap, preferably with the guard's body. If the guard to the play side is double-teaming the noseguard, the linebacker stacking quickly over the noseguard will force the guard to leave the double team and work up to the linebacker. This will free up the noseguard to throw his body into the 1 gap. Versus a play on the other side of the center with the backs taking a wide path toward the perimeter, the linebacker should fast flow over the top of all blocks and pursue the ballcarrier inside out.

When either the eagle or inside linebacker is aligned over the offensive guard to a split end surface, the linebacker is a 31 technique. When the play is at him, the linebacker is responsible for controlling the 3 gap. When the play starts to the other side of the center, the linebacker is responsible for the far 1 gap. The eagle or inside linebacker reacts to a guard pull—either to the outside or across the formation—the same as in the Eagle defense. In the 4-4-3 structure, being able to read the guards is a tremendous advantage for the linebackers.

In the 4-4-3 defensive structure, the Sam linebacker and the strong safety have mirrored responsibilities versus the run. Their alignment differs slightly. As described earlier, the Sam linebacker has his inside foot aligned on the outside foot of the widest defensive lineman to his side of the field. When aligned to the field against a pro formation (see figure 7.2 on page 78), the strong safety has his inside foot two yards outside of the widest defensive lineman to the field. Versus perimeter runs to their side of the field, the Sam linebacker and strong safety are contain players. Versus an option play, they have the pitch. Versus an inside or off-tackle running play, they should shuffle up to the heels of the defensive or rush end, take on any blocker with their inside arm, stay square, and maintain outside leverage on the ballcarrier.

If the ballcarrier bounces outside, the strong safety or Sam linebacker should be in position to contain and tackle the ballcarrier. If the ballcarrier's course is through the 5 or 3 gap, the hole will clearly declare itself. The strong safety or Sam linebacker should step up and tackle the ballcarrier. If the play starts away, the strong safety or Sam linebacker should shuffle, staying on the back hip of the ballcarrier. These two players should always clear a reverse, a bootleg, and a cutback by the ballcarrier as they pursue the ball. They will be unblocked most of the time, and they need to be in position to make the tackle if the ball penetrates the line of scrimmage.

When using the 4-4-3 defensive structure versus an offensive set with only one running back in the backfield, the linebackers will align in the 1, 3, and 5 gaps (see figure 7.6 on page 83). If the eagle or Sam linebacker is aligned to a tight end surface, he aligns in the 5 gap. He is responsible for the 5 gap whether the play is run to him or away from him. When aligned to a split end surface, the eagle or Sam linebacker is in a 3 alignment and is responsible for the 3 gap when the play is at or away from him. The inside linebacker is always aligned in the 1 gap to the tight end side.

Many coaches have their linebackers use the running backs for their read when they are in 5, 1, and 3 alignments. I still prefer to have the linebackers read the offensive linemen they are aligned over for their initial movement because of the advantages of being able to see a lineman pull. The inside linebacker, who is aligned in the 1 gap on the tight end side, reads the offensive guard on that side. The linebacker (eagle or Sam) in a 5 alignment to the tight end side reads the offensive tackle. The linebacker in the 3 gap to the split end side reads the offensive guard on that side.

Plays to a Tight End Surface

This section identifies the offensive plays that most defenses will see run to a tight end surface in each game. A description of each linebacker's read and reaction is provided for each play. If the tight end were aligned to the other side of the formation, the gaps and responsibilities for the eagle and Sam linebackers would be switched. It would be almost impossible to cover every conceivable offensive play, but the plays that follow will give you a general understanding of the linebackers' role versus the run in the Stack defense:

■ **Isolation play.** On an isolation play (refer to the figure on page 110), the offense executes a double team on a defensive lineman, opening a hole for the fullback to isolate and block a linebacker in space and launch the tailback on a downhill path to gain positive yardage immediately. The eagle linebacker will read the guard's helmet attacking the defensive tackle, and he will feel both running backs on a downhill path. When the eagle linebacker reads a threat to the 1 gap, he should attack the 1 gap with his inside arm. When a linebacker takes on a fullback, he should attack two thirds of the fullback, keeping his outside arm free. If the line-backer can't make the tackle, he must make the ballcarrier radically deviate from his path in the backfield. If the running back's path is toward the 3 gap, the eagle linebacker should attack the 3 gap, staying tight off the butt of the defensive tackle and attempting to take on the fullback with his inside arm.

The inside linebacker will read the flat course by the offensive guard attempting to execute a scoop block on the noseguard. The inside linebacker should step in that direction. As he feels both backs on a course on the other side of the center, the inside linebacker should fast flow downhill to the far 1 gap. He should work to the outside edge of the offensive center.

The Sam linebacker's initial key is the offensive tackle. When the offensive tackle's helmet is low, inside, and upfield, this tells the Sam linebacker that the running play is away from him. For the Sam linebacker in a walk position, the first reaction should be to bounce in place for a second and diagnose the play. When the Sam linebacker reads full flow away, he should then shuffle toward the play side, clearing the threat of a reverse, a bootleg pass, and the ballcarrier cutting back.

The Sam linebacker should always stay on the back hip of the ballcarrier as he pursues the ball. Overpursuit can lead to a big play against the defense. However, the Sam linebacker should be unblocked on most plays away, and he should be involved in several tackles on the other side of the ball.

■ **Power and counter plays.** These plays involve a blocking scheme designed to seal defensive penetration, create a hole off tackle with a double team, kick out the end man on the line of scrimmage, and lead a guard through the off-tackle hole to isolate on a linebacker. The counter is the same play as the power (see the figure on page 114), except with backfield misdirection. When the inside linebacker reads the guard pulling and communicates "pull," the eagle linebacker will beat the pulling guard and the tailback to the hole.

As the eagle linebacker reads the guard's helmet attacking the defensive tackle, he should simultaneously hear a "pull" call from the inside linebacker. A pull call will send the eagle linebacker on a fast-flow course to the first open seam (3 gap or wider), depending on the blocking scheme. With his shoulders square, he should beat the pulling guard into the hole. The eagle linebacker should press tight off the butt of the defensive tackle if the 3 gap is open. If the tight end blocks down inside, the rush end will close aggressively, canceling the 3 gap and spilling the ball outside. The eagle linebacker would then press tightly off the butt of the rush end. Again, the eagle linebacker should beat the pulling guard into the hole. He should keep his shoulders square to the line of scrimmage and take on the guard with his inside arm.

The inside linebacker will read the guard pulling across the formation. He should call out "pull" to the eagle linebacker and shuffle quickly across the ball. If the 1 gap is open and the inside linebacker can press the ball in the backfield, he should do so. If the 1 gap is not open, the inside linebacker should continue on an inside-out course in pursuit of the ballcarrier.

As the Sam linebacker hears "pull," he should shuffle under control, staying on the back of the ball as he pursues the ballcarrier. Before he takes a pursuit course, the Sam linebacker should always look ahead of the play to see if a reverse is coming back to the boundary. He should also be aware of a possible bootleg pass off the run action away.

■ **Trap play.** The trap play (see the figure on page 112) is designed to take advantage of an overaggressive and penetrating defensive front. A guard will pull from one side of the formation to the other in order to kick out or trap a defensive lineman. The eagle linebacker will read an outside or inside release by the offensive guard he is aligned over, while simultaneously hearing a "pull" call from the inside linebacker. When the eagle linebacker hears "pull," he should press the first open seam (3 gap or wider).

When the offensive guard across from the inside linebacker pulls, the inside line-backer will make a "pull" call to the eagle linebacker. He will also feel the fullback on a straight-ahead charge. The inside linebacker should shuffle toward the line of scrimmage in the direction of the pulling guard. He should step up and press the first open seam. In most cases, the inside linebacker will tackle the fullback.

The Sam linebacker will read the offensive tackle releasing inside. He should shuffle in that direction, staying on the back hip of the ballcarrier. If the offensive tackle releases up to the Sam linebacker, the Sam linebacker should stay behind the offensive tackle and squeeze the tackle inside, constricting the hole and staying in position to play the cutback. If the offensive tackle stays on the defensive end, the Sam should shuffle and tackle the fullback if the ballcarrier cuts back.

■ **Inside zone.** The zone scheme is both a running play and a blocking scheme for the offensive linemen. The offensive linemen all reach and block an area to the same side. Each gap is accounted for by an offensive lineman (see the figure on page 115). The zone scheme should be able to handle all defensive movement and stunts. When the defense plays straight, the offensive linemen will reach and stretch the defensive linemen, trying to get movement and working late up to the linebackers. The running back will take a path toward the offensive tackle to help widen and stretch the defensive front. The running back is looking for a hole to cut back into. The fullback takes a path in the opposite direction to cut off and seal the edge defender (in this case, the defensive end).

The eagle linebacker will read the guard's helmet attacking the defensive tackle; he should also feel the running backs separating in the backfield. The eagle linebacker will shuffle two steps in the direction of the offensive guard. Feeling the backs split, the eagle linebacker should be aware of the strong possibility of a cutback by the running back. After the eagle linebacker stacks behind the defensive tackle and draws the offensive tackle's block, he should then shuffle back inside and under the offensive tackle's block. This will place the eagle linebacker in the 1 gap. The Sam linebacker should be the first to see the backs separating. He should call out "back," which will help both the eagle and inside linebackers recognize the tailback's intent to cut back. If the tailback does keep the ball front side, the defensive tackle, the rush end, and the strong safety will be in the 3, 5, and 7 gaps and will be in position to make the tackle.

The inside linebacker will read the guard's helmet as the guard attempts a scoop block on the noseguard. He should also feel the running backs separating in the backfield and hear the Sam linebacker call out "back." The inside linebacker should shuffle two steps in the direction of the center, drawing his block. He should then shuffle back under the center's block and get in position to play the cutback in the 1 gap.

The Sam linebacker will read the offensive tackle executing a run block, and he will feel the running backs separate. The Sam should call out "back" to the eagle and inside linebackers. The Sam linebacker should bounce, staying in position to play the cutback.

Plays to a Split End Surface

Linebackers must also know their responsibilities when they encounter offensive plays to a split end surface. The most common plays are presented here with a description of each linebacker's read and reaction. If the tight end were aligned to the other side of the formation, the gaps and responsibilities of the eagle and Sam linebackers would be switched.

■ **Isolation play.** When an isolation play is run to a split end surface, the eagle linebacker will read an inside release by the offensive guard and will feel the full flow away (see the figure on page 111). The eagle linebacker should fast flow to the near 1 gap, working across the face of the offensive guard.

The inside linebacker will read the down block by the offensive guard on the noseguard. He will also feel both running backs on a downhill path at his 3 gap. The inside linebacker should accelerate downhill and take on the outside two thirds of the fullback with his inside arm, forcing the ballcarrier to cut back.

The Sam linebacker will get his initial run key from the offensive tackle blocking the defensive end. He will feel both backs flow to his side of the center. The Sam linebacker should bounce and not attack the fullback. If the fullback gets to him, the Sam linebacker should take on the fullback with his inside arm and turn the ball back inside. The Sam linebacker should be prepared to make the play if the ballcarrier bounces to the outside.

■ **Outside zone in a two-tight-end, one-back formation.** Teams will often use this formation and this play in order to execute a blocking scheme to attack the Stack defense away from the rush end and the defensive tackle (figure 14.5). This scheme involves man blocking and down blocks, with the tight end blocking down and sealing the defensive end inside. The offensive guard will block down on the noseguard. The offensive tackle and

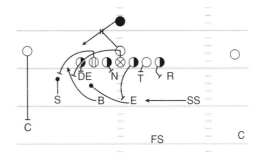

Figure 14.5 Double flanker formation outside zone versus the Stack 4-4-3 defense.

center will pull to the outside to block the Sam linebacker and inside linebacker. The offensive tackle will try to attack the Sam's outside number to execute a reach block or to force the Sam to widen, which will open up the seam off the tight end's butt. The ball is handed off deep in the backfield, and the tailback runs to daylight.

The Sam linebacker's alignment is the key to defending the outside zone. When he identifies a one-back formation with two tight ends, he should treat the boundary tight end as an offset fullback. This means he should widen his alignment to two yards outside of the defensive end's outside foot. The extra width puts the Sam linebacker in position to constrict and squeeze the offensive tackle's kick-out block by using an outside-in course (rather than an inside-out course, which would widen the running lane). The Sam should also make an "over" call to the inside and eagle linebackers. In response, these linebackers will slide their alignment over one gap toward the Sam linebacker.

The Sam linebacker's "over" call will tell the inside linebacker to align over the offensive tackle. Many teams will block down on the defensive end and pull the offensive tackle to block the Sam linebacker (as shown in the diagram). This scheme has the center pulling to block the inside linebacker. When sliding his alignment over to the offensive tackle, the inside linebacker should now read the offensive tackle. When the inside linebacker sees the offensive tackle pulling, he should immediately press the first open seam off the defensive end's butt. The center should not be able to block the inside linebacker. The inside linebacker should take on all blockers with his inside arm, sending the ball inside. The inside linebacker must press and stay tight off the defensive end's butt, allowing no room for the ballcarrier to run between the inside linebacker and the defensive end.

The "over" call from the Sam linebacker tells the eagle linebacker to align in the 1 gap to the field. When the eagle linebacker reads the offensive guard's helmet release in the 1 gap—indicating that the guard is attempting a scoop block up on the eagle linebacker—the eagle linebacker should shuffle across the ball and across the face of the offensive guard to pursue the ballcarrier. The eagle linebacker's alignment should make it impossible for the offensive guard to block him.

CHAPTER 15

Defensive Backs

All great defenses share one common component—a great secondary. Regardless of the mistakes made up front, sound play from the secondary can eliminate big plays by the offense. It is also true that a mistake in the secondary can result in an explosion play for the offense, which often leads to points scored by the opponent. On almost every play, a great deal of pressure is placed on the secondary. To prevent long explosion plays, the secondary needs to put forth great effort, be physical and sure tacklers, and play disciplined football.

Each member of the defensive backfield must be committed to the fundamentals and techniques required at his position in order to execute each defense called. A total commitment to weekly preparation is critical for continued improvement and an effective game performance. Defensive backs must be students of the game and must be willing to do whatever it takes to be fully prepared for their opponent. Studying opponent game tape will give defenders knowledge of the opponent's strengths and weaknesses, as well as the opponent's tendencies.

Communication and Game Knowledge

Communication is a necessary ingredient of successful defensive play. This is especially true in the secondary. A breakdown in communication can cause missed assignments in coverage and can easily lead to a big offensive play. When defenders are communicating, they are thinking. Communication also takes pressure off a player in the secondary who is not confident of the defensive adjustments and alerts. Communication ensures that everyone is on the same page, which greatly limits the possibility of a missed assignment in coverage or run support.

To make sure that your secondary players can communicate effectively, you should establish clear terminology, such as that included in figure 15.1. Coaches and players should use this terminology daily. Emphasize the importance of all defensive players knowing and using the same terminology. Talking is an essential fundamental to

FIGURE 15.1   Secondary Terminology

Term	Definition
Ball	The call made when the ball is thrown.
Bump	The call made to move defensive backs or linebackers from one man to another.
Cloud	A call made to indicate that a corner should provide primary force versus the run and should defend the flat versus the pass. The safety is now a half-field player.
Come to balance	This term is used to describe the body position that a defender should be in as he closes on an opposing ballcarrier. The defender should have his knees bent and his head and eyes up. His feet should be shoulder-width apart. Being in a balanced stance will enable the defender to be in the most advantageous position to make solid contact with a ballcarrier and to put the ballcarrier on the ground. In this position, the defender will allow the fewest yards possible after contact.
Crack	The call made to alert a defender that a blind-side block is coming from outside in.
Cushion	The area between a receiver and the defensive back on a pass route.
Leverage	The lateral or vertical position on an opponent that puts a defensive back in the most advantageous position to execute the defense called versus a run or pass.
Oskie	The call made when the ball has been intercepted.
Quick vertical threat	This term describes the situation whenever the number two eligible player is a wide receiver.
Skill side	A term used to denote the dominant passing threat of the offensive formation. Versus a pro formation, the skill side is the two-receiver side. Versus a one-back formation, the skill side is the side with two quick receivers.
Sky or invert	Both terms describe a safety in a walk position (usually five yards off the line of scrimmage and five yards from the widest lineman or tight end). The safety is responsible for support or contain versus the run.
Snap	The call made from one safety to another to switch responsibilities.
Top	A call made to a linebacker who is defending the curl in a two-deep coverage. This call instructs the linebacker to align over the number two receiver and to jam and disrupt the number two receiver's release.

good secondary play. The following are some of the alerts used when communicating within the secondary:

1. The free safety needs to declare the passing strength.

2. The free safety must also call the coverage check after the defense breaks the huddle. Calls must be communicated to the linebackers.

3. *Check* is a term used to indicate the coverage is changing. The coverage being checked to should be communicated by the safety after calling out "Check."

4. Defensive backs should be taught to understand formation tendencies of opponents and should communicate alerts to the other defenders.

5. Defensive backs should be alert to wide receiver splits that are greater or less than their normal alignment. Certain types of splits by wide receivers often correspond to blocking assignments on running plays or to routes that will be run if the ball is thrown.

6. "Run" and "Pass" calls should be yelled out as soon as anyone on the defense recognizes the ensuing play.

7. "Crack" calls should be yelled to alert safeties and linebackers that a crackback block is coming toward them.

8. Whenever any special play is recognized—such as a screen, draw, reverse, or bootleg—it should be communicated and echoed by all defenders.

9. "Ball" calls should be made whenever the ball is thrown. This is especially helpful when a teammate has his back turned to the quarterback while covering a receiver on a deep route or in man coverage.

10. Defensive backs must communicate with the underneath coverage to let those defenders know the type of route the receiver is running (i.e., "In," "Out," "Smash," and so on).

To communicate effectively with the defense, a secondary player must be a student of offensive football and must have an awareness of offensive formations as well as tendencies from the various formations. The free safety in particular is the quarterback of the defense. He has 21 players in front of him. He must ensure that his 10 teammates are aligned properly. He must be able to quickly determine the strength of the formation in order to set the coverage. The strength of the formation is determined by the passing strength. In a two-back formation, the passing strength is the side with two receivers. In a one-back formation, the strength is the side where there are two or more quick receivers.

When identifying an offensive formation on the field, our defenders count the receivers so that the defenders can align properly. This also helps identify which receiver each secondary defender will be reading or keying, and it assists defenders with pass route recognition and identification. We number and letter receivers starting from the strong side of the formation to the weak side of the formation. In zone coverage, we count receivers at the snap of the ball because formations often change with motions and shifts. In man coverage, we count receivers at their original alignment.

The following provides an example of how we identify receivers versus a pro formation. The number one receiver to the strong side of the formation is Z. The number two receiver is the tight end and is referred to as the Y. (If the number two receiver to the strong side is a detached wide receiver instead of a tight end, we refer to him as the H.) The number three receiver to the strong side is the running back and is labeled R. (If the number two receiver to the strong side was a detached wide receiver, or an H, and the number three receiver is a tight end, we would refer to the number three receiver as Y.)

The number one receiver to the weak side of the formation is the X, and the number two receiver to the weak side and in the backfield is a T. If the number two receiver to the weak side is a detached wide receiver, we refer to him as an O. If the number two receiver to the weak side is a tight end, we refer to him as a Y.

Identifying the offensive personnel in the game will help defensive players anticipate the potential plays that the offense will run. For example, if an offense has two tight ends and two running backs in the game, a defense should expect a power running attack. Most teams run the ball 80 to 85 percent of the time with this personnel grouping on the field. If the ball is thrown, the offense will most likely use a play-action pass or possibly a bootleg pass.

To identify the offensive personnel on the field, the defense uses two numbers to identify the eligible receivers in the game (see table 15.1). The first number identifies how many running backs are in the game. The second number designates how many tight ends are in the game. The offense always has five eligible receivers on every play. Subtract the number of running backs and tight ends from five, and that number will tell the defense how many wide receivers are in the game. As with the example of two running backs and two tight ends in the game, certain tendencies and alerts can be associated with the other personnel groupings used by the offense. Understanding these tendencies will help defenders anticipate the play possibilities for the opposing team.

The defensive secondary must also be aware of where they are on the field. Once an offense moves the ball near the defensive 20-yard line, the deep passing zones are reduced. Deep defenders should tighten up their coverage, and they never want to be deeper than 5 yards into the end zone. The closer an offensive team moves

TABLE 15.1 **Offensive Personnel Combinations**

Offensive personnel grouping	Running backs	Tight ends	Wide receivers
21	2	1	2
22	2	2	1
12	1	2	2
11	1	1	3
10	1	0	4

toward the goal line, the tighter the defenders should play the deep zones and the underneath passing routes. When the ball reaches the defensive 10-yard line, the corners should align no deeper than 7 yards from the line of scrimmage (when playing a deep-one-third technique). On the snap of the ball, they should backpedal under control and be prepared to drive on all quick passes when the quarterback takes a three-step drop. Underneath defenders should be quick to jump shallow routes. In zone coverage, all pass defenders should be careful not to drop too deep. In man coverage, defenders should take inside leverage on all receivers and should play each receiver more aggressively.

In addition to knowing where they are on the field, defenders must also know the game situation. Specifically, how many points does the offense need to win (e.g., a field goal, a touchdown)? How much time is left in the half or the game? Defenders should understand that each situation creates different expectations for the defense. In other words, the offense can be expected to do certain things in each situation. The defense should be prepared for the offensive strategies associated with each of these situations.

For example, in a two-minute situation with the offense behind in the game, the offense is forced to conserve time as they attempt to move the ball downfield. In this situation, defenders need to play smart, confident, and aggressive football. Defensive teams should practice the two-minute situation at least twice a week. Doing so will give them confidence and prepare them for all of the possibilities that can occur in a two-minute situation. It will also reinforce how difficult it is for an offense to move the ball the length of the field in a limited amount of time if the defense executes properly.

Defenders should expect conservative passes (out routes, screens, underneath routes) and an occasional draw play, particularly early in the drive. Defenders should be prepared for a fast tempo from the offense, with no huddle. They should deepen their alignments, expecting a pass. Deep defenders should be careful not to give up a deep pass. Defenders want to keep the ballcarriers inbounds and keep the clock running. Defenders must take good pursuit angles and make sure tackles. Communication and concentration become critical in this up-tempo situation. Everyone must be playing the correct defense and communicate what the offense is attempting to run.

Defensive Back Fundamentals

Mastering the important fundamentals required to play his position will give defensive backs the best possible opportunity to be consistently successful. These fundamentals and techniques should be emphasized daily with drills incorporated into practice to facilitate continued learning by the players. The following techniques and points of emphasis are essential for successful secondary play. Mastering these fundamentals will help a defensive back perform at a high level in both man and zone coverage.

- **Stance.** A defensive back's feet should be shoulder-width apart. His outside foot should be forward in an approximate heel–toe relationship. He should bend at the waist, keeping his back straight and his head up. He should also have a slight bend in his knees. His hands should dangle down around his knees (figure 15.2). The defensive back needs to be relaxed in his stance. He should be turned slightly to the inside. In most zone coverages, the defensive back's initial key is the quarterback and then the receiver he is aligned over. A safety's stance may be slightly more erect so that he can see over the linebackers and the defensive line. If the safety is aligned in an inverted position, his inside foot will be forward and his outside foot back.

■ **Initial movement.** On the snap of the ball, the defensive back should start his backpedal by pushing off with his outside foot and stepping back with his inside foot. The defensive back must be careful not to take a false step, which would be stepping forward with either foot. As the defensive back pushes off with his outside foot, he should slide his inside foot backward, keeping his weight on the balls of his feet. As he backpedals, he

Figure 15.2 Proper defensive back stance.

should maintain a narrow base and keep his chest over his thighs. His arms should continue to be relaxed, and his eyes should stay on his key. Versus a passing play, the defensive back should maintain his backpedal technique until his cushion is threatened. Versus a running play, he should maintain his backpedal until he reads the running play and reacts according to his leverage responsibility.

Coaches should watch for several common mistakes made by defensive backs. If a defensive back leans backward, he places his weight on his heels, which will hinder his ability to break on the football. If the defensive back's base is too wide, he will start to "waddle" backward and will quickly lose his cushion. Coaches should make sure the defensive back's feet remain close to the ground and do not lift too far in the air as he backpedals. Having his feet close to the ground will quicken the defensive back's ability to react.

In general, a defensive back does not want to cross his feet. He should incorporate a weave technique and should backpedal at angles. Daily practice of the proper footwork will help ensure that defensive backs do not take a false step on the snap of the ball, which is a common mistake.

A defensive back should use the buzz technique when he is going to squat in place and not backpedal on the snap of the ball. The buzz technique is useful when a corner plays a cloud technique in a two-deep coverage or when a safety plays a quarters technique when aligned over a tight end whom he is reading for his run-pass read. In the buzz technique, the defensive back should step up with his inside foot to a balanced stance and maintain a good base. He should not move forward or backward until he reads his initial key for run or pass.

■ **Change of direction.** One of the most important aspects of defensive back play is being able to react instantaneously to the play as it is unfolding. To do this, defensive backs must be able to change direction immediately with a minimal amount of wasted movement. Good athletes run in straight lines and take direct paths to the football. When a defensive back changes direction, his movements should consist of three steps: a plant step, a directional step, and a crossover step.

The plant step is used to stop the backward momentum and should be made with the foot opposite the direction the defensive back is intending to break. On the second step—the directional step—the other foot should be placed in front of the plant foot and should be pointing in the direction the defensive back wants to break. Defensive backs often round off their breaks at this point. The crossover step (figure 15.3) then serves as the acceleration step and enables a defensive back to close ground on the ball, the ballcarrier, or the intended receiver. The defensive back's shoulders must remain low, and his feet must be in constant movement, throughout the progression.

Figure 15.3 Proper execution of the crossover step.

■ **Interception.** If a defensive back has a chance for the interception, he should cut in front of the receiver and go for the ball at its highest point. If the ball is thrown above his waist (figure 15.4), the defender should catch the front point of the ball with his arms outstretched and his thumbs and index fingers together. He should look the ball right into his hands. If the ball is thrown below his waist, the defender should bend down and scoop it up with his "pinkies and palms" together. On a high and deep ball, the defender should not stop to jump for it. He should outrun the ball and then leap to catch it at the highest point.

Whenever an interception occurs, the defender intercepting the ball should call out

Figure 15.4 Interception technique for ball thrown above defensive back's waist.

a word to his teammates to alert them that their team is now in possession of the football. "Oskie," "Bingo," and "Fire" are commonly used calls. Defenders should anticipate that the ball is going to be returned to the nearest sideline and should set up their blocks accordingly. Whoever is nearest to the intended receiver must block him first. He is usually the first threat to make the tackle. Coaches should constantly remind defenders that all blocks must be above the waist and should be in front of the defender who has intercepted the ball.

■ **Strip.** A defensive back should never let a receiver catch a football without a fight. The defensive back should use his arms and hands to strip the receiver of the ball. When making contact with a receiver who is attempting to make a catch, the defender should attack the receiver high. Defenders must be aware that the receiver's most important arm in making a catch is the upfield arm. When stripping the receiver, the defensive back's first priority must be to maintain position to make the tackle on the receiver.

■ **Fumbles.** In college and high school football, fumbles can be advanced from anywhere on the field. The one exception is when the exchange from the center to the quarterback is muffed; in this situation, the fumble can only be recovered and not advanced. Defenders should always cradle, secure, and protect the football when covering a loose ball. They should fight for the ball until the official gets to the bottom of the pile. If the ball can be advanced, the defender should keep his eyes on the ball, bend at the knees and waist, and use both hands to scoop the ball. In highly congested areas, the defender must discern whether he should fall on the ball or scoop the ball up and attempt to advance it.

■ **Beat principle.** The "beat principle" applies when a defensive back is beat in coverage or is out of position. When a defensive back is in this position, he should never look back for the ball in either man or zone coverage. He should sprint to regain his position or leverage on the receiver. Once he has regained leverage on the receiver, he should then locate the ball.

■ **Block protection.** Defensive backs will face five basic types of blocks. They must be able to defeat these blocks and keep proper leverage on the football.

1. *Stalk block.* A stalk block is used by a receiver who is assigned to block the defensive back aligned over him. Versus a stalk block, the defender should attack the blocker with leverage, keeping his knees bent and his pad level under the blocker's pad level (figure 15.5). He should stun the blocker and shoot his hands to an inside position. Getting inside hand position is critical to the defender's ability to press the blocker out, gaining separation from the blocker and putting the blocker back on his heels. When a defender has a blocker in this position, the defender can now shed the blocker by ripping his arm and leg simultaneously through the surface of the blocker.

2. *Cut block.* The defender must first recognize that the blocker is trying to cut him. The defender should bend at the knees and hips and place his hands on the helmet of the blocker attempting the cut block. He should

Figure 15.5 Defensive back executing a stalk block.

then press the blocker's helmet down and into the ground. He may have to give ground slightly. The defender should then replace the blocker's body and squeeze to the ballcarrier with the proper leverage.

3. *Fullback or guard kick-out block.* This type of block is usually executed on a strong safety in a sky position who is responsible for containment. The strong safety should attack the blocker at the same angle the blocker is coming from to block the safety. The safety should not wait for the blocker. He should squeeze and constrict the area between himself and the next closest defender to his inside. The safety must be sure that he doesn't run straight upfield. Doing so would create a vertical seam for the offense. When taking on a blocker, the safety should reduce the running lane and take on the blocker with his hands. The safety's inside arm and leg should snap into the blocker simultaneously, which will put him in a position of power. It will also allow the safety to keep his outside arm and leg free. When contact is made with the blocker, the safety should hold his ground and continue to constrict the running lane. Staying square and staying on or close to the line of scrimmage will put the safety in position to make the play if the ballcarrier bounces outside.

4. *Crack block.* A "crack" block occurs when a blocker, usually a wide receiver, is flexed outside of the front seven defenders and blocks inward toward the defensive front seven. A crack block usually involves a receiver blocking a defensive safety in a sky position or blocking a linebacker. The corner or safety aligned over the receiver who is executing a crack block must make a "crack" call to alert the safety or the linebacker being cracked.

A safety being cracked must know where the ballcarrier is in relationship to the blocker. If the ballcarrier is to his inside and the safety feels that he can come under the crack block and make the play on the ball, he should do so. A corner must replace the blocker from the outside in, constricting the running lane and containing the football. If the ballcarrier is on a course to get outside of the safety or has even to outside leverage on the safety, the safety should cross the face of the receiver and work inside out to the ballcarrier.

5. *Cutoff block.* The cutoff block is executed by a wide receiver attempting to cut off a defender's pursuit on plays away from the defender. The defender should pursue the ball at top speed, maintaining cutback leverage on the ballcarrier. If the blocker chooses to run with the defensive back, the defensive back should keep a guide hand on the blocker, using it as a straight-arm to play off the blocker when necessary.

■ **Tackling.** Defensive backs must be the surest tacklers on the defense! Missed tackles in the secondary will result in explosion plays for the offense, which greatly increase the offense's opportunity to score points. Defensive backs also have many opportunities to make punishing tackles. Big hits by the defenders in the secondary ignite the entire defense and often lead to turnovers. Defensive backs should always be looking for opportunities to make the big hit. The tackling progression consists of three phases: approach, contact, and finish.

1. *Approach.* The approach is the most important skill to be learned in tackling. As the defensive back approaches the ballcarrier, he must close the distance between himself and the ballcarrier as quickly as possible, limiting the yardage gained. When the defensive back gets within four or five yards of the ballcarrier, he must gather his momentum (come to balance) and close on a course that will limit the ballcarrier's course in one direction. A defender must always know where his defensive help is, and he should fit and funnel the ballcarrier accordingly.

2. *Contact.* Ideally, the defender wants to be in the perfect football position on contact. His knees should be bent, and his weight should be balanced on the balls of his feet. His head and eyes should be up as contact is made. The defender should uncoil his body up through the ballcarrier, thrusting his arms up to move them through and around the ballcarrier.

3. *Finish.* The combination of explosive contact and leg drive as contact is made allows the defender to finish the tackle by driving the ballcarrier backward and putting him on the ground. A defensive back must always try to secure the tackle by wrapping up the ballcarrier.

All tackles by defensive backs should include the three components—the approach, contact with the ballcarrier, and the finish. Although the techniques for contact and the finish should be the same in most tackles, the approach to the ballcarrier can consist of the following variations:

■ *Angle tackle.* When the ballcarrier is on a diagonal course away from a defensive back, the defender should quickly close the distance between himself and the ballcarrier. He must attack the ballcarrier, decreasing the angle between himself and the ballcarrier. The defensive back should not sit back and wait. As the defender gets within three or four yards of the ballcarrier, he should regain his balance and shuffle, being careful not to cross his feet over (which would allow the ballcarrier to cut back across the defensive back's face). The defender should tackle the ballcarrier high, but with his knees bent, his head and eyes up, and his pad level under the pad level of the ballcarrier (figure 15.6). The defender should drive his arms up and through the ballcarrier so that his hips uncoil into the ballcarrier. On contact, the defender should accelerate his feet and drive the ballcarrier backward and into the ground.

Figure 15.6 A defensive back making an angle tackle.

The defensive back should always be aware of where he fits within the defense. Is he responsible for containing the ballcarrier and forcing him back inside? Or does he need to work inside out on the ballcarrier? All defenders should force the ballcarrier to their defensive help. In most defensive structures, the corners and strong safety are responsible for containment, and their fit on the ballcarrier should be outside in. Their head placement should be to the outside.

- *Open-field tackle.* When a defensive back is caught in the open field in a one-on-one situation, the defensive back should reduce the distance between himself and the ballcarrier as quickly as possible. As the defensive back closes in on the ballcarrier, he should regain his shuffle and regain a balanced position. He should know where his help is at all times, and he should force the ballcarrier in that direction. If the defender is close to the sideline, he should force the ballcarrier out of bounds.

As the ballcarrier makes his move, the defender should concentrate on the ballcarrier's midsection. The defender needs to be careful not to lunge and overextend his body. The defender should regain his shuffle at the last second, turning his tackle into an angle tackle. His focus should be on securing the ballcarrier first and preventing additional yardage. He should keep his head up and wrap his arms. ("Hang on. Help is on the way.") If a defensive back is chasing down a ballcarrier from behind, as he catches up to the ballcarrier, he should come down hard with his arm on the side of the ball and attempt to strip the ball out of the ballcarrier's arm. He should secure the tackle with his opposite arm.

- *Clean-up tackle*. Defensive backs often have the opportunity to finish tackles after one of the front seven defenders has made the initial contact on the ballcarrier. Defenders should always be looking for opportunities to get in on as many tackles as possible. They should look to punish the ballcarrier, knocking the ballcarrier backward. The defender should also be looking for the opportunity to strip the ballcarrier once the tackle is secured. Ballcarriers often hold the football loosely, and the football is often in clear sight of the third or fourth defender to arrive at the ballcarrier. Defensive backs should continue to keep their head up and their eyes open, making sure not to knock off one of their own teammates.

Run Support

Run support is another important part of defensive play in the secondary. The main objective when supporting the run is to always keep the ball inside and in front of the defense. Defensive backs must be hard nosed and tough when supporting the run. They should always keep the proper leverage on the ballcarrier with regard to their area of responsibility. The following five terms describe the areas of responsibility for the defensive backs versus a running play.

- **Primary force** describes a defensive back who is responsible for containing a perimeter running play. A defensive back in this role has four responsibilities. First, he should contain the football. Second, he should constrict and reduce the inside running lane. Third, he should make the tackle on any play where the ballcarrier attempts to get outside of his position. This includes having responsibility for the pitch versus an option play. Finally, when a play starts away from the primary force player, he should fold under control through the defensive backfield, staying in position to make the play if the ballcarrier cuts back. He should always clear a reverse, bootleg, or trick play that may come back to his side as he starts to fold for a potential cutback.
- **Alley support** refers to the defender who is responsible for filling the area between the primary force player and the defensive end or rush end. In most defensive structures, the free safety provides alley support.
- **Secondary support** describes a defensive back's responsibility for defending the pass first. When all threat of a pass has been eliminated, the defensive back should stack off the primary force player's fit and should support the run where needed.
- **Deep pursuit** describes a defensive back's technique when the play is away from him and he is the last man in the support pattern. The defender must take

the proper course to intercept the ballcarrier. If there is a threat of a cutback, he should adjust his course to ensure that he stays on the back hip of the ballcarrier. If there is no threat of a cutback, the defender should continue a deep pursuit course. Great effort is a must! A lack of effort by a defensive back in deep pursuit could cost the defense a touchdown.

■ **Fold responsibility** refers to the technique used by a player responsible for primary force when the play starts away from him. As he pursues the ball, he should be aware of the possibility of the ballcarrier cutting back behind his position. The fold player should shuffle through the linebacker's original alignment, staying on the back hip of the football. If the ballcarrier does cut back, the fold defensive back should attack the ballcarrier from an outside-in angle, keeping the ball in front and inside.

Before every play, each defensive back should go through a presnap thought process to ensure that he is ready for every possibility. Taking the following actions will help a defensive back prevent big plays by the offense:

1. Know the coverage called and his assignment.
2. Maintain the proper alignment.
3. Be aware of wide receiver splits that may be abnormal.
4. Use the proper stance.
5. Know whom and what he is keying.
6. Choose initial reads and movement based on each coverage assignment.
7. Know his responsibility versus the run and pass in each coverage assignment.

Zone Coverage Techniques

The advantage of zone coverage is that each defender is responsible for a predetermined area of the field. Playing zone defense allows a defensive back to have vision on both the ball and the receivers in his area, allowing him to quickly read a run or pass. Defensive backs must adhere to the following basic principles when in zone coverage:

■ If two receivers are in one zone and the defensive back is being stretched vertically, the defensive back should always cover the deepest threat. He should break up to the short route when the ball is thrown.

■ If a defensive back is responsible for an underneath zone, he should have vision on the quarterback's throwing arm. The defensive back should break on the ball when the quarterback's off hand leaves the ball as he prepares to throw.

■ In zone coverage, the defense wants to make the quarterback throw the ball in front of the defense.

■ When a defensive back is responsible for a deep zone, he should break only when the ball is thrown. He should also make sure he doesn't break forward prematurely on a quarterback's pump fake when the receiver breaks off a short route and then turns upfield vertically.

■ Zone defense allows defenders to read the quarterback's eyes and shoulders. Defenders should be aware that the quarterback can only throw in the direction his off shoulder is pointing.

■ If the quarterback scrambles, the secondary's job is to play the pass until the quarterback crosses the line of scrimmage. Deep defenders should stay deep.

In addition to these basic principles, defensive backs must be able to respond to several other key indicators that will help them read the upcoming play. Recognizing the backfield action will help defensive backs anticipate the potential play and the pass routes from the receivers in their zone. When the quarterback takes a three-step drop (see figure 15.7), the secondary should read a quick passing attack and should be ready to break on the football when it is thrown. The deep defenders should be alert for the possibility of a quick pass fake by the quarterback and a go route by the receiver.

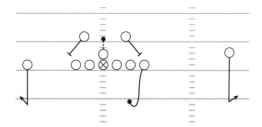

Figure 15.7 Three-step drop.

When the quarterback takes the ball off the line of scrimmage, he may hand the ball off to the running back (see figure 15.8), or he may fake the run and execute a play-action pass. The secondary should feel the tempo of the offensive line to help them with their run-pass read. The secondary players who have responsibility for a deep zone should backpedal, maintaining deep leverage on any receiver in their area, until they are certain the play is a run. The primary force players should buzz their feet and hold their position until they recognize a run or pass.

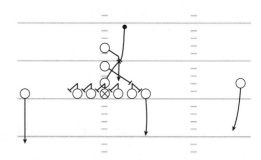

Figure 15.8 Handoff to running back.

When the quarterback drops straight back (see figure 15.9), the secondary defenders who have responsibility for a deep zone should backpedal and main-

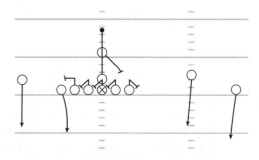

Figure 15.9 When the quarterback drops straight back, the secondary maintains deep leverage on receivers.

tain deep leverage on any receivers in their area. The primary force players should bounce and hold their position until they recognize the route being run in their area. However, versus four vertical pass routes, the flat defender will sink and carry the number two receiver vertically.

The secondary should always be aware of an abnormal split by a receiver. The split can be either wider or tighter than normal. Certain splits by the receivers will correspond to particular routes that the receivers run. Studying game tape can give a defensive back an edge when reading how a team will use the split of a receiver to set up a certain run block or pass route. Defenders need to communicate what they see.

The alignments, reads, and techniques used by the defensive backs in Cover 4, Cover 3, and Cover 2 are detailed in the following sections. Cover 4 and Cover 3 incorporate elements of the techniques used in Cover 5, Cover 2, and Cover 44. Cover 4 is a two-deep coverage to the boundary but a 44 coverage to the field. Into the boundary, the corner's technique is a deep-one-half defender but four yards off the high school hash. Cover 3 is similar to playing Cover 5 for the strong safety, but the free safety is a deep-middle-third defender. Cover 2 has two deep defenders, each responsible for one half of the field. This coverage has five underneath defenders. The corners are rolled up and are responsible for the flat zone. The Sam and the eagle linebackers are responsible for the curl zone, and the inside linebacker is responsible for the middle hook zone.

Cover 4

Cover 4 is commonly referred to as *quarter-quarter-half coverage.* The field corner is responsible for the deep one fourth of the field to his side. The free safety is responsible for his deep one fourth of the field. The strong safety is responsible for the deep one half of the field into the boundary. The boundary corner is responsible for the boundary flat (similar to when playing Cover 2).

The field corner should align seven yards deep, which will disguise whether he is in Cover 2 or Cover 4. The corner must defend two pass routes by the number one receiver—the streak and the post. Versus a normal receiver split, the corner should align one yard inside of the number one receiver's inside shoulder. Versus an abnormally wide split (referred to as an *oversplit*) of the wide receiver, the corner will line up two yards inside of the wide receiver's inside shoulder. Versus an abnormally tight split (referred to as a *cut split*) by the number one receiver, the corner should align one yard outside of the receiver.

The corner keys the quarterback (through the number one receiver) for his initial run-pass read. On a perimeter running play at the corner, the corner should anticipate the receiver attempting to execute a "crack" block on the free safety. The corner must communicate the crack block and then fit off of the free safety's leverage (as described earlier). The depth of the receiver's angle inside will give the corner a quick read on whether the receiver is on a crack block course or an inside pass route. Versus a run away from the corner, the corner has deep pursuit.

If the quarterback takes a three-step drop, the field corner should drive on the receiver. If the quarterback takes a five- or seven-step drop, the corner's eyes should shift to the number one receiver. He should read the initial course of the receiver's route to determine the route possibilities. Versus a vertical or inside release by the number one receiver, the defensive back should maintain inside and deep leverage on the receiver. If the receiver runs a shallow crossing route, the corner should work back to his deep-one-fourth zone. If the receiver releases outside and vertical, the corner should maintain his inside and deep leverage. Versus a bootleg pass at the corner, the corner should maintain his deep-one-fourth responsibility. Versus a bootleg pass away from the corner, he must squeeze the receiver and defend the post route. If the field corner is an exceptional cover corner, he can also play from a press alignment on the number one receiver. The corner can execute a press or bail technique (see page 203 for more about the press technique).

When playing Cover 4, the free safety aligns over the number two receiver. Versus the pass, the free safety is responsible for the deep one fourth of the field to his side of the ball. He should be 9 yards deep when aligned over a tight end and 10 yards deep when aligned over a wide receiver. The free safety should be aligned 1 yard inside of the number two receiver. He reads the number two receiver to the ball. If the number two receiver is a tight end and he blocks on a running play to the free safety, the free safety fits where needed off of the leverage of the widest defender on the line of scrimmage (in the Eagle defense, this is usually the Sam linebacker, who is aligned in a 9 technique and is responsible for containment). The free safety's fit should be inside the 9 technique. Versus a run away from the free safety, he should shuffle and stay behind the ball so he is in position to play the cutback.

Versus the pass, the free safety's key is the number two receiver he is aligned over. Keying the number two receiver will ensure that the free safety does not get fooled on a play-action pass. It will also allow the free safety to buzz his feet when the number two receiver blocks, putting him in position to quickly support the run.

If the number two receiver takes a vertical release past 8 to 10 yards, the free safety covers him man to man with inside leverage. If the number two receiver hooks up in the 10- to 12-yard area (known as the *intermediate area*), the free safety should cover him aggressively. If the number two receiver releases to the flat or crosses the formation, the safety looks to help the corner with the number one receiver. He should be prepared to help defend the curl route, the dig route, and the post route. If the number two receiver blocks and the quarterback fakes a running play—executing a play-action pass—the free safety (immediately after realizing he was fooled and caught flat footed) should locate the number one receiver to his side and provide deep, underneath, inside help to the corner.

Versus a sprint-out pass, the free safety should overplay the outside part of his zone, locking up on a seam route to the side the quarterback is sprinting to. Versus a bootleg pass to the free safety, he should expand with the flat route if the flat route is open, keeping his depth. If the flat route is covered, either early or late as the pass develops, the safety should then locate and cover the crossing route coming from the other side of the field. Versus a sprint-out, bootleg, or option pass away from the free safety, the free safety should rotate into the deep middle of the field. As a general rule, the free safety always wants to be aware of and defend the post route first.

Cover 2

In Cover 2, five defenders are in the underneath zones, and the two safeties align on their respective hash marks. Each safety is responsible for a deep one half of the field versus a pass and for secondary support versus a run. This coverage is typically good against a passing attack that throws the ball in one of the five underneath zones. Because the corners are now responsible for primary support, Cover 2 is not a coverage used for strong run support.

Cover 2 has five underneath defenders in coverage. The inside linebacker has the middle hook zone. The outside linebackers are responsible for the curl zones, and the corners are responsible for the flat zones. The two deep safeties are each responsible for one half of the field. Both safeties align 12 yards deep. When the ball is in the middle of the field, the safeties align on the high school hash marks (or 2 yards outside of the college hash marks). If the number two receiver is detached from the offensive formation, the safety to that side should align inside of the number two receiver. When the ball is on the hash, the boundary safety should align on the high school hash mark (or 2 yards outside of the college hash). The field safety should align 4 yards inside of the high school hash (or 2 yards inside of the college hash). The splits of the receivers to the field may also alter the alignment of the field safety.

Both safeties key the quarterback for their initial run-pass read. The safeties should backpedal on the snap of the ball. Versus a running play, the safety on the side that the ball is being run to is responsible for secondary force. He should fill outside of the end man on the line of scrimmage and inside of the corner. The safety on the side that the running play is going away from is responsible for the cutback once a run has been declared. Versus a pass, both safeties should backpedal, getting depth and working straight back.

The safeties should then key the number two receiver. If the number two receiver takes a vertical release, the safety should continue to get depth and play inside, maintaining deep leverage on the number two receiver. The safety must be prepared to defend the streak, post, and corner routes. If the number two receiver runs an intermediate route, the safety should continue to get depth and should look to help defend the number one receiver on a deep route. The safety should not break up on a short route until the ball is thrown. If the number two receiver releases flat or across the formation, the safety should continue to get depth, working straight back. His eyes should shift to the number one receiver. If the number one receiver takes an outside release, the safety should get width and play the streak route. If the number one receiver takes an inside release, the safety should work straight back and play the post, curl, and corner routes.

Versus a bootleg pass, the safety to the bootleg side should roll to the deep outside third of the field to his side. He should man up the deepest receiver in his zone. The safety away from the bootleg should roll to the deep middle third of the field and match up with any receiver who enters the area.

The corners play a jam, funnel technique. Both corners should align seven yards deep, with outside leverage on the number one receiver. The initial run-pass key for both corners is the quarterback. Versus a run to his side of the field, a corner is responsible for primary force. Versus a run away from his side of the field, a corner is responsible for deep pursuit.

Versus a pass, the corner's secondary read is the number one receiver. The corner should execute a jam and funnel technique on the number one receiver. He should squat at a position seven yards deep. The corner should buzz his feet and get his hands up as the receiver approaches his position. The corner wants to keep his inside leg lined up with the crotch of the receiver, maintaining outside leverage on the receiver. The corner should stay square and deliver a two-hand jam under the shoulder pads of the receiver. He needs to shuffle his feet while staying square and in front of the receiver. Crossing his feet would cause him to lose his base and most likely cause him to turn his shoulders. If the corner turns his shoulders, this will prevent him from jamming the receiver and will give the receiver an easy release.

When the number one receiver releases outside, the corner should get his hands on the receiver and flatten the receiver to the sideline. The corner wants to reroute the wide receiver. If the receiver gains an outside vertical release, the corner should zone turn with his back to the receiver, feeling the number one receiver. The corner should then get his vision back on the quarterback through the number two receiver. If the number two receiver takes a vertical release, the corner should lock on the number one receiver.

When the number one receiver takes an inside release, the corner should get his eyes on the number two receiver. If the number two receiver has a wide presnap alignment, the corner needs to make sure that he doesn't get outflanked by the number two receiver (for example, when the number one receiver runs a post route and the number two receiver runs a wheel route). When the number two receiver has a wide presnap alignment, the corner should not chase an inside release by the number one receiver any farther than two steps. If the number two receiver takes a normal alignment, and if the number one and number two receivers both take inside releases and then break inside at six yards of depth, the corner should squeeze the slant route of the number one receiver.

The number one receiver may also release inside and sit in the open void between the corner and the curl defender, or he may release outside and sit at a depth of approximately six yards. In this situation, the corner should open his hips at a 90-degree angle and shuffle straight back, gaining width and depth. The first route the corner must help defend is the corner route by the number two receiver. If the number two receiver is not a threat behind the corner, the corner should begin to settle and play the flat route aggressively. The corner must be aware of the possibility of a "smash" pass pattern. In this pass pattern, the number one receiver sits down at approximately six yards of depth, and the number two receiver runs a corner route behind the corner and away from the safety. The corner must communicate this pattern to the curl defender, who should then break to the receiver in the flat. The corner should sink underneath the deep corner route.

Versus a bootleg pass, the corner to the bootleg side should widen and flatten out the release of the number one receiver. The corner should then cover the number two receiver in the flat. The corner on the side of the field away from the bootleg pass should match up with the deepest receiver in his outside deep-one-third zone. In doing so, the corner should be aware of the possibility of a wheel route by the running back, who may fake the run and then release out of the backfield.

Cover 3

Cover 3 has four defenders in the underneath zones and three deep defenders. In my opinion, Cover 3 is still the best overall coverage in high school or college football. Having the free safety in the middle of the field helps prevent big plays. The eagle and inside linebackers defend the hook zone if there is a receiver in it. If their hook zone isn't threatened, they expand to the curl zone. Both the strong safety and the Sam linebacker are defenders of the curl and flat zones. They will defend the curl zone unless their flat zone is threatened, which will cause them to expand into the flat zone. The corners are both deep-one-third defenders, and the free safety is the deep-middle-third defender.

The free safety aligns 12 yards deep. Versus a pro formation, he lines up over the field offensive guard. Versus a twin formation, the free safety lines up over the field offensive tackle. The free safety keys the quarterback for ball on or ball off the line of scrimmage, and he feels the closest receiver who can threaten his zone. The free safety should mirror the quarterback. If the quarterback takes the ball off the line of scrimmage, the free safety should backpedal to his deep-one-third zone. If the quarterback keeps the ball on the line of scrimmage (i.e., for an option play or a toss sweep), the free safety should ease back and check his secondary keys for a possible sucker pass before committing up to support the run in the alley.

Versus a running play to or away from the free safety, the free safety should provide late alley support, moving inside out and fitting inside of the primary force player. On a running play to either side, the free safety should always be aware of a possible cutback by the ballcarrier. He should make sure that he does not overrun the ball.

Versus a pass, the free safety's zone extends from 15 yards beyond the line of scrimmage to the end zone. Horizontally, the zone extends to 2 yards outside both hash marks. The midpoint is the center of the goalpost. The free safety must be able to handle the seam routes from both sides of the hash marks. If both seams are threatened, he should work deep to his midpoint and break when the quarterback's eyes and shoulders indicate the direction he intends to throw (the shoulders will tilt in that direction). When doing this, the free safety will break just before the quarterback releases the football. If there is no threat of the middle zone being stretched vertically, the free safety should make sure that he can handle the post route from either side of the field. If there is no deep threat, he should level off.

Each corner's zone extends vertically from 15 yards beyond the line of scrimmage to the end zone. A corner's zone extends horizontally from the sideline to 2 yards outside of the hash mark. His midpoint is 1 yard inside of the top of the numbers. Versus a normal split, the corners align 8 to 10 yards deep and 1 yard outside of the number one receiver. Versus an abnormally wide split, the corner should align

1 yard inside of the number one receiver. The corner keys the quarterback through the number two to the number one receiver.

When aligned over a wide receiver, a corner provides secondary support versus a running play to his side of the field. If the number one receiver cracks on the primary force player to his side, the corner must communicate to the support player that a crack block is coming. He should then replace the support player's responsibility, always keeping the ball on his inside shoulder. Versus a run away, the corner is responsible for deep pursuit. Versus a pass, the corner is responsible for his deep one third of the field. Once the corner reads pass, his eyes should shift to the number two receiver. If the number two receiver is a threat deep in the inside seam of his zone, the corner should continue to get depth and work to the midpoint of his deep-one-third zone. If the number two receiver is not a threat vertically through the corner's deep-one-third zone, the corner should overplay the number one receiver as long as he remains in his zone.

When the corner is aligned to a tight end surface with no outside receivers, he should align one yard outside of the tight end and seven yards from the line of scrimmage. If the ball is in the middle of the field, the corner should adjust his alignment to a position two to three yards outside of the tight end. The corner reads the quarterback to the tight end for his run-pass read. He is also looking for a possible vertical release by the tight end. Versus a run to his side of the field, a corner is a secondary support player and should fit where needed, always keeping the ball on his inside shoulder. Versus a run away from his side of the field, the corner should pursue the ball, always staying on the back hip of the football and in position to defend against the cutback.

Versus a pass play in which the tight end releases vertically and is the only deep threat, the corner should overplay the tight end. Some pass plays may involve two threats in the corner's deep-one-third zone—for example, a wheel route where the tight end runs a skinny post and a running back starts to the flat zone and then turns up the field and runs down the sideline. When two threats are in his deep zone, the corner should work to the midpoint between the two deep routes and be in position to break on either route. If there is no threat to the corner's deep zone, he should get depth and check for a deep crossing route. The corner should always be aware of the possibility of a play-action pass. If the tight end blocks and the quarterback takes the ball off the line of scrimmage, the corner should backpedal before bouncing and supporting the run.

The strong safety aligns in a sky position to the field. Versus a tight end and flanker formation, the strong safety should align five yards deep and five yards wide. Versus a twin formation, his alignment is one yard outside of the number two receiver and five yards deep (unless there is an oversplit by the number two receiver). When the number two receiver uses an oversplit, the strong safety will align head up on the inside of the number two receiver, depending on how wide the oversplit is. The strong safety should read through the end man on the line of scrimmage to the quarterback while also seeing the near back. This is known as a *triangle read*. The end man on the line of scrimmage is often a reliable run-pass read.

Versus a run to the strong safety, the safety is responsible for primary force and containing the football. If the ball is in the alley and the wide receiver aligned outside of the safety executes a crack block on the safety, the safety can rip under and through the inside shoulder of the receiver. If the ball is already equal with or outside the receiver's crack block, then the safety should rip over the top of the crack block and pursue the ball inside out. The corner to the side of the crack block should recognize a run action by the quarterback. As the corner sees the receiver start on a crack angle in toward the strong safety or a linebacker, the corner must make a "crack" call.

When the receiver makes contact with the strong safety or linebacker, the corner should fit off the defender being cracked. If the defender being cracked fits inside of the block, the corner should replace the defender being cracked in run support. If the defender being cracked works over and outside the crack block, the corner should fit inside. The corner is responsible for a play-action pass off a crack pass or a simulated crack block, in which the receiver starts on a crack course to get the corner to move up to support the run but then releases vertically by the corner or free safety on a deep pass route. The strong safety is responsible for the pitch versus an option.

Versus a running play away from the strong safety, the safety should fold to the ball. If the football is inside of the tackle box, the safety should shuffle and maintain cutback leverage on the ball. Versus a passing play with the quarterback taking a three-step drop, the strong safety should drive out toward the flat. He should defend the number one receiver. When the quarterback takes a five- or seven-step drop, the strong safety should drive to the curl zone, 8 to 10 yards deep and 4 yards inside of the number one receiver.

If the number two receiver releases into the flat, the strong safety should drive to the curl zone, 8 to 10 yards deep, depending on the depth of the number two receiver. The strong safety should hang in the curl window as long as he can in order to buy time for the linebacker to replace the strong safety in the curl zone. The strong safety should then continue to expand over the top of the number two receiver as the number two receiver widens to the flat. If the number two receiver releases across the formation, the strong safety should drive to a vision point inside of the number one receiver, 8 to 10 yards deep. He should then square up and react to the quarterback's shoulders and eyes and to any potential receivers in his area.

Versus a sprint-out pass or bootleg pass to the strong safety, the safety should drive under the outward cut of the number one receiver. Versus a play with the number two receiver releasing vertically, the strong safety should sink with the number two receiver, protecting against the possibility of four vertical receivers against a three-deep coverage. When there is no longer a threat of four vertical receivers, the strong safety should expand to his vision point on the number one receiver.

The *cat technique* is a term used to describe the strong safety's technique for defending four vertical pass routes when aligned in a sky position against a trips formation. The strong safety should align five yards deep, with outside leverage on the number two receiver. The strong safety keys the quarterback through the number three to the number two receiver. He should shuffle back on the snap of the ball, reading the release of the number three and number two receivers. If both the number three and number two receivers push vertically, the strong safety should continue to sink and carry the number two receiver (see figure 15.10). Versus any other route combination, the strong safety should execute his responsibility for the curl and flat zones.

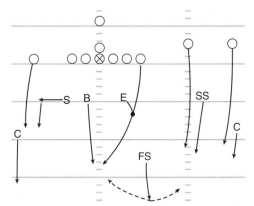

Figure 15.10 Cat technique when the number three and number two receivers push vertically.

Man-to-Man Coverage Techniques

Man-to-man coverage is an essential part of any coverage package. In man coverage, a defensive back should always know if he has coverage help. For example, a defensive back may have help from the free safety in a "man free" coverage. Or he may have help from an underneath robber assigned to help with a shallow crossing route. If the defender does have help, he should be certain of where his help is and how he should try to funnel the receiver. With or without help, the defender must know what leverage he should play the receiver with—inside or outside. Defensive backs will use four basic man-to-man techniques: cushion, press, challenge, and catch.

■ **Cushion technique.** This technique is often used with inside leverage. The defender should align with his outside foot on the inside foot of the receiver he is covering. He should be aligned seven yards off the line of scrimmage. His key is the receiver he is covering. On the snap of the ball, the defender should begin a controlled backpedal and should be ready to break on any quick pass (three-step drop by the quarterback). If the receiver presses upfield, the defender should begin to speed up his backpedal, and he should weave to maintain inside leverage on the receiver. The defender should know the break points for potential intermediate routes. He should also be alert for any change in the receiver's running techniques that could tip him off to the break point of a route (e.g., short choppy steps, a forward lean, and so on).

When the receiver breaks his steps down, the defender should also break his steps down and prepare to break on an intermediate route. Once the receiver breaks off his route, the defender should burst and break on the receiver. The defender must stay locked on his receiver and not look back for the ball. When the receiver declares his route, the defender should close the separation between himself and the receiver. When the defender gets into the proper position to defend the route being run by the receiver—which is approximately an arm's length from the receiver—the defender should turn and make a play on the ball. The defender should always play through the receiver's upfield shoulder to the ball, unless he is sure that he can cut underneath the receiver and intercept the ball.

An outside cushion is used by a defender who has deep inside help, such as a safety in man coverage on the number two receiver with a safety who is free to help in the deep middle third (along with an underneath robber over the ball to help with a shallow crossing route). The defender should align with his inside leg on the outside leg of the receiver. He should be seven to eight yards off the line of scrimmage. The technique is the same as for an inside cushion, with the exception that the defender is now playing with outside leverage on the receiver. The defender also knows that he has inside help on routes that break inside. The defender should always keep the receiver between himself and the quarterback. He should key through the receiver to the quarterback.

■ **Press technique.** The defender's alignment is one to three yards off the receiver. The defender's outside foot should be aligned on the receiver's inside foot. The defender's eyes should be locked on the bottom of the receiver's numbers. The defender's feet should be no wider than shoulder-width apart, and his weight should be balanced evenly over his feet. The defender should be bent at the knees, with a slight bend at the waist. His knees should be over his feet, and his shoulders should be over his knees. His chest and head should be up. His hands should be up and in position to deliver a blow to the receiver.

As the receiver starts his initial movement, the defender must be patient! He should mirror the receiver's release with a lateral movement along the line of scrimmage (defending the receiver first with his feet). The defender should keep his shoulders square to maintain a narrow base. He should make the receiver release around him.

Against an inside release by the receiver, the defender should execute a two-hand jam and flatten the receiver's release down the line of scrimmage. The defender needs to be sure he does not lunge at the receiver. He should work to punch the front of the receiver's chest, which provides the best surface to jam. The defender should continue to move his feet and should keep his face out of the jam. The defender should try to achieve a lockout position on the receiver, enabling the defender to maintain upfield leverage on the receiver.

The defender should stay with the receiver, keeping his eyes low on the receiver as the receiver enters the intermediate break point. The defender should match the receiver's stride. If the receiver stutters, the defender should stutter. If the receiver's strides are long, the defender should be in a full sprint. When the receiver comes to his break point, he will generally lean in the opposite direction from his break. The defender should burst out of the break and drive to the receiver's upfield arm.

If the receiver beats the defender on an inside release, the worst position the defender can be in is outside and underneath the receiver. If the defender is in that position, he should undercut the receiver and reestablish his inside leverage before regaining upfield position on the receiver.

Against an outside release by the receiver, the defender should jam the receiver with his inside hand to the chest of the receiver. He should then flatten out the receiver's release and open his hips, working to stay inside and even with the receiver. After the defender has disrupted the receiver's release, the defender should work to a cutoff position, keeping his eyes low on the receiver until he clears the receiver's intermediate break point. The defender should match the receiver's stride. If the receiver stutters, the defender should stutter and be ready to explode on the receiver's break.

If the receiver is running with long strides through the intermediate break point, the defender's eyes should rise up to the receiver's eyes. If the defender is in a trail position, he should continue to sprint and play the eyes and hands of the receiver. If the defender is in a dominant position, he should use his sideline rule regarding which way (man or zone turn) he will turn to the ball. When a corner is inside the receiver and within two to three yards of the sideline, there is not enough space for the receiver to fade away from the corner on a deep pass. In this position, the corner should zone turn to the ball, which gives him vision on the football and positions his butt on the receiver so he can feel the receiver's body. When the corner and receiver are more than three yards from the sideline, there is too much room for a receiver to separate from the corner on a deep fade pass. In this situation, the corner should maintain an inside position facing the receiver with his back turned to the football. The corner will have to make a play on the ball through the receiver's hands as the receiver reaches for the football.

■ **Challenge technique.** This technique is used when a defensive back is covering a tight end or a running back. On the snap of the ball, the defender should step laterally to secure inside leverage on the receiver. The defender should not back up. If the receiver takes a vertical release, the defender should jam the receiver. Versus all pass routes, the defender should maintain inside and deep leverage on the receiver.

■ **Catch technique.** The catch technique is used when playing man coverage with five underneath defenders and two deep safeties playing a zone technique (each responsible for one half of the field) over the top. The underneath defenders should align as they do in Cover 2 (a two-deep, five-under coverage). On the snap of the ball, the three inside defenders squat and catch the three inside receivers at a depth of five yards, maintaining inside leverage on each receiver. As the receiver makes his break, the defender should work to burst underneath the receiver's route with the confidence that they have deep safety help versus any vertical route.

The corners are aligned over the number one receiver on their side of the ball and should not expect deep help from the safety. On the snap of the ball, the corner should slide inside of the receiver to gain inside leverage. The corner should then defend the receiver man to man, maintaining inside and deep leverage on the receiver.

PART VI

Situational Preparation and Execution

CHAPTER 16

Goal Line Defense

In 1995 while I was at Northwestern University, our fifth game was on the road against the University of Michigan. In the second quarter with Michigan in front 3-0, Michigan had a first and goal at our one-yard line. On first down, we slanted correctly into the play and tackled the Michigan running back for a one-yard loss. On second down, we also stunted correctly and threw Michigan for another loss, bringing up a third down and three. On third down, Michigan passed and the ball fell incomplete. Holding Michigan to a field goal was a tremendous boost to our Wildcat team and kept 4 points off the scoreboard. We went on to win the game 19-13.

The impact of being successful on the goal line cannot be overstated. A successful goal line defense not only keeps points off the scoreboard—which we all know is critical to winning—but it also provides a tremendous mental lift and confidence boost to the entire team. A goal line stand demoralizes the opponent's offense.

Goal Line Strategies

A defense can't defend everything when they are on the goal line, but they must take away what the offensive team does best. Defensive coaches often see all of the offensive possibilities and try to design strategies to defend them all. However, when designing a goal line strategy, a coach should make sure he understands the opponent's personality on the goal line. Then the coach should design a strategy to take away the opponent's best plays, which are usually running plays and goal line passes such as the power pass.

When practicing and discussing goal line defense with our players, I often emphasize that they should never give in. The defenders should always make the offense take another snap. They need to toughen up, lower their pad level, and attack the line of scrimmage. Defenders must make a tackle for no gain or negative yardage. Linebackers should always look for an opportunity to press the ball and should always take that opportunity!

I have always believed that a goal line defense should be similar in responsibilities, alignments, and adjustments to the team's base defense. Throughout the entire season, we are only in our goal line defense for a total of approximately 10 to 20 plays during games. During the 2006 season, we were only in our goal line package 10 total times in 12 games. With this in mind, it would seem counterproductive to instill and practice a goal line scheme that is different from the team's base defense. When you stay within your base scheme, your players will be more comfortable. Consequently, they will play harder and faster.

However, no matter what scheme is employed on the goal line, it will only be successful if the front line attacks the line of scrimmage aggressively and with a low pad level. All 11 defenders must aggressively and effectively attack the ballcarrier. To reinforce the importance of great execution on the goal line, a team needs to scrimmage goal line situations (the programs I have coached in have all scrimmaged goal line situations two or three times both during spring drills and in early fall camp). Only after live scrimmage situations do players completely understand the importance of having a low pad level, attacking the line of scrimmage, and pressing and tackling the ballcarrier with perfect form and technique. Scrimmage situations also help defenders learn to read their keys and learn to react to play-action passes, reverses, and naked bootlegs.

Goal Line Schemes

For goal line situations, the defensive scheme I have used for the last 24 seasons is a split defensive front to both sides of the offensive formation. The defense is simply called *60* (see figure 16.1). On both sides of the offensive center, a noseguard lines up in a 2 alignment. A 2 alignment puts the noseguards on the inside shoulder of the offensive guard they are aligned over. They are responsible for their 1 gap.

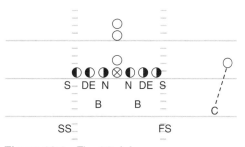

Figure 16.1 The 60 defense.

Both defensive ends are in a tight 5 alignment. The defensive ends align with their inside leg in the crotch of the offensive tackle, and they are responsible for the 5 gap. If the offensive tackle executes a base block on the defensive end, the end should be tight enough to squeeze the offensive tackle into the 3 gap. Versus a veer block, the end should squeeze and disrupt the offensive tackle, closing hard and canceling the 3 gap. If the offensive tackle executes a reach block, the defensive end's tight 5 alignment may allow the tackle to get his helmet to the outside shoulder of the defensive end. If this occurs, the end must attack and press the offensive tackle into the backfield. Doing so will turn the tackle's body perpendicular to the line of scrimmage and allow the inside linebacker to press the line of scrimmage in the 5 gap.

In this defensive scheme, a fourth linebacker—usually a backup Sam linebacker or the next best overall linebacker—replaces one of the two corners so that there are two Sam linebackers on the field. Both Sam linebackers are in 9 alignments. They align with their inside foot on the outside foot of the tight end, and they are responsible for containment to their side of the ball. They are also responsible for the quarterback versus the option. The eagle linebacker stays in the game, but he now aligns as an inside linebacker. Both inside linebackers are in a 3 alignment, which is on the outside edge of the offensive guard. Both are responsible for their 3 gap. A safety is aligned over each tight end. The corner is matched up on the wide receiver.

The coverage is a quarters concept, similar to Cover 44 (see page 94). Each safety is responsible for his quarter of the field. If either tight end releases vertically, the safety to that side covers him man to man. If the tight end crosses the formation, the safety stays home and communicates "pass" and "crosser" to the other safety. When one offensive player leaves, another will often be coming, so the safety should look for another receiver to cross into his zone.

The corner is responsible for the wide receiver and covers him man to man. If the receiver motions across the formation, the corner stays with him and must really hustle to beat the wide receiver across the formation. If the wide receiver aligns in a wing alignment, the corner can make a "Cloud" call to the safety, which makes the corner responsible for defending the flat and the safety responsible for the half of the field to that side. A Cloud call puts the corner in position to aggressively support the run to his side (as the contain player). Both inside linebackers are hook to curl defenders. Both Sam linebackers are flat defenders. When a Cloud call is made, the Sam linebacker to that side is now responsible for the curl.

When we know a tendency of the team we are playing, we may call a 60 Slant (see figure 16.2). For example, we may make a 60 Slant call if we know that the opponent usually runs to one particular tight end in a two-tight-end formation. We may also use this stunt if a team has a tendency to run to a particular offensive lineman or to a particular offensive set. When 60 Slant is

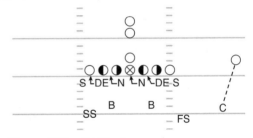

Figure 16.2   60 Slant.

called, all four defensive linemen align in their normal 60 defensive alignment, but they will slant in the direction called by the linebackers.

Both noseguards will rip across the face of the center or a guard blocking back or down. They must not get driven off of the line of scrimmage. If the tight end blocks down on the defensive end, the end should knock the tight end back into the 5 gap and beat him underneath. The Sam linebacker to the slant call should widen his alignment. The Sam linebacker away from the call should tighten his alignment and be more physical on the tight end. However, he still has the contain versus the run, and he drops to the flat versus a pass. The inside linebacker to the slant call is a 31 technique. He has the 3 gap when the play is to him and the far 1 gap when the play is away. The inside linebacker away from the call is a 50 technique. He has the 5 gap when the play is to him and the near 1 gap when the play is away. Versus a pass action to his side, the 50 linebacker would rush contain. Through the years, the 60 Slant has been an effective stunt, even when the running play is away from the slant.

The 60 Double Out is an effective defense against an outside running play and a power play (see figure 16.3). This is not a good defense versus an isolation or belly play because the middle of the defense opens up and both linebackers will have blockers on them. Versus a sweep or option play, the defensive line slanting to the outside forces the ball back into the blitzing linebackers. When the offense runs an off-tackle or perimeter play, one of the two linebackers usually comes free. On

a power play, the center will block back on the noseguard. When this occurs, the linebacker will adjust his course to penetrate over the center's original alignment and follow the pulling guard to the ball. He should hit the ballcarrier in the backfield. The key to calling 60 Double Out is having knowledge of the opponent's goal line offense and tendencies. This defense won't be effective against some teams, but it will be a great call against others.

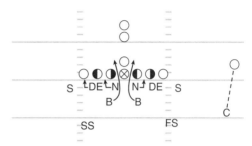

Figure 16.3 60 Double Out.

The 60 Thunder is designed to stop the run (see figure 16.4), not a pass. However, in goal line situations, most offenses will first attempt to run the ball into the end zone. In the 60 Thunder, both safeties blitz through their 5 gaps. Both defensive ends rip inside into the 3 gaps. Versus an option play, the safety has the quarterback and should take on all blockers with his inside arm. The Sam linebacker has the pitch. Versus a pass, the Sam linebacker has the tight end to the outside, and the inside linebackers have the tight end to the inside.

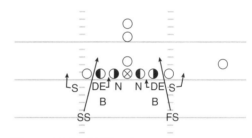

Figure 16.4 60 Thunder.

When the offense gets to the one-yard line, they will most likely run the ball between the tackles. The Pinch Run (see figure 16.5), which places a defensive player in every gap, is the best defense for stopping a run between the tackles and is also effective against a quarterback sneak.

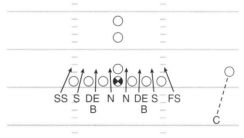

Figure 16.5 Pinch Run.

In the Pinch Run, the noseguards are in the 1 gaps, aligned with their inside shoulder on the knee of the center. The defensive ends align in the 3 gaps and penetrate the 3 gap. The Sam linebackers align in the 5 gaps and penetrate the 5 gap.

The noseguards, defensive ends, and Sam linebackers are all in a four-point stance with their helmets low to the ground and their butts in the air. They key the ball, and on the snap of the ball, they penetrate low and straight ahead, driving their feet after their initial charge and creating a new line of scrimmage. The first couple of times you use Pinch Run in scrimmages, several of the up-front players will likely attempt to enter their gap with a pad level that is too high. Using videotape to show the players how high their charge is will help them to realize the importance of a low, lunging, feet-driving charge.

Both safeties blitz tight off the edge. Versus a wing formation, they penetrate off the tight end's butt and inside and up through the wing's inside shoulder. Versus a perimeter run and a kick-out block by the offensive fullback, the safety should do his best to squeeze and contain the ball as tight to the line of scrimmage as possible. Versus a run away, the safety should squeeze flat down the line of scrimmage, keeping his shoulders square. He must be in position to play a cutback or a naked bootleg by the quarterback.

Both inside linebackers align in the 3 gap. The linebackers key the ball, and they are prepared to attack the quarterback if he runs a quarterback sneak. They should keep their shoulders square to the line of scrimmage and maintain a good base, which will keep the linebackers in position to front up and stop the charge of the ballcarrier. If the offense runs a perimeter play, the linebackers should attempt to tackle the ballcarrier inside out. This will be a challenge.

Versus a pass, the safeties should work upfield to a contain position. The inside linebackers should try to defend the tight end to their side, man to man. Realistically, this defense is not a good call against an outside running play or pass.

Versus an offense that runs an option attack, if the defense uses Pinch Run to stop an inside run on third down and one, the defense should expect an option play on fourth and one. The Pinch Run Out (see figure 16.6) may be used to defend an inside run, outside run, or option play. The defense should align as they do for Pinch Run. The front six defenders begin in their gap charge stance. On the snap of the ball, they each rip into the gap to their

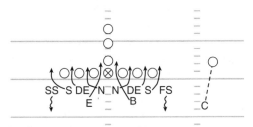

Figure 16.6 Pinch Run Out.

outside. The offensive line will fire off the line of scrimmage as low as they can to stop the penetration of the defensive gap charge. Their low, flat blocking angle allows the defenders to rip free across the face of the offensive linemen. Whenever we run Pinch Run Out, the entire line typically rips free and into the offensive backfield. Both safeties align on the line of scrimmage. On the snap of the ball, the safeties backpedal three to four yards and fit the run where needed. The inside linebackers align head up on the offensive guard and blitz the 1 gap to their side.

CHAPTER 17

Game Planning

Effective game planning hinges on the soundness of the defensive system, which must include the following:

- Good leverage on the perimeter. This means always having a support player in position to turn the ball back inside to the defensive pursuit. The support player must also be in position to take the pitch versus an option play.
- Depth and vision in the secondary. The secondary must be able to keep the ball inside and in front of the defense, preventing big plays.
- A primary focus on the defensive unit's own execution and on each defender being in the right spot.
- A method of ensuring that the number of defensive players on each side of the football is equal to the number of offensive players on each side of the ball. For example, if the offense is in a pro I formation, six offensive players will be to the field side of the ball, and five offensive players will be on the boundary side of the ball.

This last point deserves further explanation because it is a crucial, yet often overlooked, linchpin to defensive success. In the example mentioned, if the fullback were to offset to the field, the offense would then have six and a half players to the field side. (When the fullback and tailback are stacked behind each other, they count as one player—just as the quarterback and center are counted together as one man on each side of the ball, and separately as one half, when the quarterback is under the center.). When either back leaves the I, he counts as one to the side he is aligned. In the Field Eagle defense, the eagle and inside linebackers are the adjusters when running backs offset. In this case, the eagle and inside linebackers would "plus" the formation, meaning that they slide over one man to the side of the offset. Note that the back-side linebacker should never "plus" beyond the ball.

Both the eagle and inside linebackers should continue to read their guard, even though they are aligned one man away. This is critical in defending a counter play going in the opposite direction of the offset back. If the offense changes the strength

211

of their formation, the secondary does the adjusting to balance the defense to the formation.

Preparing the Defense

To ensure proper defensive adjustments, a coach should develop a checklist for preseason practices specifying all possible offensive formations. An essential step in game preparation is exposing the defense to the wide variety of looks that offenses might present during the course of the season. The defense should be drilled on these various looks until the adjustments are made quickly and properly. Defensive players should see trips formations both to the field and into the boundary, as well as an unbalanced line both to the field and into the boundary. They should also be able to adjust to an empty formation with no back in the backfield.

A defense needs to be able to adjust comfortably to all offensive formations, motions, and shifts. Sometimes that doesn't require changing from the team's base defense, but often it will. Being in proper position, regardless of how the offense aligns and shifts its personnel, will keep defenders much less susceptible to a big play.

As a defensive coach, when I examine our performance on tape after a game, I first look to see if we were defensively sound on each play. It may be easy to blame a player or players for a miscue; however, coaches must also take responsibility if they did not have their players in the right position to make the play. Coaches must make sure that the defense practices the various plays and adjustments sufficiently to give players a keen sense of how to react and how to perform with confidence.

Our defensive staff once came up short in this area when preparing our team for a New Year's Day bowl game. We failed to have our players practice enough against an offensive play where the opponent puts an unbalanced formation into the boundary and runs into the boundary versus a particular blitz. As a result, when the opposition did this in the game, our defense did not check to a zone coverage as we had instructed them to. Consequently, our boundary cornerback was run off by the wide receiver, and the running back followed him 27 yards to the end zone. I immediately knew that we had not practiced how to defend this, though our opponent ran several plays with an unbalanced attack, mostly to the field side. Yes, we had discussed it with our players, but we had not adequately practiced defending it. An adjustment to an unbalanced formation has been part of our blitz installation checklist every season since.

At Penn State, when we install our base defense and all of the variations (our stunt and blitz package), we do so in a walk-through in which players are drilled on how to make a particular defensive call versus a variety of formations. This instruction can also take place in a gym during the winter months, in a walk-through after weight training in the summer months, and during a standard practice before the first game. In any of those scenarios, it's best to limit the amount of physical work so that players can focus intently on positioning and adjustments. Variations of the formations, such as an unbalanced formation or trips into the boundary, need to be mixed into the weekly practice routine. Defenders should never be surprised come game time.

Breaking Down the Opposition

The available technology, the size and experience level of athletes, and the time that can be devoted to researching an opponent will vary from high school to college and from one program to the next. But the steps in developing a game plan should be similar for all programs. As you read through this section, try to visualize the game plan structure I present, and then consider how you can transfer those concepts to fit your structure and help your staff and team be fully prepared on game day.

Our game planning actually starts 10 days before playing an opponent. At that time, a graduate assistant coach reviews game tapes and enters data on the team we will be playing into our game-planning computer software. This begins the process we refer to as *breaking down an opponent*. We break down the opponent's previous three games and also enter data for our game against that opponent from the previous season. Although it is more time consuming, the breakdown can be completed by hand (as many of us did in our earlier days of coaching) rather than computer.

The amount of information that can be accumulated on an opponent is almost limitless. Most computer programs used for game analysis will ask for standard information about each play, such as down and distance and which hash the ball is on. Rather than quantity, the important thing is the accuracy and relevance of the input. One vital piece of information to include is the personnel grouping deployed by the opponent on each play. For instance, if they have one tight end, two backs, and two receivers, we would enter 21 for the personnel grouping. This information is critical when calling a defense.

The computer software will also request information on the formation, any shifts or motions, the play description, and the result of the play. Defensive coaches will need to know what plays the offense runs to a tight end surface and to the split end surface. The software program will often ask for the ballcarrier's number to help the defense track the frequency of how often a particular player touches the ball and how productive he is.

If the play is a pass, the pass action is recorded to specify whether it is a drop-back, sprint-out, play-action, or bootleg pass. The result of the pass should be included. Was the pass complete or incomplete? Did the quarterback have to scramble or hurry? Was he sacked? Was the ball intercepted or fumbled?

The intended receiver and the intended pass route the quarterback was throwing to should also be recorded. This kind of detail helps identify tendencies of an opponent that can give a defender invaluable clues about when to take a well-calculated risk that may lead to a big play on game day. The defensive front and the coverage are also entered for each play. This allows the breakdown to show how the offense prefers to attack certain defensive fronts and coverages.

For each play, the breakdown should also identify the quarter the game is in and the score of the game. Teams will often change their game plans depending on whether they are ahead or behind and depending on how much they lead or trail by. When designing a game plan for an opponent, you need to be aware of how these situations change the play selection and how they can give a false impression of how the opponent may attack your team.

It may not always be possible to get three game tapes on each opponent, but resourceful coaches can certainly get one or two game tapes. At the very least, the coaching staff can start with the upcoming opponent's game against their team from the previous season. That game should be broken down during the off-season.

Of course, high school programs don't have the luxury of having graduate assistants to handle the time-consuming tasks associated with breaking down an upcoming opponent. I knew a coach in Michigan, though, who trained his youngest coach and a student assistant who was interested in football to break down the game tapes of the upcoming opponents. Whatever your process, breaking down your opponents is essential during the course of your season as the team and coaching staff finish with one opponent and begin to prepare for the next opponent.

Developing the Plan

At the college level, Sunday is a busy game-planning day. Most of the staffs I have coached on meet at around 8:00 a.m. to watch and grade our game from the previous day. At this time, we grade each player's performance and make notes on personnel issues, areas where we did not make the proper adjustments, and other mistakes we need to emphasize for the upcoming week. When grading an individual player, I evaluate him in four areas: his performance on running plays to him, his performance on running plays away from him, his performance when the offense passes the ball, and his effort to get to the ballcarrier. I also record when each defender makes a tackle, an assist, a tackle for a loss, a quarterback sack, a deflected pass, an interception, and when he caused or recovered a fumble or made a great play. As we grade the game tape, we also make notes that will be helpful the following year against that opponent. We carefully critique what we did well, the areas we need to improve, and how we were attacked. Then we take a break.

We resume game planning at 1:00 p.m. At this time, if we're preparing for a team that we played in the previous season, we will view the tape of that game and review the notes we took after that game. This helps ensure that every member of the staff is on the same page regarding our assessment of the opponent and what has and hasn't been successful against them and why. The staff will then watch the opponent's most recent game tape to get a general feel for the opposition and to identify how they have changed (if at all) from the previous year.

Planning by Position

Each defensive coach is responsible for watching the opponent on his own and becoming an expert on the opponent in a particular area. The defensive line coach studies the opponent's running game and line-blocking schemes. (Having these running plays all on one tape, organized by the frequency of how many times each play was run and whether it was run to or away from a tight end, can save a lot of time.) The line coach should diagram the top running plays and how the opponent will block our particular defensive front. He needs to focus on the games the opponent has played against teams that use a defensive structure that is similar to his own.

For example, when I was coaching at Northwestern, if an opponent had played the University of Illinois, I wanted to watch that tape first because Illinois also played Eagle defense. With this tape, I could see how the opponent would block our fronts and attack our coverage.

As the defensive line coach studies the opponent's running game, he also studies the offensive line personnel—their strengths and weaknesses, how well they pass protect, where there may be a weak link, the line splits, and whether the line splits vary on an inside or outside running play. He should also analyze whether their stance and weight distribution telegraph a running or passing play and whether the offense favors running behind one side of the line or a particular player.

The defensive line coach also studies the offense's protection scheme, which is critical information for designing pass pressure. In particular, he looks for things that may help predict which side of the ball the offensive line is sliding to and which side of the ball the running back is responsible for blocking. He'll try to get the best second-level defender (usually a linebacker) matched up on the running back in pass protection. The linebacker should win this matchup most of the time.

Another coach is responsible for studying the opponent's short-yardage and goal line offense. This coach should diagram the opponent's goal line offense by personnel grouping and by formation. Special attention should be paid to whether the opponent has a strong tendency to run to a particular side of the ball. An offense will often run to their best offensive lineman or to an offset fullback. This coach should also diagram the offense's goal line passing attack and identify the top two play-action passes that the offense uses on the goal line and in short-yardage situations.

The secondary coach should diagram the opponent's passing routes by personnel grouping and then by pass action. Pass routes should be broken into five main categories:

1. Pass routes used on first down and 10 and on second down and 6 yards or less. This will typically be mostly play-action passes.

2. Pass routes used on second down and greater than 7 yards.

3. Pass routes used on third down and 5 yards or less.

4. Pass routes used on third down and 6 yards or more.

5. Pass routes used on third down and 11 yards or more.

The secondary coach should become an expert on the opponent's passing attack. He should diagram their top routes in the five areas noted and make sure the defense gets sufficient practice against these routes. He should also determine if the quarterback favors a particular receiver. Does the quarterback throw better to his right or to his left side? Does he telegraph the direction he will throw by staring in that direction? In putting together a game plan, the defensive coaches need to know how the quarterback and the passing attack in general handle five- and six-man pressure from the defense. Do the receivers get off bump coverage, and do they get open against man-to-man coverage? Are the receivers tough and will they catch the ball over the middle? Do his team's zone coverages match up well against the opponent's top passing patterns? Is Cover 3, Cover 2, man coverage, or a combination of the three the best defense to be in on long-yardage downs?

The answers to all these questions should influence game decisions. If an offense does not execute well against defensive pressure, then the defense should have an extensive game plan built around pressuring the quarterback. Nothing is more disruptive to an offense than pressure on the quarterback. To complement the pressure package, the defense should be good at showing the offense a pressure look and then backing out to play zone coverage.

The defensive coordinator should study the opponent's offense on third down. Stopping the offense on third down is critical. To do this, you must know how the offense handles pressure. Does the quarterback see pressure coming? Does he change the play at the line of scrimmage, and if so, what play does he change to? If the quarterback does change the play, is it possible to show a blitz, get the quarterback to change the play, and then roll into a coverage that will take away the pass route he checks to? When the quarterback sees pressure coming, does he throw the ball quickly in the underneath zones? Does he try to complete short but high-percentage passes? Or does he throw the ball deep, trying to make the big play?

Using a stopwatch, time and chart every pass a quarterback throws under pressure to see how quickly he releases the ball and what his completion percentage is. In addition, study the offensive protection to see how to get a defensive player free to the quarterback or get a second-level player matched up on the running back. Quarterbacks and teams that do not handle pressure should receive a lot of pressure from your defense. If the opposing team uses maximum protection and throws the ball effectively downfield, it's better to have your defense bluff a blitz and then pull out to play a zone coverage.

Putting the Pieces Together

Once the information about the opponent is accumulated, I begin to put the game plan together. We have a long grease board in our defensive staff room. On the board, we chart each play that the opponent has run, both running and passing plays. We list the plays under the formation that the offense ran the play from. Each formation is categorized by personnel grouping. It is important to list each play in its intended gap.

Figures 17.1 through 17.5 on pages 218 and 219 show examples of a condensed version of what a typical game-planning board would look like. The examples show three personnel groupings (21, 11, and 22) and five different formations within the three personnel groupings. Considering the personnel groupings allows the defensive coach to put his players in the best possible defense versus each particular grouping. An offense will only do so many things from each personnel grouping. For example, a 22 personnel grouping is a heavy run formation, favoring power football. If the ball is thrown, the play will likely be a play-action pass or a bootleg pass. A personnel grouping of 11 is generally a passing formation.

Next to our game-planning board, we have an enlarged sheet of paper with a complete listing of all of our defensive calls. The next step in our game-planning process is to go through each formation—within each personnel grouping—and make sure our defensive staff is together on how we will stop each running play in our base defense, whether it is the Eagle defense, the Stack defense, or both defenses. We then go through our defensive menu of placement calls and stunts to determine the line movement and stunts that would be the most effective in stopping what the offense does best out of each formation.

When choosing which stunts to use, you need to consider all of the plays that the offense runs from each formation. You must make sure that the stunts selected for your game plan won't put your defense in a vulnerable position and increase the chance of giving up a big play. As you grow in knowledge of your defensive package, you will become comfortable with this process. This is a healthy exercise in thinking through the strengths and weaknesses of each defensive line movement and stunt, and it will help you make effective game day adjustments. The game plan board is also a good source of information for the defensive coaches to use as they prepare to replicate the opponent's formations and plays in practice.

Based on the three personnel groupings and five formations listed in figures 17.1 through 17.5, I have put together a game plan in figure 17.6 (page 219). When an offense uses a personnel grouping of 21, Field Eagle Cover 5 has been my base defense for many years. Field Eagle allows each defender to get lined up and stay in position regardless of any motions or shifts used by the offense. Field Eagle Cover 5 should be very strong against the run.

The offense profiled in this breakdown has a strong tendency to run toward the tight end. Therefore, a Fin stunt, which calls for the defensive end to rip into the 3 gap, is included in the game plan. This stunt will help take away any running play that starts to the tight end side and then cuts back. The stunt would be called off versus any formation with a tight end into the boundary. I seldom want to rip away from a tight end. Split Eagle would be used to give the offense a different front to block when they are in a pro formation to the field.

On a Gopher stunt, the rush end, defensive tackle, and noseguard slant to the tight end. This will be a good stunt versus all of the running plays listed. The risk in using the Gopher stunt is the possibility of losing containment to the field versus a twin formation and a pass play. As you can see in figure 17.2, the offense likes to sprint the quarterback out on the perimeter in a twin formation. Cover 7 puts the strong safety in the curl zone and puts the field corner in the flat zone, which will free up the eagle linebacker to rush and contain the quarterback versus any pass action.

The game plan also includes Short Eagle Lightning Cover 3, which brings the strong safety off the boundary edge. This should be a good zone stunt versus both a pro and twin formation. Short Eagle Brave and Short Eagle Blast Cross 3 Hole (see chapter 5) are both zone stunts involving blitzing linebackers with zone coverage being played behind the stunt. These stunts should be effective against both the run and the play-action pass.

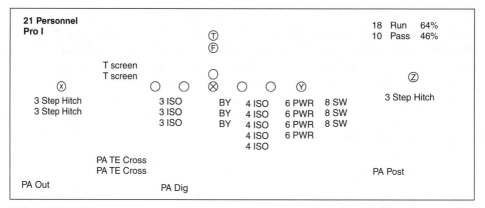

Figure 17.1

TE = tight end, ISO = isolation, BY = belly, PWR = power, SW =sweep, PA = play action

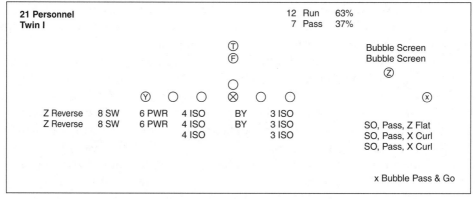

Figure 17.2

SW = sweep, PWR = power, ISO = isolation, BY = belly, SO = sprint out

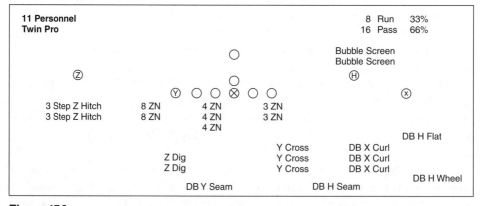

Figure 17.3

ZN = zone, DB = drop back

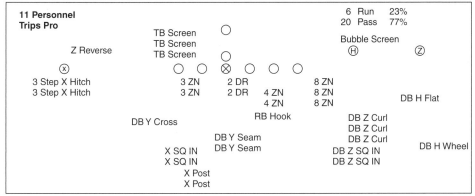

Figure 17.4

TB = tailback, DR = draw, SQ IN = square in, RB = running back, DB = drop back

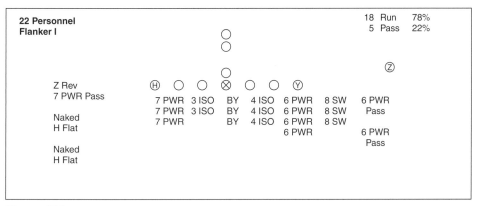

Figure 17.5

PWR = power, ISO = isolation, BY = belly, SW = sweep

FIGURE 17.6 Sample Game Plan

21 Personnel, 63 Percent of Offensive Plays are Run Plays

Field Eagle Cover 5

Field Eagle Fin (checks off if a tight end is aligned into the sideline)

Split Eagle Cover 4-7

Split Eagle Gopher Cover 4-7

Short Eagle Lightning Cover 3

Short Eagle Brave Cover 3

Stack Slant Go Cover 3

Stack Bullets Cover 0

Stack Bomb Cover 0

11 Personnel, 72 Percent of Offensive Plays are Passes

Stack Cover 3 (run situations)

Stack Cover 2 (bluff)

Stack Slant Go Cover 3

Short Eagle Blast Cross 3 Hole

Short Eagle Brave Cover 3

Stack Bomb Cover 0

22 Personnel, 78 Percent of Offensive Plays are Run Plays

Field Eagle Cover 5

Field Eagle Thunder Cover 0

Short Eagle Gopher Cover 4

Short Eagle Lightning Cover 3

The Stack defensive structure will be used to run a Stack Slant Go. Stack Bullets and Stack Bomb Cover 0 are included in every defensive game plan, and they are run in every game. (See chapter 9 for more about Stack stunts.)

When the offense uses a personnel grouping of 11, the Stack defensive structure is a better option than the Eagle defense. An offense will often use this personnel grouping on first and 10 to get the defense to play Cover 2. The offense will then run the ball against Cover 2. Playing Cover 3 on running downs and neutral downs allows the defense to outnumber the offense versus the running game. Cover 3 is also the best coverage to stop the bubble screen. Stack Cover 2 is the best coverage against all passes thrown in the five underneath zones.

Short Eagle Blast Cross 3 Hole, Short Eagle Brave Cover 3, and Stack Slant Go Cover 3 all give the defense the ability to bring pressure while playing zone coverage behind the stunt. Stack Bomb Cover 0 is our six-man blitz with man coverage behind it. Stack Bomb is called when we want to bring an all-out blitz.

I believe the Eagle defense is the best option against a two-tight-end formation. Therefore, the game plan calls for the Eagle defense when the offense has a personnel grouping of 22. The stunts selected are designed to stop the run. Field Eagle Thunder is an effective blitz versus a flanker formation. Short Eagle Lightning changes the look the offense is expecting and has zone coverage behind it.

This game plan may appear to include too many calls to practice. However, several calls carry over to more than one personnel grouping. As you plan your practices, be creative about working in your stunts throughout the practice. If you don't think the team will get enough work on a particular stunt to make you feel comfortable calling it in a game, you should take that stunt out of the plan.

The last step in the game-planning sequence is to examine each formation (within each personnel grouping) by down and distance. An offense will generally have the same tendencies on first down and 10 and on second down and 6 or less. Second and long is a situation where an offense is likely to run screens and draw plays. Third down and 5 or less is often much different than third and greater than 6 yards.

For each of these situations, the defensive coordinator should identify the defensive calls that he likes the most and should list them on the game plan. The defensive coordinator should try to memorize each situation and the calls he wants to use. As you can see, knowing the personnel in the game will help considerably. This is a time-consuming process. I like to get this done before practice on Wednesday so the team can begin focusing on our prime calls against each personnel grouping. This helps ensure that our players understand the game plan by the time game day arrives.

Every staff has a certain way of implementing a game plan into the practice and skull sessions leading up to the game. Many high school programs must play their best athletes on both offense and defense, which limits the amount of time a defensive coach has to teach and rehearse his game plan. Whatever your specific situation, you should try to prepare your athletes for success without overburdening them with details that will confuse them or be forgotten once the game is underway.

On Monday, we try to work the opposing team's runs and top passes against our base defense and coverage. We also work our Stack Bullets and Stack Bomb defenses. On Tuesday, we make sure the defensive line and the linebackers have a stunt period together, often having them line up against cones and work on ensuring that their assignments are all correct. During our team periods, we blend in as many calls as possible, along with our base defense. We run our stunts against the specific offensive plays they will be run against in the game to make sure each defender understands his role when that defensive call is made.

On Wednesday, we condense the game plan, and ensure that the defense can execute each of the calls in the game plan with precision and confidence. If a defensive call isn't making sense to your players or if they are still having trouble executing it at this point, that call should be thrown out! In this case, fewer defensive calls are better than a lot of calls your players are not comfortable with. Thursday should be a very light work day to leave time for reviewing the opponent's film and studying the defensive game plan.

CHAPTER 18

Player Organization and Critical Situations

It has been said that those who fail to plan . . . plan to fail. This chapter presents strategies for organizing and managing a team during the course of a game, including the defensive huddle, sideline discipline, and critical situations that can directly affect the outcome of a game. In addition to your goal line defense (discussed in chapter 16), other critical situations for a defense are the sudden change (when your opponent takes possession of the football inside of your 50-yard line) and the two-minute situation at the end of the first or second half. Teams should practice these situations during the preseason training camp and periodically throughout the season. Coaches at any level should never assume that the players will know how to react in a given situation.

Huddle Organization and Communication

The huddle is an important dynamic in the success of the defense. The defensive preparation for the upcoming play starts in the huddle. The huddle also brings the defense together and provides an opportunity for them to regroup in between plays. Football is a volatile and highly emotional game. Because the mind-set of the players will be influenced by the circumstances of the game—whether the team is ahead or behind, how many points they lead or trail by, and so forth—the huddle provides many opportunities for leadership.

The linebacker who addresses the huddle must have the respect of his teammates. This player should possess the qualities that a coach wants in his defensive leader. He must be a physically tough player with a great passion for the game. He must be a playmaker others will look to with confidence. He must set the pace by working hard in off-season workouts, in practice, and in games. He must be football smart so he can handle the flow of information from the coaches on the sideline. This will also enable him to make the appropriate defensive adjustments.

In addition to these qualities, the linebacker who leads the huddle needs to have natural leadership instincts. A natural leader knows when to encourage his teammates, and he knows when to look his teammates in the eye and challenge them to pick up the tempo and play harder. There are also times when he has to flat out tell

Pat Fitzgerald (far right), an outstanding linebacker with natural leadership skills, addresses members of the Northwestern University defensive huddle.

his huddle, "We are stopping them NOW!" A leader must be able to inspire others to reach down within themselves to find the will and energy to play their best in critical situations. The linebacker who is the signal caller will often reflect the personality of his coach or that of the defensive coordinator.

The huddle brings structure to the defensive unit, allowing each player to be shoulder to shoulder with his teammates. Any of the three linebackers can be a signal caller. The other inside linebacker aligns next to the noseguard in the front row along with the other defensive lineman in the huddle alignment. They line up parallel to the line of scrimmage, standing in a two-point stance with their hands on their knees and their heads up. The corners, strong safety, and free safety align directly behind the front row. The Sam linebacker also aligns in the back row, directly behind the noseguard. This huddle alignment places each player close to his defensive alignment when the offense approaches the line of scrimmage. It also allows each defender to see both the defensive signal caller and the offensive huddle.

The huddle starts the flow of information. The noseguard sets the huddle by calling out, "Huddle, huddle." He must shout this loud enough for the entire defense to locate the huddle. The noseguard should set the huddle directly over the ball and four yards from the line of scrimmage. Aligning the huddle too close to the ball, forces the linebacker calling the defense to have to sidestep the ball. Because the defense has a limited amount of time to communicate the defensive call, each player must hustle to the huddle. The players should be alert and quiet with their heads and eyes up.

The linebacker who is the designated signal caller (often the inside linebacker) will stand in front of the huddle. He is responsible for huddle discipline. The defensive coordinator signals the front and coverage calls from the sideline. The linebacker then steps up to the huddle and makes the call. The defensive coordinator then signals the coverage to the free safety, who steps up from the back row of the huddle and makes the coverage call. The linebacker then says, "Ready, break" or some word that will inspire the defense.

The eagle linebacker will call out the down and distance. He should be aware of general offensive tendencies as well as a few key tendencies of each particular opponent. For example, on second down and long, the offense is likely to run a screen or draw play. The eagle linebacker should call out each alert after he calls out the down and distance. It is often surprising how few defensive players are aware of game situations.

To help the defenders anticipate what the offense will be attempting to run at them, the strong safety will call out the offensive personnel grouping signaled from the sideline. The strong safety is also responsible for making the placement call in the Eagle defense, so the personnel information is essential. A defensive assistant should be assigned to become an expert on the opponent's personnel and jersey numbers. He should get the opponent's roster, study the personnel on game tape, and watch the opponent's pregame warm-up to confirm that he has the correct information. During the game, this coach will be in the press box and will be responsible for calling down to the sideline to communicate the personnel grouping entering the game. A coach on the sideline—other than the defensive signal caller—will then signal the personnel grouping into the strong safety.

In the course of a season, a defense may play against an offense that does not huddle after every play. To prepare for this scenario, a defensive team needs to practice all week against a scout offense that doesn't huddle. The players need to practice the communication that must occur within the defense to echo the defensive calls as they come in from the sideline. The defense needs to realize that in most cases they will have the same amount of time between each play as when they are facing an offense that does huddle. If the offensive pace does increase, the defense must be able to maintain poise and maintain confidence in each other. As the game progresses, most offenses will slow their pace down and even begin to huddle.

Sideline Discipline

The discipline stressed in football should be practiced everywhere a player goes—on and off the field. As coaches, we have little control over a player's conduct in the classroom. However, we should expect certain things while the players are on the sidelines or coming on and off the field during the game. Here are some guidelines:

1. When the ball changes hands and players are coming off the field, the players should be expected to run off the field and keep their helmets on until they reach the sideline. Nothing is worse for the morale of the entire team than to see members of the defensive unit limp off the field with their helmets in

their hands. If a player is too tired to run off the field, then he is too tired to continue playing with the intensity needed to win and should be taken out of the game.

2. As soon as players reach the sideline, they should report immediately to the defensive bench. After the defensive players on the first unit are seated, the second-unit personnel should gather around in a semicircle facing the seated players. After the second-unit players are positioned, the rest of the defensive squad gathers in place behind them. Everyone must then pay attention to the instructions from the defensive coaches. When the coach is finished with the entire unit, then the players may get drinks, see the trainer, and so on. Defensive players should then return to their designated area on the bench. They should remain in that area until it is time for them to go into the game. This ensures that the coaches can find the defensive players if corrections are needed.

3. When a defensive player is not in the game, he should offer encouragement to his defensive teammates who are in the game. The players on the bench should be the team's most enthusiastic fans. Each player on the bench is responsible for watching his position and knowing what is going on in the game. Players on the bench should read their key as if they were in the game. This is the best way for players to be prepared to go into the game, and it also enables them to offer help to the players in the game when they come to the sideline. In addition, players on the sideline should call "Pass" or "Run" when they recognize the play on the field. Screens, reverses, and draws are stopped by early recognition and communication. These plays are often identified on the sideline seconds before the players in the game are aware of the play being run. Unacceptable behavior for players on the bench would include not having their head in the game, looking off into the stands, and generally screwing around.

4. When the defense is on the bench, the defensive players should anticipate when they will be going back into the game. For example, when the offense is on the field and it is third down and long yardage, the defensive should be anticipating a punting situation. The defensive players should get up and be ready to go into the game.

5. When the time comes to go onto the field, the defensive players should *run* onto the field as a group. Defensive players should hustle to the defensive huddle as though they cannot wait to unload on the offense. They should get out of the huddle quickly and should be ready to go after the offense with enthusiasm.

Sudden Change

Sudden change is a term used to describe a situation where the opposing offense has just taken possession of the ball inside of the defense's 50-yard line, which increases the offense's likelihood of scoring points. In 1995, our Northwestern defense only gave up 116 points for the season, which led the nation in the fewest points allowed. However, 28 of those points, or 24 percent of the total points we surrendered, came from sudden change situations.

That same season, we were trailing Michigan 13-6 in a game at Ann Arbor when our offense turned the ball over at our own 23-yard line. If Michigan scored, they would increase their lead to 20-6. Playing on their home field, a touchdown by Michigan would have provided tremendous momentum for the Wolverines. Just the opposite happened. The Northwestern defense rose to the occasion and stopped the Michigan drive. Michigan also missed their field goal attempt. That missed opportunity reversed the emotional lift that Michigan had gotten as a result of the turnover. Fired up by the Northwestern defensive stop, the Wildcat offense took the ball and drove it deep into Michigan territory, kicking a field goal and narrowing the score to 13-9. Northwestern went on to win the game. The defensive stop after the sudden change was critical to the outcome of the game.

Every defense will encounter several sudden change situations in the course of a season, and they need to understand the mental dynamics involved for both teams when a sudden change situation arises. The opponent's offense will be saying to themselves, "What a great break! Their defense must be tired. Let's hit them quick before they can regroup." For the defense, the thought process is often as follows: "How could our offense put us in this terrible situation? We just got off the field, and I'm tired. I don't know if I have the energy to go out there again." Your defense has to guard against this mind-set! Defenders must believe that it is their job to stop the opponent from getting into the end zone, regardless of where the opponent gets the ball. In a sudden change, the opponent will be mentally up, and the defensive players must have the confidence and will to accept the challenge of stopping the opponent.

When a sudden change occurs, the defense should take the following actions:

1. The defense should always huddle up with a coach on the sideline before going back on the field. Some teams use a sudden change stick (about the size of a broom handle). Whenever a sudden change occurs, all 11 players grab hold of the stick before taking the field with a tremendous resolve to stop the offense.
2. Each defender needs to get control of his thoughts and get mentally up for the challenge of stopping the offense. A defender's effort should peak for a sudden change.
3. Each defender should take the field looking for the opportunity to make a big play himself.
4. Each defender needs to understand that this is not just another series. The sudden change will most likely affect the outcome of the game. A successful stop by the defense can demoralize the offense and give the momentum to the defense's team.
5. The defense should always be alert for a trick play or a play-action pass, with the offense looking to capitalize on a negative attitude by the defense.

Incorporating these actions into the training of your defense will help them recognize what is at stake when a sudden change situation occurs in a game. The defense will be prepared to accept the challenge with a positive attitude and the resolve to keep the offense out of the end zone.

Two-Minute Situations

The final two minutes of each half are a critical time in each game. Scoring in the final two minutes of the first half provides a tremendous psychological boost to the scoring team. When the score is close, the final two minutes of the game obviously decide the outcome of the game. The ability of the defense to prevent a score in these situations often determines the success or failure of the team.

Defensive players must understand the urgency of the situation while maintaining their poise and focus. They must also understand how the two-minute situation affects the defensive strategy. The following keys will help a defense achieve success in two-minute situations:

1. Each defender must play with a great sense of urgency and energy. Because the offense will not be huddling in between plays, each defender must stay poised and think on his feet. The two-minute situation can be tiring, especially for the pass rushers. All defenders must be conditioned mentally and physically to give a great effort and to flawlessly execute the defense called. The proper spacing in the pass defense and pass rush is critical to preventing big plays.

2. Each defender must know the game situation. Does the opponent need a field goal or a touchdown to win? Knowing the situation will help defenders anticipate the plays and pass routes that the offense will run. For example, with two minutes left in the game, if the offense only needs a field goal to win and has two time-outs left, they are more likely to throw short, high-percentage passes. The offense may also mix in a draw or screen pass. However, if the offense needs to cover a lot of ground quickly, the seven pass defenders should expect deeper pass routes. The defense should deepen their alignment and their drops.

3. The defense wants to expend as much time off the clock as possible. They should do everything possible to tackle the ballcarrier inbounds and keep the clock running. Defenders should take their time getting off the ground after a tackle, allowing as much time as possible to elapse after the play.

4. Deep defenders must keep the ball in front of them. They should force the ball to be thrown in the underneath zones and then break up and tackle the receiver. The flat defenders should widen and deepen their alignments and drops so that they are in position to stop pass routes in the flats and near the sideline. Passes completed in these areas may enable the offense to stop the clock. The inside linebackers should deepen their alignment to stop deep crossing or square-in pass routes.

5. The defensive front four must pressure the quarterback with their pass rush, forcing him to throw the ball as quickly as possible. They want to force the quarterback to throw to the receiver who is the first read in the quarterback's route progression. While doing so, they have to be aware of not vacating their rush lanes and letting the quarterback scramble out of the pocket. The contain pass rushers must keep the quarterback in the pocket, which will limit his ability to scramble and buy time for a receiver to get behind the defense.

6. On fourth down, when a defender is in position to intercept a pass, he should aggressively knock the ball down to the ground (unless he is in the flat and has a chance to advance the ball beyond the line of scrimmage). Too often a defensive back will intercept a fourth-down pass 30 yards downfield and be immediately tackled. In this situation, the defender's team is losing valuable field position in the last minutes of the game. Imagine the offense taking over at the spot of the interception with 1:30 left in the fourth quarter and not getting a first down. They would then have to punt the ball back to the opponent with approximately 40 seconds left on the clock. That 30-yard difference in field position would be critical. The field position after the interception may also lead to more conservative play calling as the defender's team is attempting to get a first down and run out the clock.

7. On first, second, or third down, if a defender has an opportunity to intercept a pass in the end zone, he should do so and immediately take a knee or run out of the back of the end zone for a touchback. The only exception would be if the defender is in position to intercept the ball in the flat and return the ball past the 20-yard line. Downing the ball in the end zone eliminates any chance that the defender will get stripped and fumble the ball back to the offense. Also, it is highly unlikely that the defender intercepting the ball will be able to return the interception past the 20-yard line.

Conserving Time

Another critical situation that often occurs during the course of a season is when the defense needs to conserve time. For example, this situation can occur when there are less than four minutes left in the game and the defensive team is losing. The defense must get the ball back for its offense and preserve as much time as possible. The defense must do everything possible to stop the game clock. They should do their best to force the ballcarrier out of bounds, and they should look for opportunities to strip the ball when possible. In a passing situation, the defenders should not be surprised by a draw or screen play. These are safe plays that the offense can use to keep the clock running while attempting to pick up a first down. After each play, the defense should quickly get off the ground to ensure that the official will spot the ball and get the 25-second clock started.

If a defensive player gets injured on a play, he should stay down and not attempt to get off the field. The official will immediately stop the game clock. Both teams will get off the ground and go to their respective huddles. When the injured player is removed from the field, the 25-second clock will start. This will save the defensive team 5 to 10 seconds, which could be very valuable to the team's offense as they are driving to win the game.

After each play, the defensive players should quickly look to the sideline to see if the coach wants to use a time-out. The defensive coach can also send a player from the sideline onto the field to the nearest official to request a time-out.

Index

Note: The italicized *f* and *t* following page numbers refer to figures and tables, respectively.

A

Air Force, spread option attack 26
alley, gap designation 11
alley defenders 4
alley pursuit 4, 5, 164, 165
alley support 192
angle pursuit drill 6-7
angle tackle 190-191
arm-under technique 158-159

B

back block 151-152
ball call 182*f,* 183
Barnett, Gary 121
base block 147, 149-150, 152-153
beat principle 188
bender route 99
Big Eight Conference 121
blitzing
    with best rushers 42*f*
    Eagle blended with Stack 126-127, 136-140
    man coverage mixed with run blitz 51
    momentum change in passing situation 51
    Northwestern 128, 129
    risks 51, 58
    Stack Bomb 106, 108
    Stack Bullets 106, 107
    two outside linebackers 122
blocks 18-19, 88-189
boundary, formation strength to 38-40
box call 81
bump call 182*f*
buzz technique 186

C

call side 22
catch technique 204
cat technique 201-202
challenge technique 204
cheat call 97
cheated half position 35
check call 183
clean-up tackle 192
cloud call 208
cloud technique 34-35, 49
Colorado 6, 15-16, 34-35, 121, 142, 143
communication 11, 32, 144, 156, 181-185, 223-225
competitive pursuit drill 10
computer programs, for game analysis 213
confidence 3
Connor, Dan 161-162
controlled pursuit 164
corners 18, 22, 25, 98, 125
Cover 0 51-52, 107-108, 136, 137, 220

Cover 2 98-100, 102-106, 122, 129, 197-199, 220
Cover 3 36, 38, 39, 43-44, 46-47, 49-50, 76, 89-93, 96-97, 110-117, 136-137, 139, 199-202, 217, 220
Cover 4 34-36, 38-39, 45-46, 195-196
Cover 5 24, 28, 36-37, 57-58, 59, 60, 62-69, 73-75, 217
Cover 7 38, 69-73, 75-76, 91
Cover 44 85, 87*f,* 93-96, 97
coverage adjustments
    about 31
    Field Eagle Cover 3 31-34
    Short Eagle Cover 4 34-35
    Split Eagle Cover 4-5, 4-3, 4-7, or 2-7 37-38
    Stack Cover 3 91
    Strong Eagle Cover 5 or 3 36-37
    Weak Eagle Cover 4 37
crack block 189-190, 200, 201
crack call 183, 189
cross block 154-155
crossover step 187*f*
cross sweep or outside zone 134*f*
cushion technique 202-203
cut block 188-189
cutoff block 190

D

deep-one-half defenders 18
deep-one-third defenders 18
deep pursuit 192-193
deep threat, taking away first 95
defenders
    alignment changes for Eagle with Stack 124-126
    ensuring equal numbers with offensive players 211
    in pursuit drills 7, 8-10
    role playing 12-13
    staying square 4
    in sudden change situations 227
    in two-minute situations 228-229
defending running plays
    about Eagle defense 61
    about Stack defense 109
    inside zone play 68-69, 75-76, 115-116, 116-117
    isolation play 62, 63-64, 69-70, 71-72, 110-111, 111-112
    power play 67-68, 73-75, 114-115
    sweep play 65-66, 72-73, 113-114
    trap play 64-65, 112-113
defensive backs
    about 181
    beat principle 188
    block protection 188-189
    change of direction 187
    communication and game knowledge 181-185

Cover situations 195-196, 197-199, 199-202
   fumbles 188
   initial movement 186
   interceptions 187-188
   man-to-man coverage techniques 202-204
   run support 192-193
   stance 185-186
   strips 188
   tackling 190-192
   zone coverage techniques 193-202
defensive end
   gap number 11
   in placement calls 22, 28
   position-specific fundamentals 152-155
   role playing 16-17
   stance for 5-technique 145-146
   stance in 4 eye alignment 146
   and stunts from 5-technique side 59
defensive linemen
   about 142-143
   keys to success 143-144
   pass rush strategy 156-160
   position-specific fundamentals 146-155
   spying on running back 42*f*
   stance 144-146
   stunt techniques 155-156
defensive line movement package 53-60
defensive pressure checklist 42*f*
defensive tackle
   gap number 11
   in placement calls 22, 27
   position-specific fundamentals 149-152
   role playing 16
   stance 145-146
   trapping by offense 55
dig route 99
double-flanker formation 81*f,* 179*f*
double-team block 18, 148-149, 150, 151*f,* 153
down block 151

E
Eagle defense
   defending common running plays 61
   with defensive line movements 53
   designed to stop two-running-back offense 123
   goal line package 131, 140
   linebacker techniques 167-174
   placement calls structure 23*t*
   Slant Go stunt origination 129
   Stack defense main difference from 135
   with Stack modifications 120-130
   structure 12-13
   stunt packages 41-50, 50-53
   zone stunts supplementing Stack defense 139
Eagle Gopher 174
eagle linebacker 13-14, 25-26, 136, 168-169
edge pass rusher 15
eight-man front 132
erasers 126

F
false step 163
Field Eagle Blast Cover 5 58
Field Eagle Cover 3 31-34
Field Eagle Cover 5 24*f,* 28, 62, 63-64, 64-65, 65-66,
    67-68, 68-69, 73-75, 217
Field Eagle Cover 7 69-70, 71-72, 72-73, 75-76
Field Eagle Cover 7 checks to Cover 3 76
Field Eagle Double Shoot 52-53
Field Eagle Fill 60
Field Eagle Fin 59, 173
Field Eagle Gopher 57, 60
Field Eagle G Shoot 58
Field Eagle Lightning Cover 0 136, 137
Field Eagle Shoot Cover 5 57-58
Field Eagle Slant 173-174
Field Eagle Thunder Cover 0 51-52
Field placement 22-23, 24, 28, 29
Fill stunts 60
Fin stunt 59, 85, 93, 217
Fitzgerald, Pat 13, 224*f*
flanker formation 37*f,* 38, 131, 133*f,* 135*f,* 136-138
fold responsibility 193
free safety
   in Eagle blended with Stack 125, 126
   versus pass 28-29
   in placement calls 22, 23, 24
   pursuit responsibilities 5
   as robber 24-25
   role playing 17
fullback isolation play 168, 170
fullback or guard kick-out block 189
fumbles 188

G
G alignment 54, 55
game planning 211, 212, 213, 214-221, 219*f*
game planning boards 218*f,* 219*f*
gap designations 11-12
G call 107
goal line defense 131, 140, 206-207, 207-211
Gopher stunts 43, 56-57, 217
Green call 143, 144, 157
gut call 46-47, 48, 49-50

H
Hali, Tamba 15, 142-143
handoff to running back 194*f*
Holtz, Lou 128, 129
huddle organization, and communication 223-225

I
inside linebacker
   50 gap responsibility 12*f*
   alignment, reads, and assignments 169-170
   versus pass 27
   in placement calls 22, 26
   role playing 13
   and stunts from 5-technique side 59
inside play 172

interception pursuit drill 7-9
interceptions 187-188
intermediate area 196
isolation play 55, 135*f*, 176-177, 179

J
Johnson, Jimmy 78

K
Koch, Curt 149*f*

L
landmark 99
leverage, on perimeter 211
linebackers
    about 161-162
    chosen to address huddle 223-224
    Eagle defense techniques 167-174
    gap responsibilities 12
    gaps and keys 166-167
    head on swivel 104
    plays to split end surface 179-180
    plays to tight end surface 176-179
    press technique 4-5
    pursuit 164-165
    risk in blitzing 58
    as signal callers 224
    Stack 4-4-3 techniques 174-180
    stance 162-163
    stun and separate 163-164
    tackling 165-166
    variation techniques 173-174
line movement stunts 53
Lowry, Calvin 17

M
man coverage 42*f*, 99, 101, 202-204
man coverage stunts 50-51, 51-52, 52-53, 106,
        107-108
McCartney, Bill 6
Miami 78
Michigan 206, 227

N
Nebraska 26, 121
Northwestern
    blitzing 128, 129
    defense in mid-1990s 13
    Eagle defense at 121, 128-129
    goal line defense 206
    improvement in stopping ground attack 121
    interception pursuit drill 9
    versus Notre Dame 128, 129
    players 14, 142, 143*f*
    spread option attack 26
    Stack defense added to Eagle defense 129
    strong safety in sky position 35
    sudden change situations 226-227
noseguard
    gap number 11
    in placement calls 22, 27-28
    playing blocks 19

position-specific fundamentals 147-149
    role playing 15-16
    as spy 127
    stance in 1-alignment 144-145
    and stunts from 5-technique side 59
Notre Dame 128, 129
numbered gaps 11-12

O
offensive formation 23-24, 184-185
offensive line, gap designations 11-12
Oklahoma 26, 121
Oklahoma State 121
one-back, two-by-two formation 32*f*
one-running-back offense 90*f*
open-field tackles 18, 191-192
opponents 33, 213-214, 214-216
option attack, defending 26
option play 172-173
outside zone in two-tight-end, one-back formation
        179-180
outside zone or cross sweep 134*f*
outside zone play 172
over call 84, 87
overshifted coverage 24, 36, 37, 58

P
pass call 183
pass rush strategy 156-157, 157-158, 158-160
Penn State
    alignment rules 102
    base defense walk-through 212
    versus flanker formation 135-136
    handling 22 set 133
    players 14, 15, 17, 142-143, 161-162
    preseason training 139-140
    rankings in scoring defense 2
    Short Eagle Lightning Cover 3 136-137
    Stack 4-4-3 with aspects of Eagle 131
placement calls 22-28, 28-29, 37-38, 79, 81
plant step 187
play-action passes 24-25, 51, 82, 85-86, 104
position alignments 22-28, 79-80, 80-85, 85-87
Posluszny, Paul 13-14, 161-162
power or counter play 169, 170, 172, 177-178
power rush techniques 157-158
press technique 4-5, 164, 165, 203-204
primary force 192
pro formation
    Field Eagle Cover 5 aligned against 24*f*
    Field Eagle Double Shoot versus 52*f*
    Field Eagle Thunder Cover 0 versus 51*f*
    Short Eagle Bingo versus 49*f*
    Short Eagle Blast Cross 3 Hole versus 45*f*
    Short Eagle Brave Cover versus 46*f*
    Short Eagle Cover 4 versus 35*f*
    Short Eagle Flame Roll versus 47-49
    Short Eagle Lightning versus 43*f*
    Short Eagle Shoot versus 45*f*
    Stack Bullets versus 107*f*

Stack Cover 3 versus 89*f*
Stack Cover 44 versus 94*f*
Stack Slant Go Cover 2 versus 103*f*
Stack Slant Go versus 102*f*
Strong Eagle Cover 3 versus 36*f*
pro I formation 34*f*, 37*f*, 38*f*
pull call 167
Purple call 143, 144
pursuit
   about 2
   angle of pursuit 5, 164
   controlled pursuit 164
   deep pursuit 192-193
   by linebackers 164-165
   principles 2-5
   types of 4-5

Q
quarter alert 96
quarterback
   dropping straight back 194-195
   evaluate before pressuring passing game 42*f*
   getting home to 157
   handing off to running back 194
   maintaining vision on 104
   pressure on, to defend passing attack 41
   sprint-out pass 196-197
   three-step drop 194, 195-196
quarter-quarter-half coverage 34, 46

R
Rappold, Kyle 15-16
reach block 18, 148, 150, 153
receivers, system for counting 23-24
Red call 143, 144
reduction 22
regaining shuffle 4
respect 3
Rice, Matt 142, 143*f*
rip technique 155
role playing, defensive personnel 12-19
roll coverage 49
run call 183, 226
running backs, in offensive combinations 184*t*
run support 192-193
rush call 156
rush end 14-15, 22, 26, 146, 152-155

S
safeties 86, 96
Sam linebacker
   adjuster to unbalanced line 40
   alignment, reads, and assignments 171-173
   one-back formation 27
   in placement calls 22, 27
   role playing 14
   and stunts from 5-technique side 59
   versus twin formation 27
Scharf, Tim 14
Scirotto, Anthony 17
scoop block 18, 147-148, 150

screen pursuit drill 9-10
secondary support 192
secondary terminology 182*f*
Shaw, Tim 15, 161-162
Shoot stunts 57-58
Short Eagle Bingo Cover 3 49-50
Short Eagle Blast Cross Cover 3 139
Short Eagle Blast Cross 3 Hole 44-45, 220
Short Eagle Brave Cover 3 46-47, 139, 220
Short Eagle Cover 4 34-36
Short Eagle Flame 137-138
Short Eagle Lightning 36
Short Eagle Lightning Cover 0 136
Short Eagle Lightning Cover 3 43-44, 136-137, 217
Short Eagle Shoot Cover 4 45-46
Short Eagle Thunder 52
Short placement 23, 28, 52
short-yardage situations 57
shoulder turn 159
shuffle 4, 164-165
sideline discipline 225-226
skinny post 35, 91, 96, 200
sky position 35
slant 173
Slant Go stunt 129-130
smash pass pattern 198
snap call 182*f*
speed rush techniques 158-160
split-back formation and crossing routes 94*f*
Split Eagle Blast Cover 4-7 58
Split Eagle Cover 4-5, 4-3, 4-7, or 2-7 37-38
Split Eagle Cover 5 73-75
Split Eagle Cover 7 69-70, 71-72, 75-76
Split Eagle Cover 7 checks to Cover 3 76
Split Eagle Game Cover 4-7 56
Split Eagle G Cover 4-7 55
Split Eagle Go Cover 4-7 56
Split Eagle G Shoot 58
Split placement 23, 29
spread offensive formations 121, 124
spread option attack 26
sprint-out pass 196-197
squeezing smart 43, 47, 48, 103, 104, 138
Stack Blast Tango Cover 2 Wall 104-105
Stack Bomb 105, 106, 126-127
Stack Bomb Cover 0 108, 220
Stack Bullets 106, 126, 127
Stack Bullets Cover 0 107-108
Stack Cover 3 79*f*, 81, 83*f*, 84*f*, 110-111, 111-112, 112-113, 113-114, 114-115, 115-116, 116-117
Stack Cover 44 87*f*, 93-96
Stack 4-3-4 coverage 93-97, 121
Stack 4-4-3 coverage 89-93, 174-180
Stack coverage calls 89-93, 93-97, 98-100
Stack defense
   about 78
   defending common running plays 109
   with defensive line movements 53
   Eagle defense main difference from 135

Stack defense *(continued)*
    with Eagle modifications 131-140
    handling 21 or 11 set 132-133
    handling 22 set 133-136
    position alignments 79-80
    specific coverages in 122-123
    stunt packages 101-108
Stack 4-3-4 defense 78f, 85-87
Stack 4-4-3 defense 78f, 80-85
Stack defensive alignment 33
Stack Double Dagger Drop Cover 2 105-106
Stack Gopher Go Cover 2 103-104
Stack Slant Go 220
Stack Slant Go Cover 2 102-103, 129
Stack Slant Go Cover 3 220
stalk block 188, 189f
Steed, Joel 16
strips 188
Strong Eagle Cover 5 62, 63-64, 64-65, 65-66, 67-68,
        68-69
Strong Eagle Cover 5 or 3 36-37
Strong placement 22-23, 28
strong safety 5, 18, 22, 25, 125, 126
stunts. *See also* man coverage stunts; zone coverage
        stunts
    for attacking all formations 138-140
    for attacking flanker formation 136-138
    Blast stunts 58
    choosing which to use 217
    deciding on zone or man coverage 41
    defensive linemen techniques 155-156
    as draw-, screen-, and option proof 42f
    Fill stunts 60
    Fin stunts 59
    gap numbering 12
    good in neutral situations 41
    Gopher stunts 43, 56-57
    season long practice of 42f
    Shoot stunts 57-58
    Short Eagle Lightning 36
sudden change 226-227
Sutter, Danny 13
sweep play 168, 170, 172
swim technique 158, 159

T
tackling 165-166, 190-192
taking a picture 47, 52, 102, 138
Tampa Bay Buccaneers 79
Tango 105, 107
three-by-one formation 125
three-by one set 31
three-deep coverage 49
three-step drop 194f, 195-196
three-way go 53
tight ends, in offensive combinations 184t
tight placement call 79, 81
time, conserving 229
top call 182f
trap option play 154

trap play 170-171, 178
triangle read 200
trips formation 25, 31, 33-34, 43f, 84f, 87f
trips formation to boundary 39f
trips pro formation 33, 92f, 97f, 126
trips twin formation 126
twin formation
    to boundary 39f
    and Field Eagle 24f
    and Short Eagle 35f, 43f, 45f, 46f, 47-49, 49f
    and Split Eagle 38f
    and Stack 83f, 102f, 103f, 104f, 106f, 107f, 108
    and Strong Eagle 36f
    with two running backs 95f
twin I formation 37f
twin pro formation 83f, 84f, 98f
two-back offense 45-46, 51
two-by-two formation 25, 31, 125
two-by-two set 31
two-minute situations 228-229
two-running back offense 51
two-running back pro formation 93f

U
unbalanced line 40

V
V drop 89
veer release 153-154
vertical alert 32
verty alert call 91-92

W
Wake, Derrick 14
wall 104
Wannstedt, Dave 78
Weak Eagle Cover 4 37
Weak placements 23
wheel route 90, 96
wide call 32
wide receivers, in offensive combinations 184t
wishbone option attack 26
wrong arming 172

Z
zone coverage 94, 99, 101, 193-202
zone coverage stunts
    about Eagle stunt packages 41, 43
    about Stack stunt packages 101-102
    aggression and penetration 43
    blending Stack with Eagle defense 127-130
    Short Eagle Bingo Cover 3 49-50
    Short Eagle Blast Cross 3 Hole 44-45
    Short Eagle Brave Cover 3 46-47
    Short Eagle Flame Roll 47-49
    Short Eagle Lightning Cover 3 43-44
    Short Eagle Shoot Cover 4 45-46
    Stack Blast Tango Cover 2 Wall 104-105
    Stack Double Dagger Drop Cover 2 105-106
    Stack Gopher Go Cover 2 103-104
    Stack Slant Go Cover 2 102-103

About the Author

Ron Vanderlinden has been Penn State University's linebacker coach since 2001, and he is recognized there for developing one of the top linebacker units in the nation. He coached the 2005 and 2006 Bednarik Award winners, the 2005 Butkus Award winner, two-time first-team All-American Paul Posluszny, and consensus All-American Dan Connor. Vanderlinden began his coaching career in 1978 as a graduate assistant for Bowling Green State University in Ohio, where he had earned his master's of arts degree. He has enjoyed great success in his career as a Division I coach, including stints at the University of Colorado, Northwestern University, and the University of Maryland as well as his current position at Penn State. Vanderlinden has been an integral part of four Big Ten championship teams, three Big Eight championship teams, and one National Championship team. He and his wife, Lisa, live in State College, Pennsylvania.

You'll find other outstanding football resources at

http://football.humankinetics.com

In the U.S. call 1-800-747-4457

Australia 08 8372 0999 • Canada 1-800-465-7301
Europe +44 (0) 113 255 5665 • New Zealand 0064 9 448 1207

HUMAN KINETICS
The Premier Publisher for Sports & Fitness
P.O. Box 5076 • Champaign, IL 61825-5076 USA